THE MARRIAGE FILES

THE MARRIAGE FILES

Patricia Morgan

Wilberforce Publications
London

ISBN 978-0-9575725-3-9

Printed worldwide by CreateSpace

and in the UK by Imprint Digital, Exeter

PREFACE

In January 2010 a number of organisations in the field of marriage, family, education and counselling worked together to present a consultation: "What can I possibly say?" sponsored by Anglican Mainstream. The goal was to provide resources for people who wanted to respond to those who saw no problem in advising children and young people that sexuality was entirely a matter of their own choice in the light of their own claimed sexual identity.

One of the organisations involved was the Oxford Centre for Religion and Public Life (OCRPL). The consultation revealed that much 'knowledge' in the field of sexuality was based on oft-repeated studies and research whose validity was open to question. These studies appeared to dominate intellectual discussion in the areas of gender and family studies.

OCRPL commissioned two studies of gold standard research in the fields of same-sex relationships and same-sex parenting.

Patricia Morgan, who was a senior fellow of a social policy think-tank, while not committed to our faith perspectives, has covered the available material in the field extensively. Through the sponsorship of the Society for the Protection of the Unborn Child (SPUC) she presented some of these to the House of Commons Committee reviewing the legislation for same sex marriage during its passage through Parliament in 2013. We are grateful to SPUC for their collaboration in the publication of the full research.

We wish to express our deep gratitude to Wilberforce Publications for their excellent partnership in making the results of this study available as soon as possible.

We trust that this material will be an important resource to scholars and students, church leaders and church members, and those in political and public life. We hope that, whether people agree with the findings or not, they will, as Dr Os Guinness writes, debate them as they deserve.

Dr Vinay Samuel (Director)
Dr Chris Sugden (Secretary)
Oxford Centre for Religion and Public Life
21 High Street, Eynsham, OX29 4HE
June 2014

Patricia Morgan is a researcher and writer on crime, family policy and family development. Her numerous books include *Delinquent Fantasies* (1978), *Who Needs Parents?* (1996), *Adoption and the Care of Children* (1998), *The War Between the State and the Family* (2007), *Family Matters: Family Breakdown and its Consequences* (2004) and *Family Policies, Family Changes: Sweden, Italy and the UK* (2006).

Morgan has worked for a number of think tanks and has been a frequent contributor to television and radio debates, periodicals, student texts and national newspapers. She has also contributed to *Criminal Welfare on Trial* (1981), *Re-writing the Sexual Contract* (1997), *Juvenile Delinquency in the United States and the United Kingdom* (1999) and *The Thatcher Revolution* (2005).

Contents

Chapter One

BEQUEATHING THE REMAINS: BACKGROUND AND OVERVIEW

A reformer hewing so near to the tree's root never knows how much he may be felling. Possibly his own ideal would lose its secret support if what it condemns had wholly disappeared. For instance, it is conceivable that a communist, abolishing the family in order to make opportunities equal and remove the more cruel injustices of fortune, might be drying up that milk of human kindness which had fed his enthusiasm; for the foundlings which he decreed were to people the earth might at once disown all socialism and prove a brood of inhuman egoists. Or, as not wholly contemptible theories have maintained, it might happen that if fathers were relieved of care for their children and children of paternal suasion, human virtue would lose its chief stays...
(George Santayana *Reason in Society*, 1980)

1.1   INTRODUCTION

Once, the defence of marriage by government was as axiomatic as the need for an army. As stated in 2001: marriage "as a public institution, sanctioned by law, in service to the common good, and blessed by religion, must protect its private, personal, and intersubjective dimensions." Most importantly, the procreation and education of children should remain its most crucial function.[1] But for many decades now the married family has been under concerted attack. This is despite the multiple and mounting disadvantages of marital decline and family fragmentation. Castigated by numerous academics, mocked by much of the media and targeted by demolitionists, as well as diluted by law and penalised by fiscal policy, and with reluctance among the political classes to do anything to uphold marriage, it has seemingly deserved no support or protection. To the contrary, for many Labour and Liberal Democrat activists it has been something to demolish and, as Tories have sidelined it, it has been generally discriminated against and raided to resource other priorities.

Then, in a move without historical parallel, equal or same sex marriage (SSM) completely broke with the traditional sexual complementarity that has been intrinsic to the age-old understanding of this basic unit of society. As Mark Steyn observed in the Chicago Times (July 03), a "minority that didn't even exist in a formal sense a century ago has managed to overwhelm and overhaul a universal societal institution thousands of years old." Prioritising the 'couple relationship' cast marriage adrift from the public integration of sex and love with generativity and child care and the necessity of fathers for families; leaving parenthood orphaned and alone, to fend as best it might. Was this not "dangerous and callous" to so marginalise marriage and "embrace precisely the ideas that we need to abandon" if we are to redress the "toll of suffering" that current family disintegration represents?[2] Significantly, matters of child welfare were absent from the declarations that largely passed for public debate.

It is not accidental that equal or same sex marriage (SSM) moved forward with marriage at its lowest ebb, whether in terms of reputation, recognition or participation. Being both under attack and a received part of society within human memory has meant that the conjugal family has lacked anything resembling the well-resourced pressure groups pursuing their demands and discontents. These are successful because they devote so much time and considerable resources to their cause as, in close relationship with media and government, they can intimidate and silence critics. For the badgered politicians, opening marriage to same sex partners might for some represent closure on an uncomfortable issue, or the cleansing of an institution forever threatening to contaminate any who moved too close.

Reasoning about what course is rational for a government to pursue should be related to the question of the burdens and harms that arise from encouraging or enforcing any given option. Consideration was owed to whether there are limits to what marriage could become, absorb or serve, without undergoing complete dissolution. Such a momentous change to this most basic institution certainly demanded to be approached with the utmost trepidation. It merited the greatest consideration, investigation and explanation of the nature and purpose(s) of marriage and with full ventilation of what was at stake. Instead the proposal for SSM was sprung seemingly out of nowhere and for political expediency. We have not had the right debate – or one at all – when the consequences for society stemming from the decline of marriage are all about us. The core issue *is marriage*. Stable families depend upon this critical institution, and society depends upon stable families. This is the marriage problem which should have been addressed long ago. Since 'gay' or equal marriage spells the end times for the concept of conjugal marriage, it is not just a matter of how we got here, but what further social consequences *for marriage* this portends. Some of these consequences are well on their way and others are still embryonic.

Marriage's often well intentioned reformers or revisionists may not have fully understood what they were dealing with, let alone what the consequences would be. They believed that all you had to do was to extend to same-sex couples exactly the same law as applied to existing, heterosexual marriages. Not least, they would have been sublimely unaware of the plethora of further changes that would be necessary to clear up the legislative mess created by the Marriage (Same Sex Couples) Act. Did they have any inkling that fundamental concepts as husband and wife, mother and father, son and daughter were at stake? That while they might be concerned to promote the rights of a minority, there were profound implications for those of the majority?[3] Over the last half century, as the conjugal family has been dismantled piece by piece, anyone apprehensive at this development has been paid off with the line that the particular measure at hand will not make any difference. It has been said that the change is just to iron out an anomaly, or that it is to help a minority and will not affect the rest and that everything will stay the same as before. Some may say that wreckers will always have a better grasp and more guile than any ostensibly well-intentioned reformer. A more sympathetic view might be that there is always the difficulty of seeing beyond the first post, given the tendency to believe that what is desired or imagined is what will be. This applies to so many policy considerations. If anything, it has got worse as evidence tends to become an ever more tightly closed book and less accessible to the public. Mankind's Utopian visions are eternal. The pursuit of dreams is as full of pitfalls as ever.

There is more reason then to look at marriage's purpose and adaptation over time and place – and its effects on the fortunes of men, women, children and the wider society – in order to provide the starting point for any serious debate about permutations and prospects. There may be hopes that others can be accommodated and will therefore partake of marriage's remaining benefits. But will these carry over or even survive if their incorporation nullifies or transforms the institution into something it never was nor ever can be? This returns us to the matter of marriage's adaptability, as much as to the nature and expectations of those wanting to join. If the "nub of the matter" has been "recognition – cultural and legal – for gay identity", those "who oppose it are also concerned with identity"[4] – and are not merely unenlightened people making invidious observations and distinctions.

Restrictions on free speech coincided with a climax of 'gay' rights as Government views merged with those of activists.[5] Who in 1967 could have predicted such a development? A totalitarian dispensation was effectively established that stifled enquiry and debate, extinguishing the freedoms for which people once fought and died. Speech restrictions aim at thought control. Voltaire opined: "To learn who rules over you, simply find out who you are not allowed to criticise." In little over a decade we have seen "some of the biggest peacetime assaults on British freedom in over 300 years, [as] authoritarian laws passed by former student radicals … removed ancient freedoms in the name of diversity."[6] Criticism – justified or not – was converted into 'hate speech' as self-acclaimed champions of 'human rights' and 'equality' were permitted to demonise, threaten and persecute those who challenged their orthodoxy. As well as justifying state suppression of free speech, such attributions could encourage the offended to take matters into their own hands. The result is the abuse of persons and property together with the ruin of reputations and livelihoods – something made so much easier in our technological age.

> The ability of consumers to squash offensive practices is easier to do than ever before in this age of social media and tech-savvy consumers... bringing to bear the coercive power of the state would seem unnecessary

if the market provides an adequate and swift corrective.[7]

We have been running into the dark. A 'protester's veto' over legitimate discussion has been allowed to subvert or deny investigation of matters that have important implications for everybody.

1.2   OUT OF NOWHERE?

David Cameron's apparently quixotic move to implement same sex marriage might appear to have dropped from nowhere. On May 3rd 2010 – three days before the general election – he said (on Sky News) that he was "not planning" to change the definition of marriage. Then, in the Party Conference speech, he declared that: "I don't support gay marriage despite being a Conservative. I support gay marriage because I'm a Conservative." Where had this come from? Some credit his nice wife. Activist Peter Tatchell supposedly said: "I wrote David Cameron's speech for him. That line about 'I believe in gay marriage because I am a Conservative' came directly from what I wrote." Actually, in 2006, the new Tory leader had already spoken of marriage as "something whether you're a man and a woman, a woman and a woman or a man and another man".[8]

Convinced that it would help the party's electoral fortunes, Cameron's delighted director of strategy exclaimed: "Modern compassionate Conservatism lives".[9]   Boris Johnson, Mayor of London, was soon dismissing existing marriage as 'Stone Age'.[10] Here was the "new kind of conservatism which conserves nothing, changes everything, and is guided by the very same rhetoric of equality and human rights that shapes the left-liberal agenda."[11] Significantly, the text commissioned from Cameron's favourite think tank Policy Exchange to make the case for SSM, was put together by a trainee solicitor (Roger Flint) and a *Guardian* and *New Statesman* writer (David Skelton).[12] The key to the "rise and rise of the gay marriage issue in political circles was its usefulness as a tool for political and moral reorganisation". Institutionalising gay relationships might just look like "political accommodation to the demise" of marriage and the family, emptied by "decades of assault by the cults of relativism and state interventionalism". But, as in the USA, SSM is also something from the "top down to correct the backward attitudes of the *demos*". In distancing the political elite from the 'unenlightened', it was hoped that the espousal of SSM would consolidate a support base for the Conservative Party within the creative classes and public-sector circles.[13] Parliamentary scrutiny was wholly inadequate. At Second Reading, backbench MPs were limited to four minute speeches. As the Liberal Democrats competed for ownership of the proposal, Cameron clung to the trophy despite opposition from the majority of his MPs. The fact that most MPs, activists and membership might be "appalled would only reinforce … the credibility of the Conservative Party's 'detoxification'."[14] Since in reality they turned away, Cameron was reported as having admitted: "If I'd known what it was going to be like, I wouldn't have done it."[15]

If Cameron really wanted to do something for marriage he might have prevented its discouragement by the benefits system. He could have made taxation adequately recognise, not penalise, commitment, interdependence and mutual support. Law might have more clearly distinguished marriage from other cohabitational units and created an incentive structure that encouraged norms of responsible behaviour – like permanence, fidelity and financial responsibility. Fathers' rights would stem from marrying before acquiring children, with the terms and consequences for unilaterally breaking the marital contract clearly spelt out to promote security and deter opportunists. Marriage as the preferred basis to the family would be communicated to the next generation, along with an emphasis on the importance of mothers *and* fathers. All would pay dividends. After all, family disintegration is connected to a host of costly problems which involve heightened dependence on welfare, medical/therapeutic resources and the criminal justice system. Children fare worse in virtually every aspect of development which impacts into adult life and the subsequent generation. Men not integrated into families as responsible husbands and fathers are often a threat and burden to society. But for most of the political class that would be the most unforgiveable 'moralising'. For political elites "hunting for an issue through which to express some clear sense of purpose and simultaneously distinguish itself from those who are judged to be morally inferior" this would not "demonstrate their enlightened outlook."[16]

Did Cameron really have any real grasp of what he was doing or just was he "A Man Without Qualities: passionately committed to progress, but not of any particular kind"[17] – the political moderniser of the Right ready to drop outdated institutions, as much as Tony Blair was the one to do so for the Left? Proposals for SSM had appeared in no party's manifesto before the 2010 general election, even if it was soon endorsed by all three main party leaders. Neither was it a response to the general will or popular demand, or a matter of general welfare or benefit. There was no struggle, no mass protests. The passing of civil partnership legislation in 2004 had been replete with emphatic announcements that this was *not* a gateway to SSM, and the Bill had been passed on the understanding that marriage would be unaffected. All this proved to be lies. With at least 85% having declined civil partnership, there was unlikely to be widespread enthusiasm amongst homosexuals for entering into marriage. Polling would show how only a minority believed that equal marriage was a priority and 3% might enter it.[18] At plus or minus 1% of the population and 0.2% of households, society was clearly not facing calls for marriage from legions of excluded homosexuals and the Government's "best estimate" assumed "no increase in demand" over and above that for civil partnerships.[19] Homosexual MP Ben Bradshaw insisted: "This is not a priority for the gay community, which already won equal rights with civil partnerships. We've never needed the word 'marriage'."[20]

1.3   Secret Deals and the Suppression of Dissent

Could it really be that institutions around for thousands of years are "lightly changed upon the whims of the year or the decade"?[21] When a government introduces major social legislation that will modify dozens of laws going back centuries, a Green paper should first frame the debate. This should be followed by an authoritative guide or White Paper and eventually, a draft Bill – to allow relevant information to surface and thorough public debate to take place.

Instead, a package arrived for Cameron from offshore negotiations between gay lobbyists, their political ally and equalities champion Lynne Featherstone, and Theresa May – committed to her 'modernisation' drive to rid her party of the 'nasty' label she had bestowed upon it. A pamphlet issued before the general election in 2010 and credited to May already promised to 'consider the case for changing the law to allow civil partnerships to be called and classified as marriage' under a section on 'lesbian, gay, bisexual and transgender issues'. Since bringing this to fruition through the UK legislative process threatened to be long and arduous, delivery was better from abroad.[22] As a campaign group Equal Love launched an action in Europe asking for civil partnerships to be given full marriage status, Featherstone committed £100,000 to creating an LGBT unit in Strasbourg. Together with May, she issued an official policy document 'Working for Lesbian, Gay, Bisexual and Transgender Equality: Moving Forward'. This, as Britain took over the chairmanship of the Council of Europe, ensured that same sex marriage moved to the top of the agenda. This subterfuge was in addition to the fact that little in recent political British history had entailed such a denial of free speech and bullying authoritarianism.

In March 2011, in the Foreword to a document on civil partnership registrations on religious premises, Theresa May, the Home Secretary, and then Minister for Equalities Lynne Featherstone, declared:

> During our engagement with stakeholders on these proposals it was also made clear by many that there is a desire to move further forwards towards equal marriage and partnerships. This document does not cover these further steps, but our commitment remains to consult on how legislation can develop....[23]

A consultation process or 'listening exercise' would examine not if, but how, same sex marriage would be enacted. The elite's decision was unchallengeable. The reference to 'stakeholders' is to sexual minority pressure groups. Some objected to holding a consultation at all instead of immediately forcing the measure through, where even considering impediments amounted to "a war on decency as well as on conservative sense". This would only delay "equality to members of society on shifting religious grounds and nonexistent practical [*sic*] ones" whereas "[f]uture generations of married people, straight and gay, will thank them for it." [24]

The consultation naturally concluded that a majority was supportive, even if the anonymous 228,000 who filed online might come from anywhere in the world and submit a response as many times as they liked. A UK petition signed by over 600,000 was ignored. Advertisements for this were investigated as 'offensive' and the couple who presented it at 10 Downing Street were bombarded with hate mail. Nobody in the established Church of England was asked, regardless of the profound consequences for its role and status. Despite fundamental social, ethical and legal considerations which went well beyond what 'stakeholders' might want, the possible consequences of redefining marriage for the non LGBT population did not arise.[25]

David Cameron's think-tank Policy Exchange – 'the intellectual boot camp of the Tory modernisers' – withdrew itself from a Tory conference fringe debate when it was asked to discuss its support for the measure. To help shut down debate and intimidate objectors, Nick Clegg, Deputy Prime Minister put down prospective critics as "bigots", Lynne Featherstone spoke of malign 'dark age' homophobes. For Labour MP David Lammy, opponents of SSM would have opposed the abolition of slavery..This pre-emptive assault employed the kind of negative stereotyping that rights advocates would have found unacceptable had it been applied to their own constituents. No supporter of marriage as was, or critic of SSM, operated at this level. Nor did they, as some supporters of SSM did, target the homes of dissidents, or launch death threats at MPs, bishops and even prominent homosexuals who disagreed.

The *Guardian*'s verdict that those who opposed SSM were "irrational and sinister"[26] sent the message that opponents were deviants possessed and corrupted by some hateful mental defect. They were not just wrong, but evil. A couple displaying a message that marriage was 'one man, one woman' returned to their car to find police accusing them of 'hate crime' (they could not go public because of their jobs) and a blog writer was investigated by the Advertising Standards Agency for displaying a pro-marriage advert. Dissent became a sacking or disciplinary matter, as a chaplain to Strathclyde Police found when he backed the traditional definition of marriage in a personal posting. SNP leader Gordon Wilson was voted off the board of the Citizen's Advice Bureau for asking for a referendum and Green Party councillor Christina Summers was expelled for refusing to endorse same sex marriage.[27]

The heterosexual union may be legally recognized and operating throughout the world, but to support, or *even discuss*, this merited instant suppression. A World Congress of Families event in London in early 2012 titled 'Making the Case for Marriage for the Good of Society' focused on the adverse effects of family breakdown.[4] The organiser was excluded from the Law Society – and banned from another publicly funded venue – as being contrary to diversity policy because of its opposition to same-sex marriage.

It is difficult to see how a debate could be against diversity, or how a body which regulates solicitors could forbid discussion of an institution that had been established in law for thousands of years. The Law Society had hosted a debate on (illegal) assisted dying, and homosexual activists who wish to hold events were free to do so. A prominent High Court judge was reprimanded, via the Judicial Conduct and Investigations Office[5] by the Lord Chancellor and the Lord Chief Justice, and found guilty of 'judicial misconduct'. The JCIO had taken exception to Sir Paul Coleridge suggesting that the Government had spent too much championing gay marriage, which was of minority concern, and too little supporting married couples (his independent charity, the Marriage Foundation, did not take a stance on SSM). It seemed that it was deemed unacceptably 'political' to repeat evidence that cohabiting parents broke up at alarmingly high rates. Had he expressed the established line about equal lifestyle choices, it seems unlikely that he would been placed under investigation.

This situation raises the question of whether there is any opposition left in or out of parliament, as may be necessary for a healthy democracy. Admittedly, the marriage matter has not been alone. Speaking of immigration, author and journalist Ed West claimed how: "Never in modern history has a free population simply suppressed discussion of a major issue" or, "a large percentage of the population, if not the majority, held a range of views officially considered immoral." [28] Another writer commented that, given the "preconscious and collective emotions that are propelling liberal democracies ... public debate about the most important things is now more or less impossible" and reflected that "the state will use all its weapons, and in particular the new forms of censorship, to make resistance futile." [29]

1.4   THE EQUALITY IMPERATIVE

In March 2010, a recommendation from ministers in the Council of Europe had agreed on 'measures to combat discrimination on grounds of sexual orientation or gender identity'. Focusing on Article 8 of the European Convention on Human Rights, guaranteeing 'respect for private and family life', it proposed that where national legislation recognised same sex unions, these should be given the same status as heterosexual ones. Marriage itself was not mentioned, except to propose that 'transgender persons' should be entitled to marry a person of the sex opposite to their reassigned one. While the European Court of Human Rights ruled that countries were under no obligation, Article 8's lack of definition and the 'evolutive' approach enabled this to become a driver for equal marriage.

A significant indicator of the tidal swell was the outrage over the prospective appointment of Rocco Buttiglione as commissioner for justice for the European Commission. This led to the withdrawal of his nomination in 2004. While insisting that there was no reason whatsoever for discrimination related to sexual orientation, gender or belief, he believed that the family was about children, and fathers taking care of them. European Parliament members threatened to cause a constitutional crisis by voting down the Commission. "Kick him out" wrote Matthew Parris in *The Times*: he had been "insulted". Anti-Christian discrimination was "now in order" and "superstition" could not be tolerated, even if it involved plunging "the EU into crisis".[30]

All this is distant from the 1948 Universal Declaration of Human Rights (UDHR) the primary purpose of which was to protect individuals from the coercive powers of the state, following experience with Nazism. Article 12 of the European Convention on Human Rights (1952) stated that 'Men and women of marriageable age have the right to marry and found a family, according to the national laws governing the exercise of this right'. Article 14 stated that: 'the enjoyment of the rights and freedoms set forth in this Convention shall be secured without discrimination on any ground such as sex, race, colour, language, religion, political or other opinion, national or social origin, association with a national minority, property, birth or other status.' Signatory states had discretion to make their own laws and, if a national law said marriage was between a man and a woman, this did not breach human rights. When the Convention was drafted, sodomy was a crime and 'equal' marriage inconceivable. It would have been taken for granted how the Article 8 'right to respect' for 'private and family life' would be understood, along with interference in accordance with the law and if 'necessary in a democratic society … for the protection of health or morals, or for the protection of the rights and freedoms of others.'

In recent times, states across northern Europe have encouraged widely divergent social beliefs and practices – as with multiculturalism – furthering the impetus to remove from the law the image of any particular social arrangement. Yet, paradoxically, diversity itself is threatened by the imposition of a top down uniformity aimed at eliminating differences between men and women, child and adult, 'straight' and 'gay'. Once upon a time hard cases were deemed to make bad law, and the general welfare was primary. As this position has undergone progressive reversal, emotional appeals to special circumstances or individual predicaments often drive legislation and policy making.

In a rights context, immediate injustices and satisfaction are paramount and numbers are irrelevant. This approach fits with the 'modernisation' mindset which seems to "mean looking at the world as if it began this morning."[31] It also overrides anything which might be encompassed under the rubric of unintended consequences, which might include injustices to children from moves antithetical to familial cohesion. The removal of the 'need for a father' or mention of mother and father from UK law as a precursor to same sex marriage, used the pretext that retention contravened or was inconsistent with the "wider government policy of promoting equality".[32] Equal marriage "represents equality before the law for all citizens and this principle must be upheld in a democracy."[33] This helped provide the rationale for disallowing objections, even if 'equality before the law' or 'democracy' nowhere predicates 'equal' marriage.

In the movement away from rights that provide individuals with protection for basic freedoms, groups compete for precedence and favours as equality becomes the basis for writing preferential protections into law. Threatening conflict and divisiveness, the logic of rights autonomy is towards atomised societies with eroded allegiances. Advocacy groups are shielded from criticism, and complaints are encouraged by government offshoots like the Equality and Human Rights Commission and by the various forms of anti-discrimination legislation and regulation.

As equal rights are often deemed to be insufficient, these can morph into a requirement to achieve equal outcomes, with more intervention and provisions needed so that all can fully enjoy or express their 'rights'. The state then has to acquire more control to meet the demands of competitors for power and resources. Politics is increasingly dominated by lobbyists, special interest groups and charities. It might have been imagined that "after so much struggle, all members of the human family – after generations of being oppressed by despots, oligarchs, and ruling classes – can make their rightful claim to self-determination". Now: "the new oligarchs, new ruling classes, new ruling elites ... under the guise of 'human rights', are prepared to impose regimes that erode and neutralize the exercise of self-determination...."[34]

In the USA, the campaign for same sex marriage makes its appeal to the Constitution on behalf of tax paying citizens, with parallels drawn with the laws against mixed-race marriage struck down by the Supreme Court in 1967: "Then as now, those who argued against granting civil rights spoke of morality, social tensions and protection of family values. But now, as then, the real issue is justice vs. oppression."[35] Civil rights laws were designed to protect classes of people with immutable, non-behavioural distinguishing characteristics, such as skin colour, sex and ethnicity. The logic became such that if people can no more control their sexual orientation than the colour of their skin, there is no rational basis for differential treatment. With this mindset, the freedom to marry the person one loves becomes a fundamental right.

1.5 VARIETIES OF EQUALITY

A simple *revisionist* view is often the first to confront us when we consider SSM, confining itself to recognition of the union of two people (whether same or opposite sex) who commit to loving or caring for each other. Nothing will be lost and nobody will be worse off tomorrow as "gay and lesbian people ... participate in marriage, not change it."[36] It is comfortable to think that 'so what if two men or women can get married just like a man and a woman; this will not affect me or my children or my friends' and our understanding will remain much as before.

Perhaps what we learn from history is that we do not learn from history. Liberals like to believe that many of the practices and ethics of the past were based on nothing but bigotry, ignorance and fear. They need reminding how easier or 'no-fault' divorce was sold to the public, churchmen and politicians as a modest remedy for limited injustices. It turned out to have immense psychological, social, legal, financial and moral ramifications. As the collective understanding of marriage changed in step, so did the marriages of everyone, not just the miserably married. The "wisdom of the ages is not always wrong".[37]

What on the surface may appear to be just a matter of extending a facility to a hitherto excluded group is actually highly contentious if an institution might be inherently inapplicable to those seeking entry. Is it then a case of claiming discrimination for not receiving a benefit when failing to meet the logical and objective requirements? If human beings have for millennia and everywhere taken something for granted, it is the existence of two sexes, male and female, with marriage universally defined as an opposite sex union.

Alongside the pseudo-historical examples of institutionalised same sex unions served up as precedents for emulation are the anthropomorphic fantasies of 'gay' animals from octopi to chimps. Just as groundless are claims that the lack of SSM owed itself to the arbitrary prohibitions of interfering states.

It is easier to dismantle an existing institution than construct an alternative, or one that simultaneously incorporates radically different memberships. One indicator of how equal marriage entails obliterating a great deal of legal and cultural heritage (with great monetary cost)[6] is how the word 'husband' appeared 1,003 times, 'wife' 888 times and 'spouse' 2,740 times in legislation going back to 1285AD. As marriage's redefinition rewrites language as well as law, a 'widow' becomes a 'woman whose deceased spouse was a man' or 'that person's surviving spouse' and 'partner' replaces husband and wife in a huge raft of legislation.

Measures introduced through ministerial orders have had to prevent a man becoming Queen in the event of a King 'marrying' another man or the Princess of Wales if the heir to the throne enters a same-sex marriage and similarly for a male 'partner' being referred to as Duchess, Lady or Countess.

The rejection of the traditional complementary and generative union of spouses negates the grounds for upholding marriage's constitutive norms of permanence, monogamy, and exclusivity. Matters of consummation and adultery cannot apply as people of the same sex do not unite as 'one-flesh'. The nature of homosexual proclivities raises further issues of monogamy and commitment where there are objections to being restricted by heterosexual standards. Since homosexual relations are essentially sterile, union and generativity part company. The relinquishing of marriage's gendered nature breaks with any remaining relationship to fatherhood and men's attachment to children for the first time in human history.

Rather than expanding the pool of eligible people or absorbing minorities into an established institution, the prize being sought by the proponents of SSM profoundly alters in the process – if we are not to have two distinct or parallel forms. Given how discrimination is a one-way street and homosexuals cannot fit into conjugality, convergence cannot be on heterosexual terms.

Revisionists may insist that marriage is not inherently an opposite sex relationship, but are often vague when explaining what they think marriage *is*. In turn, what were the advocates of same sex marriage seeking?

> Are they ready to assume the responsibilities that most societies attach to marriage? Do they wish to partake of an ordinance highly structured by history and religious obligation? Or are they asking to change the very nature of the institution itself?[38]

Revisionists tend to settle upon the self-defined 'couple relationship' as the basis for marriage equality. This *close relationship theory* radically relativises and privatises relationships. It rejects any criterion other than the self's subjective assessment of the self's needs. Some are bolder than others in accepting and, indeed, embracing the demise of marriage in exchange for a concept of purely personal contracts. This obliteration of any distinction between marriage and other relationships, sexual or otherwise, sweeps away the (unavoidably public) ethical and social dimensions which transfigured marriage into a unique institution.[39] To have equal marriage is to have no marriage. Irrespective of whether this might serve the interests of a small minority, to some it is the collapse of marriage long sought and planned for. At this point the aims of revisionists and iconoclasts meet, even if the former might want to dissociate from any intention to ride the course of conjugal dissolution to its predicted demise.

As marriage becomes a place for adults to pursue their self-fulfilment, does it matter what the combination of sexes or numbers are? Illustrating perhaps an obedience to lobbies irrespective of argument or evidence, legislators have little recognised how the arguments for 'equal' marriage apply to polygamous or incestuous as much as homosexual relations. Advocates may appear to be asking for little more than equality for all who 'love' one another. But, since this is bereft of boundaries or limits, there are no principled grounds as to who and how many can be in a union.

Arguments for allowing two men or two women to marry equally apply to groups comprising all and any combination of genders, with three, four or more person unions for bisexuals. This may be brushed aside as irrelevant scaremongering, but the augurs are not good – with no end to the forms marriage, or its substitutes, may take.

Entangled with considerations of what is being done to marriage are matters of why equal marriage was ever wanted. The debate is perhaps at its most heated amongst homosexual activists without the reticence and innocence often shown by heterosexual bystanders. This leads directly to a conundrum, given how activists have long been fervently opposed to the heterosexual conjugal family. What started with the 1971 Gay Manifesto's call for abolition of this "rotten, oppressive institution", is followed by a big long literature arguing that we "denormalise heterosexual monogamy as a way of life" and rectify "past discrimination against homosexuals, bisexuals, polygamists, and care networks."[40]

Seeing an opportunity to overhaul marriage on terms that keep homosexuals in the forefront of a new sexual order, some in the liberation vanguard joined the campaign for inclusion. Activists moved from appeals to "include within marriage an oppressed minority whose sexual orientation is some unchanging essence…" towards a change in society's "entire understanding of the organization of the sexual life cycle – a change that could usher in a new flexible bisexuality that would transcend the poles of homosexual and heterosexual…."[41] Marriage capture could represent the end game of the long pursuit of eradication. Children and the reproduction of society are irrelevant. What *transformers* want is to settle old scores and deliver the death blow to the hated institution at the core of 'heterosexist' society. Same-sex unions are weapons with which to radically transform or implode the repressive, heterosexist prison 'from within'.[42]

The route to annihilation may be via a garden of diverse sexual delights. Same sex marriage could be seen by some as a key to undermining sexual exclusivity and promising to open up heterosexual relations to more experimentation or a 'diversity agenda'. Over time, the sexual extravaganza has for some become a more mature promise of untrammelled choice and joyful expression or a 'pure' pattern of human relationships that will finally free humanity from the shackles of restrictive demands. The role of marriage in underpinning human bonds is irrelevant, along with the often dismal reality of lives freed of commitment and obligation. The future looks gay and bright.

A more refined version of the transformative power of same sex relationships views them as modelling egalitarian twenty-first century living, where opposite sex relations are cleansed of patriarchal remnants like household divisions of labour and sex role distinctions.

1.6   PRACTICAL CONSIDERATIONS

Same sex marriage will impact on all the major socializing institutions of society – schools, universities, media, social services and employment. This portends an increased infusion of 'gay' issues throughout compulsory subjects in the name of the legal duty to promote equality – there is no prospect of challenging the content or the insistence on attending. Since the move to power of the LGBT rights movement has been so inextricably bound up with censorship and the curtailment of liberty, this points, if anything, to the intensification of the persecution of dissidents and doubters, instead of exemptions, let alone protection, for those who may have conscientious objections. Businesses and public premises are likely to be 'tested' for discrimination. People may need to choose between their conscience or their livelihood, as public or private sector employees are up against their employers' 'public sector equality duty', with teachers in the front line. All the "countless tentacles of the state", whether at national, local or quasi-government or quango level, now have their 'equality and diversity' statement and must meet equality guidelines.[43] Non-compliance or any questioning of LGBT criteria merits 'diversity training' along with dismissal or demotion, as firemen found who refused to take part in a gay pride event.[44] Refusal to publicise LGBT events and go to Stonewall presentations constitutes 'institutional homophobia' and resources will be removed. All is reminiscent of the Red Guards in China or Pol Pot's cadres in Cambodia, dedicated to rooting out thoughts, suggestions or terms that might run counter to their doctrines. Other exposed groups are businesses big and small, charities, and chaplains to the military, prisons and hospitals, even if they act outside work time, along with bodies which use premises provided by local authorities for all manner of functions. If we follow New Zealand's Government Charity Commission example, then family rights groups that do not support SSM will be considered to serve no 'public benefit' or interest. The wedding industry faces bigger challenges than with civil partnerships. Promises that those holding traditional views would be protected have so far largely proved to be meaningless – such as how adoption agencies that did not want to place children with homosexual parents could coexist with others who believed the contrary.

At least a quarter of all weddings take place in the established church. If religious institutions refuse to conduct same sex weddings, this implies different forms of marriage in register offices and at church for the first time in history. Since the canons of the Church of England have been part of English law for centuries, it may not be possible to sustain for long one saying something different from the other. If homosexual unions cannot have full sacred accreditation, is this not discriminatory for suggesting that these unions are inferior? Churches might be better protected from hostile litigation if the established church's obligation to marry any eligible persons in England and Wales was ended, or if the rights of religious bodies to conduct marriages were terminated. Courts have already determined that the 'orthodox Christian view of marriage' is not a 'core' part of Christian belief.

The Deputy Prime Minister made it clear in 2012 that any exemption might be temporary and the 'evolutive approach' indicates that, once states institute SSM, protection will end. Any exemptions or conscience clauses await challenges under human rights and equality laws, given how the European Court has powers to override national legislators. The European Court of Human Rights recently quoted a non-binding resolution from the Parliamentary Assembly of the Council of Europe which said that, in the event of SSM being legalised, it will place a state under an obligation to "ensure that [the] rights and obligations [of homosexuals] are equivalent to those of heterosexual couples in a similar situation."[45] Sweden made it mandatory for all churches to conduct same sex marriages. Some 'faith' groups were no longer "willing and able to continue to act as a state agent in the form of religious ceremonies of confirmation". The Church of Sweden grumbled but complied in this highly conformist society and created a 'gender neutral' liturgy'. The state is supreme and "once the applicable legal framework has been established, this framework is alone decisive".[46] Similarly, churches in Denmark were obliged to carry out same sex weddings in 2012. If individual priests refuse to carry out the ceremony, the local bishop must arrange a replacement.

The moral authority of religious institutions will further retreat in favour of a narrow secular ideology, particularly since behaviour at odds with traditional norms is encouraged and advanced. Some may hope that compulsion for churches to perform same sex weddings will sever church and state and further push Christianity out of public consciousness.[47]

As other intimations of things to come, the introduction of SSM in Canada (2005) has meant severe curtailment of freedom of speech, conscience, and religion, with jobs lost and hundreds of cases of litigation against those expressing support for traditional marriage. In Ontario, where teachers must undergo training in 'gender diversity' and 'sexual orientation', a government minister announced that if the Catholic Church did not approve of SSM it would "have to change its teaching."[48] This was hailed as a 'world first' but it was similar to moves recommended by the UK Home Office in 2006. The Quebec Department of Justice launched a 'Register of Homophobic Acts', where the names of those anonymously accused of 'any negative word or act towards a homosexual or homosexuality in general' will appear for life. In British Columbia, phone apps enable children anonymously to rat to the police on 'guilty' fellow pupils, parents and teachers. Reminiscent of how the Soviets induced children to betray their parents, the potential for persecution, intimidation and blackmail is infinite. Going further, making what might be considered offensive statements about homosexuality merits a prison term in Sweden, and the European Court of Human Rights has ruled that this does not constitute any rights violation.[49]

1.7 THE OTHERS

It has to be remembered – particularly by those who use statistical trends as ammunition for farewells to the conjugal family – that married hetero-sexuals form a very large proportion of the adult population. Nevertheless, there is a long retreat as the married section of the population falls steadily. This has a host of adverse repercussions which impose a massive charge upon the public purse as well as eroding social cohesion, social continuity and social order.

The origin of so much harm can hardly be better brought home by research than it already has, but the problems arising from the change to the institution of marriage have not been addressed in the public arena, given the widespread antipathy to conjugality. With marriage the ghost at the multi-billion extravaganzas to counteract poverty, educational failure, crime and childhood disadvantage, there are legitimate interests in wishing children to grow up in the most favourable or optimum conditions – begotten where parents are bound to each other and their offspring by the ties of morality and law as well as nature.

While the conjugal family might be a "morally loaded concept embodying an ideal image or model of relationships to be strived for and supported",[50] this has been incessantly set up as an object fit for disparagement and deservedly on the way to extinction. Marriage has suffered many blows in recent times from law and public policy. Interdependence and mutuality have been targeted for eradication as outworn and even oppressive, in favour of spousal and parental self-sufficiency, with the tax and welfare systems increasingly tipping the odds against two-parent families. As marriage, parenthood and child-rearing were eased apart, and husbands and fathers progressively lost from homes, the self-sufficient or stand-alone mother has largely become the focus of policies affecting families. A fundamental task of marriage has always been to make a father, but if it is deemed that children do not 'need' one, then marriage can be seen as superfluous, and not relevant to how children should be born and raised. If androgynous 'parenting' is acceptable, officialdom has to construct its own clumsy and constantly evaded procedures to involve 'parents' or 'stake-holders' with their offspring.

The received wisdom may well have been that, when it comes to people's decisions about marriage and family behaviour, external suggestions and incentives are irrelevant. Those actively engaged in dismantling the conjugal family's supports have denied that their actions have any effect, even in the face of the changes they have themselves cultivated.

In the midst of the worsening inter-generational consequences of marital disintegration, the recent preoccupation with SSM seems somewhat arcane. It is not accidental how those who would never have sought the elimination of conjugality are some of SSM's biggest champions. It is doubtful whether SSM would have been implemented if the drive to eradicate the conjugal family had not emerged from the counter-cultural maelstrom of the

1960s/70s. The depletion of marriage prepared it for homosexuals, just as extending marriage to homosexuals promises to abolish conjugality. For some proponents of SSM, their aversion to traditional marriage may be overcome when it is open to a different clientele.

Since marriage has been so deracinated by law and social policy, the demands for equality to relieve the exclusion of minorities might resemble speculation on a falling market. This hardly makes it appear as if outsiders are given the accolade of marriage because it is worth anything or because they deserve to be admitted to a noble institution. Reduced to another 'lifestyle choice' for couples, it is further robbed of any status worth having.

Those who claim a more conservative respect for marriage have endowed same sex unions with a redemptive role, believing that homosexuals will re-brand and rescue marriage. Optimistic predictions of a re-vitalisation or even 'no damage' are vapid. How same-sex marriage will be a boon for society is scarcely explained, beyond suggestions that the newcomers are somehow better people than those heterosexuals who have so far only devalued the institution. The dissolution of two-parent families along with marriage continues in Scandinavia. In what have been more 'family friendly' countries like Spain and the Netherlands, equal marriage has been party to a more belated process of dismemberment, accompanied by a marked downturn in the numbers of people seeking marriage.

Marriage also promises to be an answer to a spectrum of homosexual woes which would be invidious to deny. Family fragmentation has imposed a heavy cost on individuals and society without having had any impact upon policy making. In contrast, laying the causes of homosexual tribulations – from self-harm, to depression, to HIV, to suicide, to drug abuse, to a lack of gay footballers – at the feet of society's bad treatment or insufficient enthusiasm has been immensely successful in winning attention, influence and resources. Justifiably or not, victim status also provides protection from challenge or criticism. Social engineering schemes involving a flood of supposedly therapeutic measures throughout education for making 'gay' youngsters comfortable with (and the rest of the child/adolescent population happy to admire, accept and adopt) homosexuality have abounded. Pressure groups are dictating educational content and the school environment to a degree hardly seen elsewhere.

Homosexuals have more than their fair share of sexually transmitted disease, conflict, violence, transient relationships and addictions. The thinking is that if marriage can make their lives happier and healthier, why not? By assuming that heterosexual norms are transferable, expectations are expressed that marriage might impose controls on self-destructive behaviour and introduce mutual care over the long term. This may be wishful thinking. It might also be politically unacceptable if it implies that there are aspects of behaviour which need to be curtailed, or if it is perceived that a jealous world is trying to stop people having fun.

Otherwise, the adversities of homosexuals are directly attributed to homophobia or to the result of society's non-acceptance, stigmatisation and victimisation. Irrespective of behaviour change, the existence or possibility of SSM promises to diminish vulnerability and improve well-being by enhancing self-esteem. So far, there is little indication that the prevalence of generally more 'gay friendly' environments in education and elsewhere do much to ease or reverse same sex tribulations. Consideration needs to be given to whether more might be exposed to avoidable dangers, given the immense repercussions of SSM for (not least) what schools teach. In education, the interventions to equalise 'sexualities' and promote different 'family forms' merge into comprehensive drives to rid society of heteronormality and heterosexism, along with sexual distinctions. This illustrates how equal marriage is unlikely to be the last of demands given the existence of a powerful propaganda machine built on perpetual victimhood and the crushing of free speech and thought, given claims that opposition is not simply unconscionable but damaging. To some, the "implications are [already] clear ... believing what every human society once believed about marriage – namely, that it is a male female union – will increasingly be regarded as evidence of moral insanity, malice, prejudice, injustice, and hatred."[51] Again, the promises that equal marriage will not impact anyone but a few couples who want to marry are hollow given how the European Court of Human Rights maintains that it will not protect anyone who might disagree.[52]

Most importantly, dismantling connections between marriage and family gives the state freer access to intrude into the private domain – despite the brag that equal marriage denotes 'limited government'.[53] As family life is conceived and ordered to suit 'degendered' relations, the to-ing and fro-ing of 'couple relations' and peripatetic parenting, the freedom of individuals to regulate themselves within simple and proximate associations is reduced. While it might be agreed that those who legislate:

> … same-sex unions do so in the name of high ideals: fairness, justice, compassion. I do not doubt their sincerity. To take the already troubled institution most responsible for the protection of children and the continuation of society and to gut its most basic presumption in the name of furthering adult interest in sexual liberty seems to me morally and socially cavalier.[54]

Homosexuals are not the only people affected by SSM and significantly, matters of children's welfare have been missing from its pursuit. This was to be expected, as the social significance of marriage as the means through which "the work of one generation is dedicated to the well-being of the next" was essentially terminated.[55] No apology need be made for having regard to the multitude that marriage has served and continues to serve, and to those with the task of rearing further generations more than for the minority grasping a prize. What has to be recognised is that while exponents of SSM "use equality to promote the substantive value of transforming society to embrace and support homosexual relationships", others desire: "to protect the interests of children, families, and society by preserving the integrity of the foundational institution of social order."[56] This book is concerned with outcomes for general well-being, upon which the future of all depends.

Chapter Two

THE FORTUNES OF MARRIAGE

2.1   CONJUGAL ORIGINS

Marriage has been present in some form in every culture and as far back in the human record as it is possible to ascertain. Before the 21st century break with past ages and peoples, marriage was, in essence and by definition, a union between man and woman. As much or more than for the mutual benefit of husbands and wives, it was indivisibly allied to the bearing and rearing of children and therefore central to generational cohesion and continuity. Matrimony, literally 'defence of the mother', derives from the Latin words 'matri' (of the mother), and 'munium' (fortress or defence) and holds the biological parents responsible for each other and any offspring they engender. Without children, a society perishes.

With their prolonged helplessness and dependence, human young need a lengthy process of care, together with the transmission of the skills, knowledge and possessions essential for survival and success. Reproductive alliances between the sexes, with male parental investment, gives access to more resources and protection for child survival and development. They also provide for the efficient pooling of resources and division of labour, as acknowledged by Aristotle. If humans reproduced asexually and offspring were self-sufficient, marriage would never have existed. The view of theologian Thomas Aquinas – whose sacramental view of marriage has so influenced Christian marriage theory – coincides with that from modern evolutionary psychology and sociobiology. In both, the male is joined to the primordial mother-infant dyad given the long period of human dependency.

The judgements of Minister Lynne Featherstone and London Mayor Boris Johnson that conjugal marriage is 'dark age' or 'Stone Age' are in line with 17th century enlightenment philosopher John Locke's characterisation of mankind's 'first society'. In ancient Greek and Roman society the family resembled a religious cult, with the father as high priest tending the family altar where the ancestors were manifest. Membership of the early 'polis' or city was itself inseparable from an association of families, all with their own particular heritage.

A design for what might best protect the interests of children coming into the world would best incorporate the act for generation into an institution for their upbringing – even if, by natural accident or otherwise, no children were born from a given union.[1] To exist, marriage has had to be sealed or consummated by the same reproductive act that reflects the complementary natures of male and female. As a condition for a 'proper' marriage, it ties the unique generative act essential to new life practically and symbolically to the institution for rearing children. In the context of intimate personal ties children are provided with the concepts and values which generate the self and help to root them in a particular place, language, culture and history. Otherwise, "you expose children to the risk of coming into the world as strangers, a condition in which they may remain for the rest of their lives."[2] Without modern state welfare, survival is imperilled, and everywhere investment and affiliation is weakened or undermined.

Motherhood is an indisputable fact, but fatherhood has to be socially established or created and this has been universally accomplished by marriage. When this reliably joins the begetter of children to the woman who brings them into the world, this ties a man's position in the wider society to the performance of family duties. While sexual dimorphism and reproduction precede the emergence of human species, fatherhood is likely to be coterminous with the appearance of cultural beings. With huge consequences for child development, the place of males in society and social structure, there is no parallel for other primates. The 'principle of legitimacy' is seen universally where, according to Bronislaw Malinowski, the founder of modern anthropology, the "most important moral and legal rule" of kinship has been that no child should be brought into the world without a man as guardian, protector and connection to kin and community. Turning sperm donors into parents provides for paternal involvement over the long term, where: "the necessity for imposing the bond of marriage is ...practically and theoretically due to the fact that a father has to be made to look after his children."[3] Fathers are important to child development and in ways which cannot be easily deleted or reduced to that of subsidiary mothers, or equated with maternal involvement and characteristics.[4] This even has physiological implications – as in relation to the timing of female puberty.

Along with mutual assistance and sexual exchange with the mother(s), men are more likely to care for the young if they have a high degree of certainty that a child they are supporting and nurturing is really their own and continuous with their own biological existence.[5] While modern feminists might regard this as patriarchal oppression, would women like to be made to rear or provide for anybody's children that are imposed upon them? Apart from difficulties arising where progeny (not of their own) are knowingly or unknowingly looked after by husbands, a mother's continual pursuit of mates might put the welfare of the young at risk, or expose them to males bound by none of the responsibilities and prohibitions which apply to biological fathers. If men randomly sired children instead of being responsible for those of a particular woman, who then knows who is related to whom? Would there be any reason why a father should care about his son or the son about the father or brothers about one another? Such a lack of affiliation is likely to foster endemic antipathy and even violence.

Ties to a particular woman reduce the likelihood that the resources of fathers, emotional and material, will be subdivided across many households – or none. Without agreement about who belongs to whom – 'till death do us part' there is little to contain disputes over sexual access or jealousies. The incitement to conflict is perhaps reflected in the increased levels of domestic violence and abuse experienced by cohabiting and single (compared to married) women.[6]

Certainly, as Plato warned, families bring threats of nepotism, unfairness and favouritism, which socialists use to justify replacing personal attachments with one to 'the people' in abstract. While justice generally may involve curtailing kin absolutism, it has as much or more – until recent times – entailed the protection and enhancement of kin investment and allegiance.

2.2   Promiscuous Paradise Lost

It has for long been part of some Utopian aspirations that children should be nursery reared, like lettuces or chickens. As much as ensuring full equality, this frees all adults for productive work and sexual adventures. Some states in the twentieth century tried this out. Modern governments' support for universal, full time child care aims to free all women to earn unimpeded. Ending collaborative interdependence, all mothers may then be fully self-sufficient. Whether values are drawn from socialism or the market, both see 'production', being 'productive' or having a 'productive role' in terms of efforts that enter the money economy. In reality, the massive contribution that domestic work and collaboration makes to actual productivity would be extremely costly for state or market to provide.

Often lurking in the background is that image of a lost matriarchy that supposedly constituted primeval society and to which it has been imagined we might return. In such prelapsarian myth, people invariably lived in a community where all were equal, free and owned nothing. Without private property, everything was shared according to 'need' among female kin and their offspring by unattached males – raising questions about what these were doing meanwhile. Much is owed to notions traceable to 19th century theorists like Friedrich Engels (Karl Marx's collaborator) that fatherhood is only a recent development in human history. He drew upon Lewis H Morgan's *Ancient Society* of 1877 and Bachofen's *Mutterrecht* (Mother Right) of 1861, which offered a history of the family in terms of descent through the female line and a gyneocracy which he believed characterised all peoples of antiquity. Men subsequently invented marriage to acquire the children women produced so that there was someone to inherit their possessions – a flint axe or two? This is still being recycled: "Marriage…is an institution designed to ensure paternity and keep the resources of the wealthy within the family" says Nicola Barker in 2013.[7]

Prior to this male usurpation of 'mother right', relations were promiscuous: "In the beginning, people were already born married – married to an entire group of the opposite sex" while, "society looks after all children alike".[8] Here, "brothers and sisters, male and female cousins of the first, second, and more remote degrees, are all brothers and sisters of one another, and *precisely for that reason* they are all husbands and wives of one another." With this went sexual intercourse between parents and children and Engels cited tribes where this purportedly occurred. Back in 1761, Rousseau's disciple Dom Deschamps spoke of eliminating envy and jealousy with a community of goods. All art, books and writing would go, with vegetarians living together in one hut, working together on simple tasks, and sleeping in a big straw bed.

Would transitory sexual bonds be enough to curtail conflict and coercion in these sexual explorers' relations, let alone ever be strong enough to hold people together? To sexologist Havelock Ellis in his *New Spirit* of 1890, true morality was "the normal activity of a healthy organism", external to tradition, education or rationalism. No social demands would intrude upon pure, natural, loving expression where, if humans lived fully fulfilled, silly bourgeois emotions such as jealousy and possessiveness would vanish. Before him there was John Humphrey Noyes who founded the Oneida community in New York State around 1846 and which lasted until 1879. Noyes believed marriage "provokes to secret adultery, actual or of the heart. It ties together unmatched natures. It sunders matched natures. It gives to sexual appetite only a scanty and monotonous allowance…" producing poverty, narrowness, meanness and jealousy. Therefore, it must be replaced by love of the entire community or 'communism in love' – group marriage or multigamy – plus a 'children's house' to restrict the influence of parents – something tried in the Israeli kibbutzim in the 20th century until undermined by mothers' insistence on being with their own children.

Might all this, as in Plato's ideal society – which held 'women in common' – just mean swapping the husband's tyranny for that of the male peer group? Engels provided an example of existing 'group marriage' among the Gilyaks, a tribe on the island of Sakhalin, where women apparently practiced sexual intercourse with the brothers of their husbands and the husbands of their sisters. But where was 'woman power' when every man had the right of a husband to the wives of his brothers and to the sisters of his wife or when a widow passed under tribal direction to one of his brothers? Similarly, Gilyaks were reported to be virtually free of murder or theft and lacked motives of personal gain, yet kin groups guaranteed their members security through blood revenge – something being suppressed by Russian rulers. Engels also identified remnants of group or mass marriage among the Australian Aborigines where a man with several wives shared them with his guests. Since the women belonged to the marriage group of the stranger and were his from birth, they apparently gave themselves without resistance or resentment. They had better, a spear through the thighs hurts.

The reality of experiments with sexual liberation has tended to be ignored. In the Oneida community the theory was that a woman was free to accept or refuse a man's advances. In practice, a small number of men had privileged access to a harem of females (some as young as ten), who were obliged to service their elders. Oneida dissolved when its founder fled to avoid rape charges. Dreamlands open the way to charismatics or the dominating force of inspiring leaders who wield judicial, executive and legislative power – the savage solution to problems of governance and a recipe for tyranny. These leaders tend to amass women for their use, and whether Aborigines, Bushman, Polynesian chiefs, and rulers in empires from Egypt to China, Mexico to Mesopotamia.

Roger Sandall in his *Culture Cult* finds it significant that in many of the guilt free sexutopias following on from Jean-Jacques Rousseau, no fathers and mothers or even children are mentioned, and certainly no daily routine of child care. However, a persistent fantasy has been that society looks after all alike, where:

> The child would still form intimate love relationships, but instead of developing close ties with a decreed 'mother' and 'father', the child might now form those ties with people of his own choosing, of whatever age and sex. Thus, adult-child relationships will have been mutually chosen – equal, intimate relationships free of material dependencies.[9]

According to Germaine Greer: "If necessary the child need not even know I was his womb-mother, and I could have relationships with other children as well".[10] To another feminist: "if no one had exclusive relationships with children, then everyone would be free for all children. Their natural interest would be diffused ... rather than narrowly concentrated on one's own."[11] Where everybody cares indiscriminately, no-one would be "involuntarily stuck with" any particular child and, with affection impersonal, nobody would ever be called upon to make sacrifices for anybody else. The child may have "ties with people of his own choosing" but is otherwise independent and makes no particular demands.[12] When not relinquished to the commune, children are free to bring themselves up with their peers. Then too, a new generation of women will grow up who, according to Engels, will have never known "what it is to give themselves to a man from any other consideration than real love...." Men and women "will care precious little what anybody today thinks they ought to do; they will make their own practice and their corresponding public [*sic*] opinion about the practice of each individual – that will be the end of it."[13]

In practice, the modern replacement for the caring, sharing anarchistic commune adopted by 20th century socialist states and present day Western societies is for children to be in state-run or regulated group care. As Engels himself insisted, the first condition of the liberation of the wife is to bring the whole female sex into public industry where the care and education of the children becomes a public affair. This demand that society assume responsibility for children attacks the family as the basis of their own oppression and a central buttress of class exploitation.

> If one takes normal parental attitudes to be a mere perversion, a bad habit of bullying possessiveness, the apparent chance of establishing everybody on a new, antiseptic, independent footing looks like the only hope for mankind.[14]

Following on are those postmodern notions that the characteristics we attribute to children are just social and historical mechanisms of control and coercion, rather than inherent in the human condition. According to these ideas, children are no more dependent or ignorant than adults, but rather carriers of 'rights' with political autonomy who can determine their own conditions and futures. Not as we have hitherto known them, children do not need looking after – giving hope that parents can be abolished.

In no society have women cared for any and everybody's children or men not given priority to their own kin. How can mutuality be built into relationships "without committal", or is love an "impersonal commodity" that drizzles over all? Alongside questions of how anything gets done, or how disputes get settled without insults, fists and worse, if all relationships are voluntary, who provides for the children nobody 'feels' like caring for at any particular moment? What happens to a child nobody likes very much, or who tries to attach to someone uninterested in its care? As Aristotle exclaimed, "That which is common to the greatest number has the least care bestowed upon it ... How much better to be the real cousin of somebody, than to be a son after Plato's fashion!" The reality on the ground throughout human culture is that children are dependent, and the younger they are "the more care and protection they need, and the less liberty they can use."[15]

2.3 ALLEGIANCE

What we *do* have in human society is a reverse process to one where impersonal, diffused 'love' is meant somehow to glue social relations. People's impulses to care and to attach themselves to others, as in the relationship of mother to child, are instead the raw material upon which law, morality and custom go to work. These organise the attitudes and activities through which these inclinations can find appropriate application and consistent, enduring expression. This transforms biological processes into morally and legally validated institutions. It also exemplifies the rule making and rule following without which no culture is possible.[16] Altruistic obligation is "morally binding in its own right, as regardless of feelings of affection, or of likes, or dislikes, or of familiarity, as of reward" and, as such, is unrenounceable and unconditional. Almost without saying, 'rights' have little or no place here. As something simply owed in recognition of filial ties, altruistic obligation does not establish claims to equivalent returns and nor must it be seen as accruing costs that might be better spent elsewhere. It is just assumed that the beneficiaries will act in a similar way in similar contexts. There are those who, if they turn up on your doorstep, you *have* to take them in. That baby may be getting on your nerves, you may be exhausted, but you *have* to look after it. You may hate getting up to go on the hunt, up the ladder or down the sewer, but your family *must* be provided for.

Marriage not only entails intimate relationships between spouses, whether or not emotionally charged, and regulates sexual and procreative behaviour – it also creates in-laws. It has been important to ensure that children have a complete set of relatives and can be properly placed in terms of their affiliations. This tells children and everyone else who they are and where they belong. It also channels the flow of resources and care across and between generations by uniting sets of strangers as kin. In comparison, even relations between close friends tend to be contingent and conditional.

Humans are distinctive in that both sexes maintain lifelong relationships with kin (even when separated for long periods), regardless of which sex leaves its birth group or whether both sexes do (as has been the custom in Britain). Apes might have habitual attachments between mother and offspring and perhaps with siblings, but no lineage or ties across and through generations and so there are no grandfathers, uncles, cousins and nephews or even their female complements. Through the joining of families, as Ruth says to her mother-in-law in the Bible, "your people shall be my people".

The term 'prescriptive altruism' refers to values generated in family and kinship relations and, while distinctive of this domain, also work to maintain the mutual trust underlying social relationships.[17] Eighteenth century philosopher David Hume spoke of "the observance of promises [which have] become obligatory, and acquire[d] an authority over mankind." Therefore, the family is the primary moral domain and, to Emile Durkheim, it was the key link of the social chain of being, which mediates between individuals and other institutions.[18] Simon Schama describes how scholars in the 17th century Dutch Republic endorsed Cicero's claims that: "The first community ... is that of marriage itself; thereafter in the family household with children, in which all things are common."[19] Marriage means that you are prepared to undertake a commitment not just to another but to the wider community as a "model of the intersection between private and public responsibility."[20] The ability to recognise a transcendent bond is transferred "from hearth and home to place, people and country". Recognizing its legitimacy, the citizen is predisposed "to bestow authority upon the existing order"[21] Familial ties extend beyond individual interests to "a commitment of continuity with the past generations in the presence of whom you make that declaration, and to the future generations that your union may produce."[22] To Greeks and Romans marriage was the foundation of the republic and the private font of public virtue. To Church Fathers, marital and familial love was the 'force that welds society together'. The almost universal custom is to identify altruism with brotherhood, where the development of moral character is "along the axis of the widening range of imaginative identifications" – not *vice versa*.[23]

In Roman Catholicism, God not only bestows sanctifying grace on husband and wife but their bond blesses the Church itself and the wider community. As with Eastern churches, marriage as the beginning of all is the first blessing bestowed upon humans after creation; serving society through encapsulating altruism, co-operation, love and patience. In the Anglican Book of Common Prayer, it is 'an outward and visible sign of an inward and spiritual grace ... ordained by Christ himself' – for the procreation of children as well as the remedy for licentious behaviour and the provision of mutual comfort and society. As an inter-generational alliance, the family is inextricably linked to three great ethical concerns: the welfare of dependents; education or the handing on of accumulated wisdom; and concern for the fate of the world beyond our own lifetimes.[24]

To report these understandings is not to wax lyrical about any golden age. Nor are they to be dismissed and discussion closed by unnecessary references to wife beating or child abuse, or the differential powers of spouses in times past.[25] Despite great change over time, some things are constant. Moreover: "misery has innumerable shapes" and the vices of possessiveness, cruelty and avarice occur throughout human institutions and can poison any association or relationship. They are not "essential features of the abstract 'family'... or even of the 'nuclear family'" – which mandate its obliteration – "rather than just human failings."[26]

The social role of kin altruism is a grounding assumption for the theory of subsidiarity, where the state and the market should support the solidarity and social order represented by the family and marriage. These have a commanding role in controlling unstable natural tendencies and cultivating dispositions which make people more capable of self-governance over the long term. Rights themselves have little purchase in the absence of such social attachment and the meaning which is induced by relationships of responsibility and commitment that together sustain civil society and civic virtue. Government endeavours to undermine or replace them are destined to be forlorn and disruptive.

The Western conjugal unit has enjoyed considerable freedom compared to those societies where it is subordinated to wider kin or absorbed into extended families. This went with a heightened emphasis on loyalty and the indissolubility of the marital bond. Marriage vows constituted a covenant, or a promise at large, to all witnesses, including God, that the promise (for better or for worse) would be lifelong. The tight regulation of marriage and the difficulties of dissolution in the past may seem oppressive today. But it is no coincidence that the mutual responsibilities of the couple were if anything heightened along with the development of individualism. Moreover, the confirmation of the Western conjugal family as an intimate zone is related to the separation of the household from industry and its emergence as a protected locale for child rearing.

2.4   IMPOSED OR RECOGNISED BY THE STATE?

Cultures have seen fit to regulate the relationships of actual or prospective parents to each other and to any children that they might have, bringing laws, norms and rules that reflect the interests of society at large to bear upon sexual and reproductive behaviour. In turn, religion recognised, but did not invent – even if it might refine and adapt – a pre-existing institution. People pass from one social condition to another and do it publicly where "[r]ites of passage are conducted in the presence of the ancestors... presided over by the gods ... [where] the long-term interests of society may animate the short-term interests of its present members."[27]

This applies to advanced as much as simple societies, where states have taken an interest in marriage on account (not least) of goods like child rearing and property ownership, as well as bonds across and down generations – which are fundamental to social stability. Marriage plays an essential role in maintaining order and continuity – which gives reasons for many leftists to reject it. In turn, civil society cannot be without a state to protect its citizens and ratify the institutions which contribute to the common good. There is no spontaneous order upon which well-being can depend, whether the market, 'forces' of history, animal instinct or evolution. The fate of institutions is: "one aspect of the fate of persons, and the fate of persons is inseparable from the history of the institutions which form and nurture them." As social arrangements acquire the mantle of sovereignty and law, this removes the:

> ... arbitrariness from custom and agreement. ... the family, the club, the firm, the government and the state itself, cease to be mere contracts between private persons for purposes of their own and become recognisable entities ... the individual expands his own capacity for action, and acquires also an expanded image of himself, as a bearer of functions and roles. No civil society can persist in stable form, unless

these collective entities become institutions, with personality, agency and the capacity to survive their present memberships, and to acquire a history and an identity of their own. ...the state is inevitably selective, providing protection for some institutions (for example, the family), and removing it from others (for example, from the private army).[28]

It is argued that same sex partners, for example, have not had access to marriage because the state took "a step to interfere with the liberty of its citizens" – an "interference which should be stopped".[29] The reasoning is that it "is not right for one person or the state to impose his or her beliefs or ideas on another unless identifiable harm is caused". The then "current definition of marriage in the Matrimonial Causes Act [as of 2012] represents ongoing and unnecessary interference by the State".[30] However, since nowhere in human history was sexual difference other than essential to marriage, nowhere did the "state" step in to prohibit something that was inconceivable and non-existent in the first place.

It is somewhat incongruous to argue against state interference, since this is precisely what those extending marriage to various other relationships besides that of a man and a woman use. No wonder others see "a statist assault upon the independence of marriage as a pre-political institution" rather than interfering governments preventing homosexuals marrying.[31] Ironically, this might seem to receive confirmation from Equalities Minister Lynne Featherstone's contradictory statement in 2012: "Some believe the Government has no right to change it [marriage] at all ... I want to challenge that view – it is the Government's fundamental job to reflect society and to shape the future."[32] This sounds in line with the majority opinion of the Massachusetts *Goodridge v. Department of Public Health* decision mandating same sex marriage where, since the state creates marriage, it can redefine it at will.[33] Believing that what the state creates, it can re-make in any shape or form clears away any problems that might be posed by 'pre-existing' institutions.

Of course, the state *has* "intervened" historically:

... introducing civil marriages; by allowing Jews, Quakers and Catholics to marry under their own faith; by introducing divorce reform legislation; and by ensuring that marriage moved away from being an institution of male dominance ... With each change the institution has retained its power. [34]

As Quaker, Jewish and Catholic marriages involved opposite sex partners, this is no riposte to objections that marriage equality fundamentally changes marriage's nature. Nor are references to Disraeli's support for the Second Reform Act, the legalisation of trade unions, votes for women, and reforms instigated by Joseph Chamberlain and Harold Macmillan. In some societies marriage was confirmed when the spouses' parents decreed that it should, or when the first child was conceived or after a requisite period of courtship, but all involved opposite sexes. Divorce reform (in the late 1960s/70s) is an unfortunate citation of how "marriage has changed and evolved over time ... without losing its unique character or its power as an institution". This is justifiably indicted as having been a devastating blow against marriage, children and society. The institution did not "retain its power" or "unique character" – far from it.[35]

Paradoxically, marriage has to be recognised by the state in order to create a protected locale or a legitimised zone of privacy where the state's intrusion is minimised. The same applies to property laws and contracts, like the deeds to a house. All prevent the kind of chaos and conflict that would result where nobody had an exclusive right to anything and everybody could help themselves to whatever was around. This would benefit the strongest and most coercive, until others came along to cast them out. The family has certainly been an impediment to the free run of the state to pursue its own educational objectives. Where guaranteed boundaries fall, freedom is lost. The sociologist Carle C. Zimmerman wrote in the 1940s how modern states will always strive to eviscerate the family and sponsor anti-family intellectuals as they seek supremacy to pursue their own political and educational objectives.[36] This was understood all the way back to Plato's somewhat totalitarian vision. It was practised in (not least) Bolshevik Russia and Nazi Germany and, more (comparatively) carefully and comprehensively, in contemporary Sweden. [37]

Where parenthood is not produced by marriage, it has to be separately recognised by law and society in legal and administrative terms. Or it has to be fragmented into genetic, social and legal aspects which have to be somehow allocated or distributed among 'parents', guardians, 'carers' or 'care-managers'. Multiple interests, goods and wants which are otherwise met in protected relations are elevated to the status of rights or entitlements that must be provided by the state. Any retreat of marriage mandates increasing official involvement through overseeing child rearing or creating substitutes for familial care and socialisation. Along with bureaucratic complexity, lives are opened to unprecedented intrusion.

2.5 AN INSTITUTION IN DECLINE

Although married couples with children are still the most common family household, their numbers went into decline in the latter part of the 20th century. More relationships broke down and fewer people married. At the end of the first decade of the 21st century, married people in England and Wales numbered approximately 20.4m (200,000 fewer than a decade before), while cohabiters rose to nearly five and a half million (from four a decade before). Single adults stood at eleven million, having risen by three million over two decades. In 2013 around 60% of over 25s were married, compared to nearly 80% in the early 1980s. On present projections, the married proportion will fall to 42% by 2033. By 2013, 24% of children were living with a lone parent in Britain and nearly a half of 15 year olds had experienced parental separation. Of those children who will still be living with their parents at their fifteenth birthday, only 5% will have unmarried parents. Overall, cohabitations are four times as likely to break-up as marriage (nearly six-fold in a child's first five years), accounting for 19% of couples with dependent children yet 50% of family breakdown. Almost half of births in England and Wales are now by unmarried mothers or a record 47.5%. The size of the married family has contracted as that of lone parents expands. More couples have only one child compared with the two or more even a decade ago, and single mothers have children in sequential relationships.

Insofar as marriage might still haunt the moral understanding as a special sort of contract expected to be permanent and not to be repudiated without just cause or profound consideration, it is one which the law now barely enforces. The decline began with the watershed reform in 1969/70 which marked the transition to 'no fault' divorce. The 1956 Royal Commission on Marriage and Divorce was appointed in response to attempts to extend the grounds for divorce beyond that of the matrimonial offence or fault. Its report insisted that "people have good and bad impulses and we conceive it to be the function of the law to strengthen the good and control the bad."[38] Bodies from the Catholic Union to the atheistic Ethical Union emphasised how the first function of marriage was to uphold general standards and protect the institution of the family as the assumed and approved foundation of society by confirming life-long union.

These were the last sighs of an ethically grounded approach to law and public policy which held that law must reinforce cultural norms and align individuals with the long term consequences of their behaviour. Into its place was rushing free choice, guided only by a deterministic naturalism. To progressives, 'institutionalists' who held that marriage had a value in its own right, were sacrificing people to meaningless abstractions. Divorce was "neither good nor bad, but should be judged in much the same way as one judges the decision to resign from a job."[39] With the realm of morality rejected as unreal and invalid, the law appeared burdened with the irrationality of historical tradition. As with SSM, reformers could seek solace in the fact that opponents would soon die off.

A tremendous appearance of rectitude was combined with a failure to grasp that, even if there might be nothing beyond individuals as the sources and subjects of moral rules, values exist insofar as they are externalised or objectified. Social beings create institutions to embody and carry on systems of meaning, which are experienced as existing outside individual consciousness and provide authoritative reference points. Some change in divorce law was widely desired, but the 1969/70 reform did not reflect popular demand as much as the design of those anxious to promote a new liberality.

As would become the pattern for many subsequent upheavals, anxieties were eased by assurances that nothing would really change. The doctrine of 'irretrievable breakdown' promised to make divorce purely responsive and regulative: a tidying up process, whose task was the 'decent burial' of already 'dead' unions. It was artfully promoted and innocently accepted by archbishops and politicians as something that would take out a few 'hollow-shells' and leave the rest – and everything else – exactly as before. As the law would declare defunct what had naturally ended, it might even revitalise marriage, not least by allowing for the legitimisation of 'hole in the corner' unions. Marital breakdown would be identified by 'experts' (who proved to be non-existent) with a speciality in diagnosing marital mortality. In practice, there was fall back onto matters like separation, 'unreasonable' behaviour or 'breakdown' – now subjectively defined. Marriage was terminable without much, if any, intervention by the state other than what might be involved in the division of assets.

To many it seemed such a good idea: a pathway to happiness with a negligible downside. The reality was that:

> In our rush to improve the lives of adults, we assumed that their [children's] lives would improve as well. We made radical changes in the family without realizing how it would change the experience of growing up. We embarked on a gigantic social experiment without any idea about how a new generation would be affected.[40]

Some, like Maggie Gallaher, have placed this among the boldest social experiments in history where, without public discussion of the possible consequences, laws were enacted across Anglophone jurisdictions that effectively ended marriage as a binding legal contract. More than the removal of government from enforcement of the contract; it allowed the government to enforce the abrogation of the contract. Regardless of the terms by which a marriage is entered, government officials might, at the request of one spouse, simply dissolve it (and the household created by it) and without penalty to the leaving party.

As people began to operate according to a new paradigm, this changed the marriages of everyone, not just the 'hollow-shells' as, in its aftermath, divorce rates soared and marriage rates began their downward slide. The law sends out messages. That is what law does, whether meant to or not. If criminals are not punished, people become demoralised. Feeling that they cannot expect justice, criminalisation of the population spreads and with it, for those in a position to enforce their will, reprisals and revenge. The option of divorce if happiness was not forthcoming, and the possibility of improved chances with a new partner, gnawed away at the belief that marriage was a life-long commitment. People were faced with a contract or agreement whose terms were obscure and unpredictable – breaking it did not much matter and, in doing so, a person might even benefit from their fault, since resources were to be distributed according to 'need', not desert. As the promise of security became a source of trepidation, refuge was increasingly sought in even more insecure and informal unions of convenience. There is no trial run for commitment. But, without commitment, relationships lack pointers to the future and structures to hold them together in difficult times.

A persistent mirage of the 'good divorce' promised that, if only it was made ever easier, acrimony and destructive behaviour would disappear. People would make better choices if they could be set free from earlier 'mistakes'. Avoiding anything adversarial or judgemental might stop 'conflict' causing 'damage' and people might glide effortlessly out of relationships, hardly knowing what was happening. This reached its apotheosis under John Major's government's legal change (which was not implemented) where divorce would be automatic a year after an application without the need to mention anything at all. Helped out by therapeutic mediation, it was imagined that people would speedily and tidily sort out financial and child arrangements. This owed much to the Law Commission (significantly influenced by feminists) which saw little reason to support marriage beyond 'any other living arrangement'. As it transpired, mediation was more likely to foster than eliminate 'conflict'.

To complement this process, rights extended to cohabitants diluted those of marriage. Ironically, these may impose conditions that the parties are trying to avoid, as when a Supreme Court ruling in 2011 brought the property rights of married and unmarried couples closer together in the event of dissolution. Kite-flying for the following civil partnerships legislation, Lord Lester introduced a bill in 2003 to remedy an 'ancient injustice' whereby people living together, and whether of the same or different sexes, would enjoy the same rights as married couples. Baroness Hale, a member of the UK Supreme Court and the top female judge, also called in 2012 for cohabiting couples to be given more legal rights – to pensions, property, etc. This was not to impose upon unmarried couples the responsibilities of marriage, but to redress the losses flowing from their relationships since, as more people cohabited, law 'failed' to reflect the way people 'choose' to live. However, the ability to leave a relationship with no strings attached is why individuals may 'choose' this arrangement. If those who 'choose' to avoid commitment obtain benefits without responsibilities, marriage is further devalued. The drift towards a time limited agreement is perhaps even more explicit where pre-nuptial agreements specify arrangements in the event of divorce. Separation becomes almost a fulfilment of marriage.

Is there any point to marriage when it is so devalued? Back in 1982, when she was the barrister Brenda Hoggett, Baroness Hale was already writing how: "Family law no longer makes any attempt to buttress the stability of marriage or any other union" and how "we have reached a point at which, rather than discussing which remedies should now be extended to the unmarried, we should be considering whether the legal institution of marriage continues to serve any useful purposes."

Just as "people are less disposed to assume the burdens of high office when society withholds the dignities and privileges which those offices have previously signified", so too for marriage when society fails or refuses to recognise its "uniqueness, the value, and the sacrificial character...."[41] Ideally, virtuous conduct may be logically independent of incentives. Practically, in this flawed world good behaviour is often a function of the costs and benefits of various courses of action. People will often go with an incentive structure that rewards opportunistic behaviour, even in the most intimate aspects of their lives. After all, in the commercial sphere promises have to be backed by the whole panoply of legal requirements however honourable the participants may be. If legislation offers suggestions and provides incentives and disincentives, so too do economic measures send out critical signals about what is worthwhile and deserving and what is not.

By the 1970s the state was moving in to meet the housing and financial support of lone parents – first, as 'casualties' of marital breakdown and then as single mothers. As well as being prioritised for social housing and guaranteed a basic income, their concessions and extras accumulated in the 1980s/1990s. Attempts to make estranged fathers pay child support and thus reduce the benefits bill were effectively abandoned in the face of protests and the bureaucracy involved. The mother came to keep any contributions on top of her benefit allocations while, for couples, fathers' earning are counted against entitlements.

Poverty statistics consider the number subsisting on a household income when calculating living standards, while taxation and welfare makes no allowance for two adults compared to one. Since a couple's entitlements have been the same or lower than for a lone parent, they must earn far more to avoid poverty. The married couples' allowance (half the basic personal allowance) was cut as an 'anomaly' by Chancellor Kenneth Clarke and removed by Chancellor Gordon Brown. The withdrawal of tax reliefs which had been given for the support of dependents has left resident husbands and fathers taxed as much or more than single, childless men. Local taxation was reduced (by a quarter) for sole adult occupancy introduced after the failure of Margaret's Thatcher's poll tax (which charged couples double). The child tax allowance, once worth as much or more than the personal exemption, became a universal 'child benefit' in the late 1970s, to be subsequently whittled away in favour of means tested or 'targeted' benefits. Since these have to be withdrawn as more is earned, means testing has undermined incentives for the 40% of families entitled to its credits. The Marginal Effective Tax Rate (the percentage removed from each extra pound earned) was 73% in 2013 and will be 76.2% when Universal Credit arrives in 2016.

Relative measures of child poverty increased from the 1970s onwards. With the focus on lone parents, couple families below the poverty line have largely been disregarded. Yet, even in 2012, 1.6 million children lived in couple families with income before housing costs below 60% of the median and 0.7 with lone parents. All has not been helped by the changes to male employment following from the fundamental economic restructuring in industrial countries, happening at the same time as the tax burden shifted onto two parent families. International comparisons show that UK married couples with children now face a tax burden 42% above the OECD average – leaving them with the highest taxation in the world. In particular, the one earner family saw a substantial increase in taxation in the new millennium, compared to that of lone parents, singles and double income couples. Ninety-five per cent of all singles with children would incur a 'couple penalty' if they married or lived together, with 10% losing a third of their income.[42]

Means tested welfare means that the state outbids husbands and fathers - transforming them into liabilities. While ONS figures show that there are nearly two million lone parents in England and Wales, according to HMRC there are an extra quarter million (means tested) tax credit beneficiaries. Because of significant penalties for staying together, couples have to pretend to be separated to avoid penalisation. Theodore Dalrymple relates how:

> … a young Londoner [said] that he loved his family, but had concluded that the best thing he could do was to leave them…. Without him, his wife would have her housing costs covered and qualify for a suite of

other benefits. The state was ... substantially outbidding him for the responsibility of supporting his wife and children.

It's easy for ministers to denounce such people as cheats. ...they might do better to ask what type of incentives they have created when thousands of mothers are pretending to be single, and husbands are sneaking into their own homes in the hope that they're not reported by their neighbours.

Made such an unattractive proposition, the effect has already been largely to wipe out marriage from the lower income reaches of society. In 2013, further means testing pushed the couple penalty into areas of the distribution where it previously did not apply, or only to council tax. Anyone entitled to child benefit and whose spouse has an income exceeding £50,000 now has this clawed back (1% for every extra £100 of income) until all is removed. One-earner couples with two children already paid tax of £13,829 compared to £8,217 for a two-earner couple on a combined £60,000 and, in 2013 this rose to £15,565 (or 89% more than a double earner couple).

Exit one parent and the state must not only move in as economic provider, but substitute for the missing parent's functions and make good the loss of social capital for the children. It endeavours to mimic or even exceed the family's role in nurturing those personal skills which sustain communities. It is questionable whether official bodies can ever discharge such functions adequately, especially in circumstances where the client group rapidly increases and support must constantly expand at the expense of productive society. Interventions range from 'working with' the 'most troubled families' to early years schemes like New Labour's SureStart to transform children's development, and to promises that: "What all families have a right to expect from the government is support"... including "safe streets; strong communities... We are striving to deliver this."[43] The state might strive, but it is hardly going to substitute for the absent fathers who are a primary cause of unsafe streets and weak communities.

The married family is probably the best welfare tool but, given that so many obstacles are placed in the way of couples at the starting line, this is bound to impact on poverty and inequality. This is borne out where, for example, using census data and some simple modelling, stimulations are made of what might happen to poverty rates under different assumptions about work, marriage, education and family size.[44] Children whose parents remained single had higher hospital admissions, alcohol and tobacco consumption, truancy and vandalism, early school leaving and poor attitudes to education. Even a doubling of current benefit levels did less to reduce poverty than any of the simulations of behavioural change relating to work, marriage and education. This did not even take into account how increasing cash benefits undermine incentives to work, marry, complete an education and limit family size. All is paralleled by other evidence from both Britain and the US – one with a large welfare state, one without – on how children's lives progress between the ages of five and thirteen.[45]

The policy answers have long been that getting lone parents into work is the answer to these families' drawbacks – and to fulfilling the socialist feminist dream of the fully functional independent mother. According to New Labour feminists, the assumption that men are financially responsible for families "… is at the root of women's disadvantage", and thwarts the ability of "women alone to provide adequately for themselves and their children."[46] With over a third of lone parents completely workless, even in 2014 a Policy Exchange report was reiterating how "high levels of unemployment among them should be a 'key focus' of ministers'" approaches to "addressing the reasons [sic] behind the high-proportion of lone parent households".[47] There was a lack of awareness that this had been tried and tried since the 1980s, not least on an extraordinarily costly scale by New Labour. If lone parents work it is for the minimum number of hours for the maximum amount of wage and child care subsidies. Either the state pays an income or provides for children's care, or both, subsidising people whose earnings are often less than the cost of minding their children.[48]

2.6   AN INSTITUTION DESPISED

Inseparable from the dilution of marriage in law, its penalisation in the tax and welfare system, and the increasing dissipation of its remaining rights, is the denigration and dismissal of the conjugal family in social and political commentary. This has reached levels where any presumption that children have or need two married parents is described (1990) as a "morality from the fairy tales which has to change", or as existing only as "unreal expectations from a mythical past."[49] A statement of values for schools is praised by the *Guardian* (1996) because it did not promote the "traditional cornflake version of a heterosexual married couple and their children".[50] It was irrelevant that this was still the most common as well as the most beneficial kind of family. The Labour Government's *Supporting Families: A Consultation Document* of 1998 poured cold water on the idea that the conjugal family was of much use since, in a roll call of the clichés: "There never was a golden age of the family" and "Lone parents and unmarried couples raise their children every bit as successfully as married parents". What we "need to acknowledge is family structure has become more complicated..." without "trying to turn the clock back...."[51] Family defenders are indicted with setting up an ideal, when 'family' or marriage is precisely a model to be strived for and supported. Instead, whatever is, is right, and right is whatever is.

The tacit consensus of academics, children's charities and public bodies has long been that nothing should be said about the manifold implications of changing family structure, unless it be to cheer it all on. Restrictive definitions of the traditional family to show how unrepresentative it is have proliferated since the time when disintegration of the family was a fraction of what it was later to become. An example might be a boy and a girl both under five, a father in full time work and a completely non-employed mother. The 10,000 in civil partnerships with dependent children made up 1.6% of the LGBT population in 2010 and 0.017% of the UK population. In contrast, these have not been dismissed or insulted for being so few, or received anything remotely approaching the abuse levelled at the conjugal family.

The British Association for Adoption and Fostering is the central organisation for advising and coordinating UK adoption and fostering services, to which all local authority and other adoption agencies belong – providing advice, training and support. Guidelines idealising 'gay' parents (2005) dismissed the two parent conjugal family as invented to further "nationhood and colonial expansion", with no practical purpose apart from being a tool of white male imperialism. Even then it only existed as a "metaphor" for "fixing ideas about reality" and existed, at most, as just a transitional phase in some people's lives,[52] prompting questions about how the majority lived. Does this imply that historically most people never married and had children? Or is family living only a 'transitional phase', because people go through childhood before setting up their own households, are single before they are married and are likely to live widowed at the end of life?

Other accusations had it that only "society presumes heterosexuality as the norm... based on myths and stereotypes" where even gender is "a social, cultural, psychological and historical construct" with people programmed to become or behave as male and female according to how "society perceives their sex".[53]   This raises questions about societies with multiple genders and why everybody has always been so mistaken about two existing sexes with the complementary means to engage sexually and reproduce. This is redolent of postmodern nihilism which, having made its way through the universities, research bodies, leading charities and government organisations, turns to mopping up outliers like adoption agencies.

Ed Straw, chairman of Relate (a relationship counselling service) and brother of Labour's Home Secretary, claimed that marriage was a 'turn-off' for young people, and that traditional family campaigners were 'nuclear family supremacists'. Funding for National Marriage Week (2002) was removed, and subsidies to gay pressure groups and support for non-marital relationships expanded. Relate was anxious to distance itself from its previous being as the Marriage Guidance Council and re-invent itself as something for all and any 'relationships'. The Marriage Research Council was converted to One Plus One. The term 'marital status' was abolished in most government-supported family research in 2003. Statistics now referred to 'couple parent families' and someone who 'lived with the mother' and this might refer to a lodger as much as a spouse. With 'husband' and 'wife' subsumed to 'partners' by businesses, officialdom and media, the most casual of liaisons are elevated by a term that voids relationships of exclusivity and permanence. Even a man sleeping with the grandmother of a girl he is accused of raping and murdering is described as a 'partner' and a 'step-grandfather'.

A reason for ignoring marriage and marital status, along with the accelerating removal of long standing provisions for marriage support and services, is related to their perceived irrelevance, or distraction, from the direct prioritisation of children's well-being. Instead, there is 'parenting' as might exist independently and irrespective of any 'family form' or adult relationship. Jane Lewis, prominent family researcher at the National Centre for Social Research opined: "whether parents are together is only a small part" of how it is "all about children and healthy lives in the broadest possible sense." Beverley Hughes, the Minister for Children (*sic*) declared that "What children need is not marriage" but "love, stability, financial well being and positive parenting." The shift in focus is illustrated by the Green Paper *Every Child Matters* (2003) and the Children Act 2004 which legislated to support the 'needs' of all children and young people – placing their welfare at the heart of services provided by the state. There was total denial of any connection between adult relationships and the well-being of children. As one researcher purportedly explained: "parent to parent relations are too uncomfortable… Anything to do with 'traditional family values' – the department won't go there."[54]

In turn, new 'family forms' have constantly been identified – akin to how 19th century anthropologists sought out lost tribes. Alternative 'families' include those 'living apart together' (LATs) – mostly under 25 and what would have been once described as boy and girl friends or courting couples.[55] The plurality that was ratcheted up in order to slight the conjugal family can be simply stages in the life cycle – or where anyone happens to be at any point in time. We are told:

> There are more opportunities and more choices: marriage and re-marriage, cohabitation prior to or instead of marrying, lone parenting, non-heterosexual couples and families, young people and the elderly living alone.[56]

Trumpeting how 'Traditional family structures are no longer the norm' the five types of household 'tribe' or 'alternatives' that will be coming near you are apparently:

> … the Waltons – three generations living under the same roof; the MEcos – environmental friendly, health-conscious couples living in eco homes; the Tumbleweeders – wealthy people with one or two houses whose children have grown up… (*Sunday Telegraph* 02.03.2014)

And so on goes the nonsense. How does having a grandparent living in, the children growing up, or possession of solar panels, make for non-normative family structures? How does being young, getting old or living alone equate to "more opportunities and more choices" as part of the growing battalions of families of 'all shapes and sizes'? As academics and commentators cast around for different 'family forms', so the concept of family, like a sponge, covers virtually any association, whether "two friends who live together (as with Rent Act protection), the people who work in the office, the local unit of the Mafia, and the family of Man."[57] Demoted to a 'get out of jail' pass, a cat and a boyfriend is a 'family' according to a 'human rights' interpretation to avoid deportation. For those in favour of diverse family forms, on the upside:

> ...the life course is full of exciting options. These include living in a commune, having a group marriage, being a single parent, or living together. Marriage is one life-style choice, but before choosing it, people weigh its costs and benefits against other options. Divorce is part of the normal family cycle and is neither deviant nor tragic. Rather, it can serve as a foundation for individual renewal and new beginnings. Marriage itself should not be regarded as a special privileged institution; on the contrary, it must catch up with the diverse, pluralistic society in which we live....[58]

The future is one exemplified by 'blended families' or a shifting cast of presences in the home who effortlessly combine and separate as will and whim take them. In this world, all is a matter of happenstance. Demographic movements purportedly arose from a multitude of spontaneous personal moves uninfluenced by incentives, disincentives, opportunities, example or suggestions – bubbling up from forces "deep in the fabric of society" (Lord Chancellor Mackay's divorce proposals, 1994) that are conveniently beyond comprehension or control. The cumulative removal of the legal, financial and general support for marriage and married parents is presented as being no more than coincidental. By extrapolating statistical trends, a projection becomes a prophecy and, with 'cornflake' families dead and gone, the future is with 'diverse' pluralism. Change is proof of rightness and possesses an authority of its own that we are obliged to serve since, by reading standards off from trends, an 'is' becomes an 'ought' which we must welcome and expedite for no more reason than that it is happening.

2.7   GOOD FOR CHILDREN

The disparagement of the two parent family and dismantling of marriage has occurred at the same time that evidence has relentlessly piled up showing how marriage's children have better outcomes in virtually every category of life compared to those reared by single, divorced, cohabitating couples, step-parents or with foster families and in institutions. A multitude of large-scale, well-conducted studies demonstrate how those born and raised in an intact marriage with two original parents are, on average, far more apt to avoid abuse, criminality, homelessness and psychiatric problems; to truant less and achieve more educationally, become gainfully employed and, in turn, successfully to raise the next generation – after controlling for economic status and other factors. Boys raised outside of marriage are more likely to be delinquent and girls to be young unwed mothers. The findings have been constantly repeated, are in one direction and have altered little, if at all, over time. For example, for 17,110 under 18s from the longitudinal National Health Interview Study there was a 40% to 95% difference between children with both biological parents compared to those with previously or never married mothers or in step families when it came to school based problems like expulsion, suspension and behavioural referrals. Parental marriage is associated with a much reduced risk of infant mortality and better physical and mental health for children, compared to other types of household arrangement. For behavioural and emotional problems there is a threefold difference.[59]

This applies across the world and in societies which have striven to make one parent families fully functional. Swedish boys with lone parents are five times more likely to die from drug or alcohol abuse and more than four times from violence. Girls are more than twice as likely to die by suicide and three times more from drug or alcohol abuse. Overall, risks of psychiatric disorder, suicide, suicide attempts and self-injury are more than double and more than threefold for addictions.[60] Children who have been through family dissolution show similar rates for lower educational attainment, raised morbidity (overall 50% greater for boys) and reduced life expectancy to the UK and US.[61] This is in the face of confident assertions that: "Swedish evidence suggests that if there is a difference between the children of lone mothers and those of couple families with the same social and economic circumstances, it is that the former are more mature and self-sufficient."[62] This assumption might reflect the belief that developed welfare states such as Britain and Sweden must make the role of parents less important, since money compensates for 'deprivation'. However, that family structure is as or more important in Sweden than in the US or UK underlines its importance for upbringing – regardless, or in spite of, the largesse of welfare.

While most adverse outcomes usually have roughly double or treble the prevalence among children not with original married parents, the exceptions are abuse and homelessness, where rates are vastly increased. A classic study found that preschoolers in step parent homes were estimated with a 40-fold risk of being abuse victims as same aged children with two natural parents.[63] All is at its worst in homes with 'multi-partnered fertility' where mothers have offspring in transient relationships with a sequence of uncommitted men.[64]

Deteriorating home circumstances are reflected in the rising care population and those considered to be 'at risk' (numbers on child protection registers or the subject of protection plans in the UK increased to 50,552 by 2011 – from 32,492 in 2006). Most children who enter the care system come from lone parent homes and a significant proportion of young prisoners, teenage parents, addicts and prostitutes come out of the care system.

There are indications of a substantial rise in psychosocial disorders – or conduct, hyperactive and emotional problems – affecting young people over the past 50 years.[65] The samples used are adolescent sweeps of the 1958 National Child Development Study, the 1970 Birth Cohort Study, and the 1999 British Child and Adolescent Mental Health Study. Conduct problems have shown a particularly strong rise and have long term implications – affecting socio-economic matters (benefit dependency, unemployment, homelessness, early parenthood etc.), poor health and contact with the criminal justice system.

Children's immediate environment might, in turn, interact with factors like the greater availability of drugs, involvement in early sexual relations and deviant gang cultures which generate feedback loops that increase exposure to all manner of risks. Fatherless girls not only tend to fare poorly academically,[66] but to mature and reproduce earlier. Father absence often indicates a stressed or highly conflicted childhood environment. This may be combined with the presence of unrelated men which, in turn, can mean very early sexual development and experience, often coerced.[67] Boys with absent fathers are more likely to have had at least one child by their early 20s.[68] Along with early sex and motherhood for girls goes the 'Young Male Syndrome' of father free boys, where aggressive, risk-taking males have sex with as many females as possible. Gangs offer the immediate social comfort and protection that families, schools or welfare departments cannot provide.[69]

Boys thrive far better with men at home. Involved fathering is: protective against depression or suicidality (thoughts and attempts); imparts views of what is right and wrong, encourages boys to consider being a father themselves and to appreciate how both parents have responsibilities and deserve respect. In one of the more accessible studies, those labelled 'Can-do' boys reported 'Highly Involved' men in their lives (91%) compared with only 9% in the 'Low Can-do' group. In contrast, 72% of those with 'Dad Deficit' were 'Low Can-do' boys.[70]

A quarter of boys with involved fathers had one or more problems, such as an anti-school ethos, depression and trouble with the police. None had all three, compared to more than one in ten of the 'Dad Deficit' boys, where two-thirds had one or more problems. 'Dad Deficit' is reinforced by a lack of constructive compensatory male models to show boys ways of being a man. A spell in jail might be the first time a boy spends with adult males.

2.8   GOOD FOR GROWN-UPS

The costs imposed by men growing up without a constructive place in society are not only well attested by the tribulations of fatherless boys. As well as leaving more children with inadequate supervision, compromised security, fewer adult role models, and less inter-generational relationships, societies in which men are peripheral pose daunting problems of cohesion and control. Those deprived of their role as providers and protectors may become predators themselves. Marriage is the variable with the strongest influence on male crime rates and the foremost reformatory influence.

The longest longitudinal study of crime in the world – based on the lives of 500 criminals who were in institutions in 1930s/40s – identified three factors which led men into law-abiding life – a steady job, a spell in the armed forces and marriage, the greatest of all. Marriage reduced reoffending by 40% after controls for a multitude of other factors. In contrast, cohabitation reinforced or increased criminality.[71] By embodying a set of norms, responsibilities and binding obligations, marriage connects men to the larger community and encourages personal responsibility and altruism. Otherwise, male disengagement from family and work are primary causes of the disintegration of neighbourhoods and areas with concentrations of fatherless families are particularly dogged by problems.

Such findings are part of a similar body of research to that for children, demonstrating the advantages of marriage for adults with large nationally representative, longitudinal studies. All show benefits in terms of lower all-cause mortality compared to the single, separated or divorced, with better physical and mental health, less addiction and exposure to violence.[72] This applies to all ages and both sexes, even if there may be a greater effect for men and especially in mid-life, where the difference approaches threefold.[73] It is seen throughout the economic and ethnic spectrum. Controlling for personality and health risk behaviours reduces but does not eliminate the impact of marital status.[74] A meta-analysis examining 641 risk estimates from 95 publications providing data on more than 500 million people showed how this has been both modestly increasing over time and more rapidly for women.[75] Divorce and separation may have negative health consequences because, not least, fear, hostility and disturbance may affect cardiovascular activity and the immune system.[76] People who live alone are particularly prone to excessive drinking, smoking and drug use, but even non-smoking, non-alcoholic divorced men have twice the mortality rate of married men.[77] Even after taking personality and risky behaviour into account, marital status still affects survival into old age.[78] Not only does single living or being unmarried increase serious risks to health, but the prognosis worsens for both sexes regardless of age and treatment.[79] Men and women separated at the time of cancer diagnosis have the lowest survival rate, followed by the widowed and never married.[80] Marriage is associated with shorter hospital stays and fewer visits, as well as reduced nursing home admission.

Healthy, well-adjusted people are more attractive prospects and may be better able to cope with problems and sustain relationships. However, selection is only likely to be part of the explanation. Marriage's health benefits are significantly reduced the second and third times around.[81]

Again, despite Sweden's reputation as a welfare and equality pioneer, lone mothers' health is as bad as Britain's – with rates of limiting long-standing illnesses between 50% and 60% higher than those for 'couple' mothers, who have the lowest deaths from suicide, assault, homicide or alcohol-related causes.[82] The less than good health of poor lone mothers increases over time and declines for poor mothers in a couple.[83] Since married mothers everywhere have lower rates of depression compared to the single or cohabiting, this has implications for children's welfare.

The UK suicide rate has significantly increased in recent years. There were 4,552 male suicides in 2011 (18.2 per 100,000 population) and 1,493 female suicides (5.6 per 100,000). Patterns by marital status tracked over time show rates among married people to be consistently lower than for unmarried people of both sexes and all age groups. For single, divorced and widowed men aged 25 and over, these were three to four times higher than for married men between 1983 and 2004. For single women the differentials have increased to about threefold even if, for the widowed, these are fairly constant at about two and a half times higher. Similarly, 25% of divorced men have ever had suicidal thoughts, compared with 9% for married men, and 2% of married men ever attempt suicide compared with 9% of divorced men. Among divorced women, 28% and 11% respectively ever had suicidal thoughts or made a suicide attempt, compared with 13% and 3% for married women.[84]

Unsurprisingly, increases in divorce and declines in marriage are the demographics most consistently associated with rises in suicide.[85] Danish studies have looked at time trends over a century (1906–2006), the longest period studied to date.[86] A 1% increase in divorce increased suicides by 0.52% and 1.12% for males and females: a one percent increase in marriages reduced suicide by 0.77% and 0.63%. When factors such as employment status, income, ethnicity, psychiatric history and the clinical history of relatives are included, being unmarried is still a risk factor for both sexes.[87]

Other work using European cross-national comparisons and follow-ups (covering 99.5 million person-years aged 30 plus and 25,476 suicides in Austria, Belgium, Denmark, Finland, Turin, Madrid, Norway and Switzerland) found that while non-married, lower educational groups had a greater increased risk compared to the highly educated, marriage had a generally protective effect for those more exposed to economic vicissitudes and stresses.[88] Stronger welfare policies lacked any buffering effect, although involvement in public religious practices is associated with lower levels of suicidality (ideas and attempts) through the high levels of social support provided by religious communities.[89] This is paralleled by a time-series analysis using available suicide, social, economic and health data which focused on two age groups for whom trends have diverged in England and Wales, or 25–34 and 60+ year olds.[90] Having a child lowers female risk, signalling the importance of attachment and responsibility for others.[91] Expectations that the differential suicide levels of the married and single should have reduced in recent years given the big increase in cohabiting have not been realised.

These and other results offer strong support to a social cohesion model consistent with Emile Durkheim's[92] theory of normlessness and alienation from social structures. The recently increased suicide levels for younger males, probably relate to the declining levels of social integration and recognition, which have not adversely affected older generations to the same degree.[93] There is a failure in Western societies to provide appropriate sources of social identity and attachment for (particularly lower status) males along with tendencies promoting unrealistic expectations of freedom and autonomy.[94] As suicides for men in the 30–44 age group (23.5 deaths per 100,000) have recently overtaken those younger, there may be a 'cohort effect' as a particular generation was most exposed to significant social changes like the decline of male jobs and lifelong marriages. Unemployed and lower skilled men are ten times more likely to kill themselves than affluent men. It is here that unwed births, rising divorce and cohabitation, lone parent households, solo living and 'partnering and de-partnering' with all their stresses and lack of established status or position are concentrated.

None of this denies that suicide rates and suicidality are also associated with personal circumstances and characteristics. There are the family histories and exposure to suicidal behaviour by others and in the media, as well as the availability of means.[95] Most people (estimates of 70–90%) who die by suicide have psychiatric problems – depressive, substance related, anxiety, psychosis, and personality disorders – with comorbidity common and self-harm a major risk factor.[96] This may be an adequate explanation. However, personal afflictions do not negate how suicide is more likely during times of strain or crisis. This is particularly true where there is a lack of social support, and relationships generally have a positive effect through practical and emotional help and can control personally harmful behaviour.[97]

At the most beneficial end of a sliding scale of relationships, marriage focuses social support and constraints in the intimate environment not least because commitment profoundly alters how people deal with each other. The uncommitted are less likely to accept another's control, or change their behaviour at another's expectations or request when no public promise has been made. Although cohabitation has rapidly become an alternative to marriage, it is less advantageous in all dimensions of mental and physical health. Conditional and provisional, with no forward trajectory, it may be entered precisely so that the participants can keep a foot out of the door and be prepared to opt out if times get tough or a better opportunity comes along.

The effects of family structure continually emerge although such a substantial body of evidence is routinely ignored by government and despite the negative ethos of publicly funded university, charitable and other research organisations. It is perhaps surprising, considering the erosion of marriage, and the opposition and disbelief that it has faced, how the advantages for health, longevity, communities and children have endured at all.

Chapter Three

ABOLITION

3.1   ABOLITIONISTS

If the conjugal family is so advantageous, why the antipathy? Even acknowledging the supportive evidence is apt to be ruled out as 'judgmental' and offensive to those who don't fit this pattern. As such, the process of dismantlement, along with the animosity and discrimination that the married family has suffered from the 1960s onwards, is inseparable from the condemnation of marriage as patriarchal and outdated, and as something that traps humanity in an oppressive structure with manifestations which are all and everywhere evil. Rather than a template for sympathetic identifications and attachments which extend beyond their confines, we should instead believe that filial loyalties are the product and prop of malevolent forces. Paternal responsibility is seen as egoistic tyranny and a licence for abuse.[1] Anyone unconvinced suffers from 'false consciousness':

> The institution of marriage has the same effect the institution of slavery had. It separates people in the same category. It disperses them, keeps them from identifying as a class. The masses of slaves did not recognise their condition either. To say that a woman is really 'happy' with her home and kids is as irrelevant as saying that the blacks were 'happy' being taken care of by ol' Massa.[2]

The ideological rationale was largely an amalgam of neo-Freudianism and Marxist revisionism, bequeathing a form of analysis where explanation amounts to revealing how a practice or institution like the family functions to the benefit of an alien, exploitative or controlling class or power.[3] The Frankfurt School (including Theodor Adorno and Herbert Marcuse, 'father of the New Left') inverted Sigmund Freud's claim that civilization necessarily involved repression, principally of sex. For the New Left, history became not so much a struggle between warring economic factions, as a fight against the repression of instinct. As much as the negation of notions of free sex and relationships were thought to stymie the revolution by making the workers docile, so heterosexual marriage was held responsible for "the crucial issue …the intrinsic sickness of society…"[4] The post family future included living communally, gender subversion and multi-partner open relationships, and the abiding necessity to liberate the sexual impulse from its conventional constraints, imploding Western civilisation. Those debating in the 1960s and 70s how to 'smash the family' became tomorrow's teachers, professors, social workers and politicians. One at Goldsmith's College, London, teaching courses in Teacher Education and Women's Studies was in no doubt that "heterosexuality … I would argue that it is the key institution in and through which male power is produced and maintained."[5]

The attack provided the crucible for the emergence of an influential group to replace the hopeless proletariat. This did not just seek equality and the end of discrimination, but challenged the legitimacy of heterosexuality and sought confrontation with it. The opening paragraph of the Gay Liberation Front Manifesto back in 1971 stated how the primary and "long term goal" was:

> …to rid society of the gender role system which is at the root of our oppression. This can only be achieved by the *abolition* of the family unit, with its rigid gender role pattern, by new organic units such as the commune … Children must be liberated from the present condition of having their role in life defined by biological accident….[6]

We saw how Engels demanded that the monogamous family be abolished so that women understand how this economic unit at the heart of class society is basic to their subjugation. Now, not only was there, "the man in charge, a slave as his wife, and their children on whom they force themselves as the ideal models", but the "very form of the family works against homosexuality". Nearly two decades on (1988), Marxist Simon Watney of the Terrence Higgins Trust Policy Group, refers to the conjugal family as a "murderous myth",[7] and a colleague agrees that:

> All workers are victims of the economic, legal and ideological bonds that pressure us to live in nuclear families. All workers are victims of the repressive sexual code imposed by our rulers.[8]

Later, in 1996:

> Marriage is an institution that evolved primarily to ensure the sexual control of women by men, and to regulate the conception and rearing of children. Tailor-made for an old-fashioned, patriarchal version of heterosexuality, it's irrelevant to the vast majority of lesbian and gay people (and to many liberal minded straights too) ... being queer frees us from the rules and rites of hetero culture.[9]

Their 'polymorphous perversity' put homosexuals in the vanguard of the revolution to sexually liberate all humanity. Guilty of none of the sins of heterosexuals, yet persecuted for threatening the gender system, queer males did not have to subjugate women and neither were lesbians dependent upon men, economically, emotionally or erotically. As the Manifesto put it: "we are already more advanced than straight people. We are already outside the family...." Unburdened by exclusive attachments or commitments, homosexuals could pursue sex without constraint, seeking out the randomization of sexual relations and outlets. They met the counter culture command that the individual be 'the centre of my own world' through the self-absorbed hedonism that symbolised an unrepressed, unbounded ego that challenged anything in its way. In the new century, 'gay' films like *Raspberry Reich* perpetuate this genre by combining hardcore pornography with manifesto statements like: 'Heterosexuality is the opium of the people.'[10] This must be replaced by the primal pursuit of inconsequential sex and involved a transformation of intimacy as might subvert modern institutions as a whole. Given that Western civilisation's identity and ways of life are inextricably formed by and fused with Christian values, gay revolution has recently re-allied itself to militant atheism. The link ever was, as when 'Act-up' groups in New York invaded St. Patrick's Cathedral and trampled the sacred Host.

The origins of the condemnation of marriage may now seem arcane, but have to be recognised as foundational to decades of hostility. Over time, attitudes are loosened from their sources, however bizarre, and become incorporated in customary ways of perceiving and reacting to the world. Consider the insistence of Friedrich Engels that the abolition of the nuclear family will make women "understand that it is the monogamous family as an economic unit at the heart of class society that is basic to their subjugation."[11] Then: "the first condition of the liberation of the wife is to bring the whole female sex back into public industry" where the "care and education of the children becomes a public affair: society looks after all children alike...."[12] This will "suffice to bring about the gradual growth of unconstrained sexual intercourse and with it a more tolerant public opinion in regard to a maiden's honor and a woman's shame."[13] Consequently, what has grown ever stronger over the years is an assumption that domestic divisions of labour or household interdependence are unacceptable. All women, including mothers, must work to the same degree as men or more, and be no more or less involved in caring for children who, in early life, should be in state run or regulated group care.

Observing how "social institutions can be oppressive" and that "people can be enslaved not only by ignorance and poverty, but also by conformity", Deputy Prime Minister Nick Clegg's example is "a particular version of the family institution, such as the 1950s model of suit-wearing, bread-winning dad and aproned, homemaking mother".[14] This encapsulates the hated object and suggests the moves necessary for its eradication. Never mind that the "suit-wearing, bread-winning dad" was dutifully supporting the family with his labour, not abandoning it to the welfare system. Predecessor Alan Johnson, Labour Education Secretary, similarly mocked fathers and mothers at Sunday lunch. Would we be better without family meals?

Even those with no particular ideological grudge against the conjugal family have recoiled from association with such a distasteful subject. Governments have disingenuously claimed how they could not afford to restore the resources that families have lost, while responding to pressure groups and guilelessly maintaining that they were acting in concert with inscrutable trends beyond all human influence. More aware of the power of policy to engineer change have been those like the following feminist academic specialising in family studies who spoke (1984) honestly of how:

The idea of abolishing marriage may sound as attractive as the classical communist call to abolish the family, but such demands are probably as [generally] unpopular as they are unrealistic. It would be far more effective to undermine the social and legal need and support for the marriage contract. This could be achieved by withdrawing the privileges which are currently extended to the married heterosexual couple. Such a move would not entail any punitive sanctions [sic] but would simply extend legal recognition to different types of households and relationships, and would end such privileges as the unjustified married man's tax allowance. Illegitimacy would be abolished by realizing the right of all women, whether married or single, to give legitimacy to their children. Welfare benefits and tax allowances would also need to be assessed on the basis of individual need or contribution, and not the basis of the family unit....[15]

Deprive the plant of light and water, and cut the roots. Much was achieved by this time. The measures to come included removal of the married couples' tax allowance, the extension of legal recognition to different types of households and relationships, the end of illegitimacy (1987 Family Law Reform Act) and dismissal of fatherhood. What remains today is, ironically, how welfare benefits given on the basis of the "family unit" are heavily tipped against two parent families. In a familiar pattern, this professor's opposition to "the married heterosexual couple" did not stop her enthusiasm for same sex marriage. Those who so hate the original are only able to support marriage if it is emptied of its former associations, purposes, or (in their terms) its heterosexist and patriarchal constraints.

Using same sex marriage as part of the conjugal family's death by many cuts might hardly suggests that homosexual relationships are much esteemed for themselves. For many on the left intending to obliterate the family and sexual differentiation with any weapons at the state's disposal, including 'equal marriage', gay rights is a flimsy fig leaf. This is an area full of disjunctions and incoherence. Nick Clegg's castigation of 'nuclear' families as a pathogenic 1950s charade went along with his insistence that the homosexual flag fly over Whitehall. As a de-toxifying force, 'gay' marriage enables people to recognise or 'be at ease' with an otherwise tainted institution – as for the authors of *Tory Modernisation 2.0* (David Willetts and Francis Maude, 2013). Overhauling marriage for "those who never traditionally wanted it, and who in many ways are not suited to it reflects the lack, not presence, of value ascribed to marital commitment and the socialisation of future generations."[16] At the same time as any support for conjugality or two parent families might seem somewhat pejorative or divisive, cities (like Liverpool) put homosexual emblems on street signs, erected monuments despite expenditure constraints (a diamanté encrusted rhino in Birmingham to mark the entry to the Gay Village area) and universities celebrated 'Queerweek'.

Significantly, same sex unions made their appearance in Scandinavian countries as the end game of a long sustained assault on marriage which had dismantled this in all but name. Authoritarian and dogmatic, it is true to say that "in no other nation has a reforming party of the political left held such a grip on the state apparatus and on the public perception of policy choices".[18] The politicians' and planners' 'ideology of neutrality' (*sic*) amounted to about the most concerted attempt in history to engineer a liberated sexuality along with freedom of women from child rearing and the demise of interdependence through economic manipulation, social pressures and massive public re-education.[19] All "legislation and all social policy must support a shift from man-the-breadwinner and woman-the-homemaker to a society of independent individuals and of partnerships in which all tasks were shared."[20] There must not be a 'right to choose', since people did not know their own minds and were 'culturally conditioned' into an impoverishing mould. Divorce was available on request and needed no reason(s). The withdrawal of support for two parent families, penalties on non-working 'partners' and very high taxation ensured it was impossible to live on one wage.

Sweden almost brought to fruition what French feminist Simone de Beauvoir desired – that no woman should be able to stay home to raise her children since, were there such a choice, she might take it. The word 'custodian' designated the person closest to a child, a licensed supervisor or agency acting on behalf of the state. By the 1980s Sweden was "moving faster than most other advanced industrialised counties toward a society of cohabiting individuals, temporary families, and single individuals with and without children."[21] Socialised child care turned out to be the most unimaginably expensive and inefficient way to look after children and full time maternal employment sent births plummeting. In response, parental leave expanded – under the euphemism of a 'career break' – with compensation for lost wages not support for parental child rearing.

In Britain the process has been less overt or simply haphazard, leading to claims that the "sheer intractability of the UK's real marriage problem may help explain the bizarre focus on same sex marriage: it is what Freud called displacement activity." Having fixed upon this "pseudo-injustice", this exempted not necessarily hostile, but reticent policy makers from recognising, let alone addressing, a genuine and incomparably more formidable one.[22] It certainly might seem easier, less contentious and cheaper (at first glance, anyway) to earn some accolades by giving homosexuals marriage than to address the wider policy areas which have been consigning marriage to a tortuous demise. David Cameron and some of his allies must have thought so. By the new century, the process of undercutting and dismantling conjugality was accelerating not only with further moves to distribute whatever remained of marriage to others but radical moves which laid the foundations for the transformation to come.

3.2 Advancing Equality

Alongside the dissolution of the conjugal family, homosexual equality moved swiftly forward in the 1970s/early 1980s, was pulled back somewhat in the late 1980s, and by the mid-1990s took off at accelerating speed. Some reforms had little or no bearing on family developments while others – like civil partnerships and removing the need for a father from legislation – had significant implications. Originally, the drive for homosexual rights linked up to socialism and feminist antipathy to the conjugal family. By the new century, adherents had positions in the political establishment that gave them key policy making roles. There was also a profound change of strategy on the part of activists. A tide of recrimination now had it that LGBT people suffered from a host of afflictions, the origins of which lay in the anguish caused by heterosexual society's intolerance, intimidation and discrimination. This brilliant move helped to deliver virtually any demand and meet any complaint, simultaneously engineering a clamp down which censored and then effectively closed down opposition.

The Sexual Offences Act 1967 decriminalising homosexual behaviour (for those over the age of 21) both opened up the public arena to sexual minority pressure groups and was a cause of outrage by reinforcing inequality. In its 'Equality 2000' campaign launched in 1997, Stonewall listed its aims of achieving the following goals by the end of the century: equal recognition for lesbians, gays and bisexuals; an end to homophobic bullying, and the repeal of Section 28 of the Local Government Act 1988.

That notorious Section 28 was characterised as an abrasive and insultingly discriminatory measure, for which politicians have been profusely apologising ever since. To Neil Kinnock, Labour leader, it was a "pink triangle clause produced and supported by a bunch of bigots". It decreed that a local authority shall not: "(a) intentionally promote homosexuality or publish material with the intention of promoting homosexuality; (b) promote the teaching in any maintained school of the acceptability of homosexuality as a pretended family relationship." Promotion had to involve "active advocacy ... towards individuals in order to persuade them to become homosexual or to experiment with homosexual relationships". No action must: "be taken to prohibit the doing of anything for the purpose of treating or preventing the spread of disease". It did not prevent the discussion of homosexuality in classrooms, ban books with homosexual themes, inhibit the discouragement of discrimination, or restrict homosexuals' rights to public services, or prohibit organizations which provided facilities for youngsters who were, or believed they may be, homosexual. Since public bodies 'over interpret' legislation to be on the safe side it largely succeeded in halting or diluting 'gay' campaigns throughout education.

A couple of decades on and it is easy for people to believe that Section 28 along with Section 46 of the 1986 Education Act were stupid bits of legislation dreamed up by Tory backbenchers. In reality, both moves were secured by parents and private members trying to staunch the (publicly funded) anti-family rhetoric and sexually libertarian position of left wing local authorities – often under the umbrella of HIV/AIDs education. As Christie Davies observed: both measures were largely "provoked by verbal attacks on the family by radical homosexual activists, which had dismayed most homosexuals who, above all, wanted social acceptance". It was equally wrong to "assume that the defense of family values was an important source of hostility to male homosexuality in Britain before the 1980s."[23] Repeal of Section 28 was achieved in Scotland in 2001 and England and Wales in 2003. Tony Blair insisted that no child was going to be forced to take part in homosexual role playing as the clause would not be formally repealed until alternative guidance was in place. Activists added demands for an equal age of consent for sodomy with heterosexual intercourse and the repeal of the offence of gross indecency; protection from discrimination in the workplace, in education, and in supply of goods and services; and equal recognition and respect for same sex partners and for homosexual parents and their children.[24] The lowering of the age of consent to 16 (which happened in 2001) was hastened when the European Commission on Human Rights deemed that unequal ages breached the Human Rights Convention, with the Government invoking the Parliament Acts to bypass opposition in the House of Lords. There was a view that 'gay' boys did not need legal protection but, like heterosexuals, more advice on how to do sex 'safely'.[25]

3.3   THE COMING OF GAY UNIONS

Justified on the basis of concerns that there was no legal protection for unmarried partners in circumstances of death or break up, by the end of the last century businesses and services were already starting to provide 'domestic partnership' benefits ranging from pensions to free travel and rights to inherit tenancies. Rights in the occupation of the home in the case of domestic violence were provided under the Family Law Act 1996.

The Civil Partnerships Act granted same sex partners the remaining rights of marriage in terms of property, pensions, tenancies, next of kin and so forth. Those with any qualms about this leading to marriage were told not to worry – the purpose was simply to remove the inequalities that homosexual partners suffered under existing law.[26] In 2004, Lord Filkin, spokesman for the Department of Constitutional Affairs and Parliamentary Under secretary of State, stated that: "The concept of homosexual marriage is a contradiction in terms, which is why our position is utterly clear: we are against it, and do not intend to promote it or allow it to take place." Civil partnership was not "…a drift towards gay marriage. We see it as having value, merit, meaning and purpose in its own right."[27] Back in 1999, Home Secretary Jack Straw stated that his Government had no plans for same sex marriage. Since: "[Marriage is]…about a union for the procreation of children, which by definition can only happen between a heterosexual couple. … I see no circumstances in which we would ever bring forward proposals for so-called gay marriages".[28]

Experience is that granting civil partnerships increases or precipitates pressure for equal marriage, leading cynics to suggest that Government assurances to the contrary were "akin to saying 'no surrender' whilst waving the white flag".[29] Boris Dittrich, a former Dutch politician, explained in 2013 how he successfully introduced gay marriage by softening public opinion by first introducing registered partnerships.[30] Gay rights groups in the UK were also fully aware of the significance.

> As civil unions for gay couples become acceptable in Britain gay rights campaigners will have the strength to eventually push for gay marriage. As Peter Tatchell said at the introduction of the bill, civil partnership will increasingly be seen as 'marriage lite for queers'… activists will claim that straight unions are no different from gay partnerships. The idea of marriage as a ceremony reserved just for straights will come under fire.[31]

Civil partnerships provided further rationale to purge conjugal terms from public discourse where the Women and Equality Unit joined with local authorities in 2006 to remove marriage references in register offices to ensure equality. As signage changed and venues advertised Civil Ceremony and Civil Partnerships licences, marriage suites became 'suites' and 'ceremony rooms', with pictures of brides and grooms disappearing to pre-empt complaints of offensiveness. Redefinitions are public events which change meaning for everybody. In agreement with gay rights groups, amendments to the Matrimonial Causes Act 1973 replaced 'husband' and 'wife' with 'parties to the marriage'.

Straw's comments on marriage and civil partnerships in 1999 bear comparison with introductions to the Children Act 1989 and the 1991 Adoption White Paper in England and Wales, arguing how it would be wrong to exclude arbitrarily any particular groups as prospective adopters. However, some adults' chosen way of life may mean that they are not able to provide a suitable environment for a child's care and nurture. No one had the 'right' to adopt or foster and 'equality' or 'gay rights' or other adult 'rights' issues had no place in children's services. Decisions must centre exclusively on children's welfare.

After 2005, when the Adoption and Children Act (2002) was

implemented and homosexuals acquired the right to adopt, local authorities' duties to 'safeguard and promote' the welfare of 'looked-after children' ran to affirming same sex relations, applying to carers of infants as well as adolescents and young adults. Prospective adopters and foster parents with reservations were struck off the books. The British Association for Adoption and Fostering now judged children's services by how effective they were as agents of social change, by "promoting equality" or "working in a way that challenges discrimination".[32] Agencies and professionals were urged to recruit lesbian and gay carers, avoid words like 'husband' or 'wife' and 'challenge' any 'homophobic' assumptions of families and panel members. After the passing of the Equality Act in 2010, adoption agencies had to serve same sex couples, or close – which some did, and disproportionately those with considerable experience and world leaders in finding permanent homes for even the most difficult to place children (as was acknowledged by the Government, both on the floor of the House, and in Select Committee Reports). Massachusetts, USA, saw a parallel movement forcing Christian charities to relinquish adoption services.

The old 'hallmarks' of the desirable adopter – married, with 'sound moral values' and 'unimpeachable character' – were moribund, even if those who came close to this ideal made good parents and reared well balanced, successful children. Guidelines that older children and birth parents should be consulted over placement, or that there must be as close a match as possible to origins, like those for race or ethnicity, did not apply to same sex adoptions.[33] Magistrates and specialists on adoption panels requesting to be allowed to abstain were dismissed or obliged to resign. The same applied to counsellors who might be uncomfortable providing sex therapy for homosexuals (one lost at an employment tribunal and the Employment Appeal Tribunal and was refused permission to take his case to the Court of Appeal).

3.4   THE HEALTH IMPERATIVE

It might be imagined that homosexual groups would have found it difficult to get into schools after the backlash which led to Section 28 and similar moves in the USA. However, by the first decade of the 21st century, the Sex Education Curriculum CGP Key Stage Four PSHE was providing detailed accounts of anal sex; informing 14–16 year olds about a gland called the prostate near the rectum which provided super exciting sex when stimulated.[34] Peter Tatchell's *Safer Sexy* guide was endorsed by leading medics and, until recently, the NHS page for Young People directed them to the Terence Higgins Trust's *The Bottom Line* and *Below the Belt*. These described a range of same sex activities, many of which are unfamiliar to the general public and which carry a high health risk – such as those involving faeces and urine. Action man dolls presented gay sex in breezy, juvenile terms which connoted adventure and fun: 'arse play without tears'. After some unwelcome publicity, the NHS switched to GMFA (The Gay Men's Health Charity) with much the same 'judgment free' advice for how "to have lots of sex and stay safe."[35] The Terrence Higgins Trust (claiming to be 'the leading and largest HIV and sexual health charity in the UK') now has at least £10m a year from the government to distribute 'health advice'. In 2011, there was an extra £200,000 plus to train 'Sexual Health Champions' aged 14+ to advise fellow pupils.

How was this change of fortunes achieved? Activists in the UK had previously depended heavily upon sponsorship by far left politicians and officials with a revolutionary agenda. As Kevin Jennings, founder of GLSEN (Gay Lesbian Straight Education Network) reported in his 'Winning the Culture War' speech to the Human Rights Campaign Fund Leadership Conference back in 1995, if the opposition could "succeed in portraying us as preying on children, we will lose. Their language – 'promoting homosexuality' is one example – is laced with subtle and not-so-subtle innuendo that we are 'after their kids.'" (GLSEN was previously known as GLSTN, or Gay, Lesbian, and Straight Teachers Network, an organization working to take homosexuality into schools.) The chances of retrieving and building on the educational work of the 1980s or advancing anti-discrimination agendas would be best advanced by using "the opponent's calling card – safety" and explaining "how homophobia represents a threat to students' safety by creating a climate where violence, name-calling, health problems, and suicide are common."

Thereafter, the key to circumvent opposition and gain entry and respectability lay in 're-framing the issue' as either or both a fight for 'social justice' and for health, where accusations of driving LGBTs to mental illness, self-harm and suicide began routinely to accompany complaints about any lack of rights, recognition, resources, or manifestations of disapproval.

Activists became champions of health and campaigners for equality and justice rather than heralds of counter cultural sexual liberation anxious to cast off moral restraints. The GLSEN report: *Making Schools Safe for Gay and Lesbian Youth* threw opponents on to the defensive. With strategy now "linked to universal values that everyone in the community has in common. ...no one could speak up against our frame and say, 'Why, yes, I do think students should kill themselves': this allowed us to set the terms for debate."[36] As succinctly put:

> In any campaign to win over the public, gays must be portrayed as victims in need of protection so that straights will be inclined by reflex to adopt the role of protector. ...The purpose of victim imagery is to make straights feel very uncomfortable; that is, to jam with shame the self-righteous pride that would ordinarily accompany and reward their antigay belligerence, and to lay the groundwork for the process of conversion by helping straights identify with gays and sympathize with their underdog status.[37]

Heart-rending accounts of victimhood to gain attention in the media and public sympathy have, of course, been employed elsewhere by activists using emotive appeals which capitalise on people's compassionate concern. The suicides highlighted by rights groups may have helped attempts to make estranged fathers pay towards their children's upkeep being kicked into the long grass, but the well-tuned strategy of gay activists was more impressive.

What was stunningly influential was *After the Ball: How America Will Conquer Its Fear and Hatred of Gays* in the 90s.[38] Its authors presented their publicity strategy as one of taking any opportunity or venue to confound bigoted stereotypes by putting positive images to the public. Homosexuals would become as founders of civilisation, with a 'gay Athena' theme involving Socrates, Leonardo da Vinci, Isaac Newton and others – whose contributions are enhanced by operating in hostile worlds. They must also be shown as victims of unfairness and prejudice who cannot help how they were born and whose plight is both a civil rights and a health issue. Especially through targeting naïve audiences like children and playing on maternal sensibilities and sympathies, heterosexuals may come to adopt the role of protector. Critics must be silenced by demonising them as bigoted, 'jamming' any negative information, and mobilising political campaigns –

as would happen with opponents of same sex marriage. Confronted with stories of youth who had suffered, opponents would have to attack people who had already been victimized, which put them in the bully position.

Nonetheless, this strategy was not without risk. After the American Psychiatric Association removed homosexuality from its diagnostic list of mental disorders in 1973, the consensus among professionals as much as activists was, and often still is, that evidence had conclusively shown that homosexuals did not have abnormally elevated symptomatology compared with heterosexuals.[39] Actually, what had been shown was that homosexuality did not equate with mental illness, not that homosexuals, on average, were *just as* psychologically healthy as heterosexuals.[40] Publication of research suggesting otherwise was discouraged. An unforeseen consequence of the HIV/AIDS epidemic was the proliferation of material on the health status of men who have sex with men (MSM),[41] and much evidence accumulated on the downside.[42] Drawing upon a mounting number of studies, a scientific consensus emerged that: "Homosexual orientation . . . is associated with a general elevation of risk for anxiety, mood, and substance use disorders and for suicidal thoughts and plans."[43] Purportedly, no other social group of comparable size experiences such intense and widespread pathology, whether physical, mental or emotional and covering a wide range of disorders. This is unrelated to any notion or re-classification of homosexuality *per se* as a mental disorder.

It is apparent from any perusal of the existent mass of literature that the matter of same-sex tribulations in terms of their existence – let alone cause(s) – is incredibly various, complex and difficult to estimate. There are problems gathering a reasonably representative sample due to low population representation, along with questions about what qualifies as homosexual or homosexuality. Matters are complicated by the abundance of advocacy research aimed at politicians, legislators and practitioners which, despite poor scientific credentials, often makes the media and contains strong recommendations for policy and legal changes. Tellingly, it is in those areas where differences between the well-being of heterosexuals and homosexuals have been most highlighted and used for political effect – particularly suicide – that information is simply missing (sexual orientation is not on death certificates).

When the better conducted research is sifted out, higher rates of mental disabilities for sexual minority populations are demonstrated across the globe and in large scale longitudinal studies that have followed the same people over the life course. Higher odds of any lifetime disorder are usually more consistent and pronounced for sexual minority men than women and for bisexuals. Behaviour has the highest association with morbidity, compared to 'orientation' or 'identity' *per se*. A meta-analysis from 1999 to 2005 which met rigorous inclusion criteria covered totals of 214,344 heterosexual and 11,971 non heterosexuals. The prevalence of mental disorder, substance misuse, self-harm and suicide attempts was from one and a half to over four times that for heterosexuals in the recent past and over a lifetime. For England and Wales, rates of self-harm and levels of psychiatric morbidity as defined by the Clinical Interview Schedule (CIS–R) are 42% for homosexual men, 43% for lesbians and 49% for bisexuals compared with previous community surveys of (predominantly heterosexual) people which recorded 12% for men and 20% for women.[44] The very high rates recorded here might owe something to biases inherent in sampling; other figures for lifetime prevalence put mental health problems at two thirds for homo/bi-sexual adults in the UK compared to one-third for heterosexuals.[45] The highest comparative rates of mental abnormality are found in the longitudinal New Zealand Christchurch Health and Development Study – a 21-year long project involving a birth cohort of 1265 individuals (the small proportion of LGBs limited the precision of this study).[46] Other results from recent nationally representative household surveys whether in the US, Australia or elsewhere, show homo/bi-sexual men with a 3-fold or more increased risk of major depression, high levels of distress, substance use disorders and self or other-ratings of 'fair' or 'poor' for mental health.[47]

Significant differences between homosexual and heterosexual health ratings can decline depending on the scope and representativeness of the studies and perhaps also with the subjects' ages. There will be many homo/bi-sexual people who experience few or no problems.

Although the health outcome differences referred to above represented a significant departure from earlier insistence that homosexuals and heterosexuals were equal in health status, it coincided with the advancement of a *minority stress* hypothesis.[48] This holds that excess morbidity is caused by homophobia and generally discriminatory social conditions – ranging from threats to civil rights to criticism or unwillingness to accept same-sex behaviour as healthy and normal. The 'minority stress' hypothesis:

> ...extends stress theory by suggesting that conditions in the social environment, not only personal events, are sources of stress that may lead to mental and physical ill effects. Social stress might therefore be expected to have a strong impact in the lives of people belonging to stigmatized social categories... [inducing] changes that require adaptation and can therefore be conceptualized as stressful.[49]

It is unselfconsciously explained how this "conceptual framework for understanding this excess in prevalence of disorder in terms of minority stress" has been adopted as "the basis for a review of research evidence, suggestions for future research directions, and exploration of public policy implications."[50] One study states that: "Due to stigmatization, isolation, abuse, and violence, psychological problems are more common among persons whose sexual orientation is homosexual."[51] Its own data fails to bear this out and nor does other work it quotes.[52]

The minority stress hypothesis starkly contrasts with the stance of earlier gay rights warriors and radical agitators of the 1960s/70s that the state and the 'moral majority' should not interfere and let them get on with whatever they wanted. However, appeals to 'minority stress' avert the risk that, by reporting negative health outcomes for a minority group they, or aspects of their lifestyles, might become (re)pathologised. It also suggested that homosexuality now had to be present and reflected throughout all social institutions if destructive 'myths' were to be dispelled and youth made happy with a homosexual orientation as 'natural' and 'normal' as a heterosexual one which now included 'proper' marriage. These developments drew the gay movement "into an ever closer, increasingly needy relationship to the state, since the cultivation of lifestyle 'identity' requires continual external support and flattery".[53] With LGB people "at risk for excess mental distress and disorders due to social stress" it follows that "psychologists, public health professionals, and public policymakers [must] work toward designing effective prevention and intervention programs."[54] In one study, homosexuals are immersed in such a swamp of intractable problems where, in a convoluted sequence, discrimination and the 'internalized' homophobia that it purportedly generates is responsible for HIV/AIDs:

...lifelong effects of social marginalization or stigma may work to create high occurrence of psychosocial health problems among urban MSM, problems that in turn function in an additive manner to raise levels of high-risk sexual behavior and thus HIV infection itself.[55]

Elsewhere, claims are made that, despite "millions of pounds being spent on HIV awareness" there are rising rates among young homosexuals because this cannot overcome the legacy of children "growing up fearful of being terrorised just because of the way they were born". To stop their self-esteem being undermined parents, school governors, local councillors or former pupils need to go to their local school and get them to "tackle this insidious form of bullying".[56]

To stem the toll imposed by homophobia, social toleration of homosexuality (or other alternatives) is insufficient, considering how this is compatible with moral disapproval. Since targets of homophobic bullying are assumed to be the same as those with same-sex orientation, they can be helped by organisations able to ensure a positive transit into the 'gay' world.

Encouraged to label 'sexual minority' pupils, the Primary School Sex & Relationships Education (SRE) Pack tells teachers and school governors that "at least 5% of the children in your school" are "gay or lesbian". Teachers and parents are recommended to put their queries to activists as recognised 'experts'. If the latter are up to date with the latest output on homophobia, they will have been informed how those growing up with "autonomy-thwarting parents... may be prevented from exploring internally endorsed [sic]values and identities and as a result shut out aspects of the self perceived [sic] to be acceptable."[57] Confused about their orientation, young people may embrace the views of their elders.

Under guidelines from the Department of Education on sex and relationships involving 'affirmative' teaching, there are also proactive measures which include the incorporation of gay themes into the broader curriculum and wider school environment, from sport to books to posters to prize giving: celebratory events like 'gay history month'; hardening sanctions for instances and indications of 'homophobic' bullying and more help for pupils and parents with 'coming out'. It is reinforced by Section 149, Equality Act 2010 (reinforced by the Equality and Human Rights Commission in 2012), where the Public Sector Equality Duty requires educational authorities to advance 'equality' for gay, lesbian and transsexual pupils. With 'due regard' to the need to eliminate discrimination, schools are required to publish information demonstrating their compliance – parallel to the monitoring of pupils' commitment to equality and diversity, and mandatory training of staff and governors under anti-racist educational directives. This has given Stonewall a free pass to go into schools and create LGBT supportive environments.

Nick Clegg emphasised back in 2008 not only how schools must tackle homophobia, but that Ofsted – or the 'independent and impartial' official unit for 'inspecting and regulating services which care for children and young people' – should assess how well schools were managing the problem. Ofsted obediently set out to investigate and advise on bullying in its report *No Place for Bullying*. No other form of bullying apart from the homophobic variety seemed to merit concern and there was even a complaint that some schools' programmes were 'too general' for failing to focus specifically on 'incidents of homophobia'. This mainly seemed to relate to young children casually using the word 'gay' (meaning trashy) and failing to see it as a matter of much concern. The sample of 1,060 pupils revealed factors centred on families, names or background, race or religion. Serious bullying centred on appearance – red hair, being tall or small, 'fat' or 'skinny', wearing glasses or (more in secondary schools) clothes, hairstyle or accessories such as unfashionable bags. (The all-Party Parliamentary Group on Body Image and the Central YMCA has recommended putting 'appearance-based discrimination' on the same legal basis as race and sexual discrimination. Calling someone fatty would be a 'hate' crime.) This is the greatest cause of bullying, featuring prominently in known young suicides, and is the form that appears to be growing. Elsewhere, Mencap claims that 82% of those with a 'learning disability' are bullied.[58] For six out of ten it means being physically hurt, sometimes badly, with some afraid to leave their homes.

Since Ofsted could only find three primary and five secondary pupils seemingly bullied over sexuality, it mused how friendship and appearance issues "may mask issues around perceived or actual sexuality". Whether words should or should not be used is one matter, so is whether this is equivalent to intimidating or attacking others, or whether the subjects or bystanders become mentally ill or suicidal. Bullying now covers: "somebody said something I did not like."

The gay affirmation policies purporting to prevent everything from suicidality to sexual disease by attacking endemic homophobia lack any legitimate medical basis or accreditation, and groups such as the Samaritans are not involved. As elsewhere, little or no empirical evaluations are conducted involving issues promoted by pressure groups. Moreover, it goes unacknowledged how the 'gay rights' movement is hardly a *bona fide* human rights movement and nor does it represent all people with homosexual tendencies, but is an ideological and political force.

Others condemn the way that education as a "most effective instrument for solving the problems of society has acquired the character of an unquestioned dogma" and that it has become a place where "anti-intellectual and anti-traditionalist sentiments of curriculum engineers have converged with the instrumentalist and managerial ethos of ... social engineering policy-makers."[59] The manipulation of feelings and attitudes of school children is an intrusive and coercive indoctrination project. Teachers are subservient to a growing body of external managers and 'experts' from advocacy groups, whose emphasis on 'compulsion' is characteristic of their engineering objectives, whether promoting self-esteem, guilt over global warming, or dealing with drugs, crime, obesity, racism or homophobia.

As health came to have such an important role alongside equality in the drive for same sex unions and other recognition, it also played a major part in building the bulwark against free speech which more or less eliminated public discussion at the introduction of SSM. As the job of the police and the courts turned to preventing people having their feelings hurt, 'hate speech' can be perceived as a particularly serious matter if this threatens to harm the minds or mental health of minorities – or even kill them. It is easier to close down debate, cut off dissent or expressions of opinion that some people may not like if it is for a benign purpose and attractive to 'right-thinking' people who want to help minorities and save them from opposition or abuse.[60] C.S. Lewis observed that a tyranny sincerely exercised for the good of its victims may be the most oppressive. The emphasis on sexual 'orientation' itself helps to put critics into a position where they are seen to attack other people rather than specific behaviours.

Shifting "the lens of pathology away from the same-sex-attracted individual and toward the individual who holds ill will toward her or him",[61] accusations of homophobia mark how opposition or disagreement is seen not merely as prejudiced or morally wrong, but sick, insane or otherwise indicative of pathology. Martin Kantor described *homophobia* as "…a phenomenon closely related to, or in some instances exactly like, emotional disorder or mental illness."[62] After all, a phobia is an irrational fear, or abnormal response to everyday circumstances or objects, like open spaces or spiders. Consequently, it is necessary to "uncover and treat the raging psychoneurotic tide" by recognising that the "culture of homophobia is as much a product of the individual as individual homophobia is the product of its culture." With chilling analogies to Stalin's Russia and Mao's China so, using "clinical judgment", consideration "must be given to the homophobe's current reality, such as where he lives and where and with whom she works."[63] However, unlike claustrophobia, arachnophobia or any of a multitude of other irrational fears, homophobia is not recognised as a mental ailment or illness. Instead, homophobes are wicked and liable to be sent for re-education or prosecuted, rather than pitied as sick and inconsequential – bearing resemblances to beliefs about demonic possession. Its capacity to make its objects ill and put their lives at risk is akin to casting the evil eye.

As much as recognition and approval of homosexual lifestyles are needed lest sickness ensues, victimhood justifies abuse and even tyrannous reactions to the slightest non-conformity. The British Association for Adoption and Fostering called critics 'retarded homophobes' in its *Pink Guide to Adoption for Lesbians and Gay Men* and on the Be My Parent website since, coming from the perspective of a homosexual 'carer', it reflected the strength of feeling against homophobia. (BAAF apologised to people with 'learning disabilities'). A columnist was accused of 'inciting hatred' against transsexuals because she defended (in the *Observer*) a colleague who made a crude joke. Ex-minister Lynne Featherstone demanded the sacking of both the journalist and the paper's editor.

Following on from civil partnership legislation, the Sexual Orientation Regulations (SOR) introduced in 2007 had criminalised discrimination in the provision and delivery of goods and services on the basis of sexual orientation. Stonewall attempted to attach a speech hatred clause, banning any jokes, discussion or criticism which might offend homosexuals – which could result in seven years imprisonment. It was defeated in the House of Lords with Lord Waddington's free speech clause then and on further occasions when the Labour Government tried to re-introduce it. Labour promised to reverse it, by invoking the Parliament Act if necessary. Angela Mason from Stonewall set up the Equality and Human Rights Commission, aimed at developing a single Equality Bill, and this emerged in 2009. Other provisions accumulating over time enable action to be taken over unacceptable speech. In 1986, legislation from 1839 was revisited to remove the requirement for there to be an *intention* to cause a breach of the peace. Abusive or insulting behaviour might be penalised if it was within the hearing or sight of anybody likely to be caused harassment, alarm or 'distress' even if they did not themselves complain. There is also the Malicious Communications Act of 2003. Material need not even be within sight or hearing of *anybody at all,* as would happen when a housing manager was downgraded and had wages slashed for posting a comment on his personal Facebook page – outside of work time – criticising proposals for same sex church ceremonies as 'An equality too far.' His employers worried about losing their gay rights charter award if he went unpunished.

The term 'insulting' was removed (2013) from the 1986 legislation due to concern over the trivialities targeted. (A tipsy student spent a night in a police cell for calling a horse 'gay'.) But other options remain for pursuing grievances in law and, as or more importantly, throughout employment and service provision. The Equality Act 2010 made it unlawful to harass, victimise or discriminate against anyone because of their race, gender, sexual orientation, age, or disability. As the lives and integrity of minorities have come to receive special protection, this represents retreat from principles of equal and fair treatment before the law which were defended for centuries in the Anglophone world. The creation of categories to which special sensibilities and rights are attached gives some a higher 'blood price' than others. Like old status differentiations between slave and freeman, serf and lord, personal attributes are more important than the fact of being human.[64] There is no limit to the subcultures or individual proclivities or features that might be similarly privileged. Moreover, offence was no longer a matter of objective fact, but *subjective* evaluation.

So it came to be that only the strictest adherence to gay or LGBT perspectives might be tolerated throughout education, media, social and political elites. In a Sovietised "current climate of opinion in Europe … no politician, no journalist, and no churchman can risk inviting this [homophobia] charge."[65] Like racism, any questioning of the orthodoxy on homophobia is proof of homophobia. Ordinary people are also ill equipped to confront the onslaught of propaganda and the threat – if not reality – of legal force and workplace coercion.

3.5   DELETING FATHERHOOD

As developments in the tax and welfare system made marriage a material liability for child rearing and officialdom progressively deleted recognition, the next step was to separate parenthood from pairing and rewrite both as little more than legal convention.[66] Jack Straw may have commented about same sex marriage being an oxymoron since marriage was about procreation which only opposite sexes could accomplish. However, marriage would be extraneous to making fathers once they were no longer needed. Officially, they were already being eased apart. A man might still be acknowledged as a father if he is married to the mother of the child, but other ways of registering an interest were now available, like simply signing a birth certificate. This did not involve him in any commitment to the child's mother, let alone living with or supporting it. If Maggie Gallagher already failed to see how legalising same sex marriage might weaken an institution that has already been legally 'abolished' or a contract that was now unenforceable in law, how could it be refused if paternity became irrelevant?

Severance of fatherhood from marriage was certainly attractive to those for whom fatherhood, as a central feminist grievance, was just patriarchal capture. New Labour feminists were inspired by the works of Martha Albertson Fineman, a leading authority on feminist legal theory and family law, directing the Feminism and Legal Theory Project which she founded in 1984.[67] Assuming that the conjugal family was already a thing of the past so, following Engels, she insisted 'society' be responsible for children's welfare and sustenance. She is one with Matthew Parris in wishing to downgrade what was left as the 'sexual family' – and whether the parties were married or unmarried, 'gay' or 'straight' – to liaisons involving, at most, private contracts. Whatever Jack Straw and others might say, agitation to move from 'inferior' civil partnerships to 'real' marriage began with the Department of Trade and Industry where Patricia Hewitt, for whom marriage 'doesn't fit any longer, particularly not in Britain', resided as its Secretary. Hewitt had appointed radical activist Angela Mason from Stonewall as Director at her Women and Equality Unit, with links to those like the academic Carol Smart (mentioned above) and Polly Toynbee on the *Guardian*. The Family and Parenting Institute arose on the ashes of the research body The Family Policies Studies Centre. Under Katherine Rake from the Fawcett Society, the emphatic message was that policymakers must not try to encourage 'traditional families' but seek ways to support 'different types' of family.

Contraceptives, abortion and commercialism may also have helped to separate childbearing from marriage, leaving males expecting 'no-strings' sex and absolved of responsibility for untoward pregnancies – 'it's her fault, she should have....' In turn, something put about in every form of media and throughout education is that sex is a recreational activity and nothing to do with making babies. If an AI (artificial insemination) child is missing a father – so are all those children of divorce and temporary affairs. Since contraceptives allowed heterosexuals to pursue sex as an end in itself, divisions or categories of relationships looked increasingly artificial with heterosexual patterns of behaviour seemingly becoming more and more like those of homosexuals.[68]

In 2008, the Parliamentary Committee charged with considering the government's Draft Human Tissue and Embryos Bill recommended that the 'need of a child for a father' be removed from the Human Fertilization and Embryology Act 1990. Section 13(5) stated that 'A woman shall not be provided with treatment services unless account has been taken of the welfare of any child born as a result of the treatment (including the need of that child for a father).'

Allegedly the first in the world, it was part of the same paradigm shift that excluded adoption agencies which insisted on placing children with a mother and father. The recommendation reflected how it had not simply become discriminatory to deny homosexuals a 'right' to make a family from donated gametes, but how the homosexual lobby now led or formulated policy affecting families. Design must override biology, gender and kinship, as gay experience with 'families we choose' delinked family from gender, blood and kinship. In vitro fertilization, surrogacy, gamete intrafallopian transfer, and the possibility of cloning would bring procreation to singles and same sex couples. It might institutionalise the way that, in Foucauldian jargon: "Post-modern living arrangements are diverse, fluid, and unresolved, constantly chosen and rechosen and heterorelations [*sic*] are no longer as hegemonic as once they were".[69] Angela Mason had already cast lesbian and gay parenting as heralding the appearance of the *scientific baby and the social family* that would kill off patriarchy and genetic parenthood by overriding sexual reproduction and biologically based ties.[70]

Law signals what is believed to be in the interests of children generally, not only those being adopted or engendered artificially, and influences the way present and future generations think about children, families and parents. The 'need for a father' might have been only casually observed by some organisations offering assisted reproduction to women, but replacing fathers with 'supportive parenting' (resembling 'stake holder') was a momentous step to delete the key rationale for opposite sex parenthood.[71] A 345 page consultation document contained ten pages of legal jargon defining mother, father and parent, and another four of explanatory notes since "[s]taff working in fertility clinics need clear guidance on the many different scenarios they may encounter..." as it tiptoed around a minefield trying to redefine categories once self-evident.[72] Prefiguring the central argument for same sex marriage, the pretext for removing the 'need for a father' or any provision that mentioned a mother, a father or the sex of a parent, was that retention contravened or was inconsistent with the "wider government policy of promoting equality".[73] Symptomatic of a 'me first' society, and for the "presumed interest of a tiny minority of adults and children in non-standard households, it insisted that understandings of parenthood for *all* children must be changed".[74] A child would no longer have any "right to be raised in a society whose legal, religious and cultural institutions intentionally promote, and do nothing to compromise, the principle that children should be raised, as nearly as possible, by the parents who conceived them."[75]

The health minister Lord Darzi resorted to the familiar excuse of historical inevitability. He considered it "unnecessary, inappropriate and out of step with practice in society" to take account of a child's need for a father as a social standard, and particularly since many homes now had missing fathers. The majorities opposed to removal were "from the older generation" whose opinions were invalidated by their age.[76] To Evan Harris the legal need for a father was judgemental and anachronistic and an "unjustifiable discrimination against gay people and single women".[77] If, according to the UN Convention of the Rights of the Child, Article 3, 'In all actions concerning children…the best interests of the child shall be a primary consideration', Parliament appeared to suggest that children were better off without fathers and certainly that "[a]bolition was an essential measure in ensuring that the child came first".[78] Harris insisted how "research evidence shows that it is the quality of parenting that counts, rather than gender" or family structure. How might that be? He pointed to one small study, conducted by researchers closely involved with lesbian parenting – and how this suggested that "children do very well brought up by lesbian couples and solo parents, so good riddance."[79]

Initially, this study involved 70 children in all, or 21 solo DI (donor inseminated) mother children and 46 DI married family children. After drop-outs, the solo sample was at most 17, too small to yield results of any value.[80] The study purportedly showed how solo DI mothers were better parents because their two-year old children had lower levels of problems and more competence than those of married DI mothers. Even the researchers made the study's limitations abundantly clear and how "it is plausible that differences went undetected due to the relatively small sample size of solo DI mother families." Moreover:

> …all the measures were parent-reported, which creates a real possibility of social desirability bias (Colpin, 2002). This may be particularly likely to occur among solo DI mothers, who have chosen two controversial pathways to parenthood: solo motherhood and DI.

The solo mothers had actually shown *lower* levels of interaction and sensitivity when the babies were one year old.[81] There was a refusal to acknowledge that a tiny study based on self-reports from a few prosperous mothers does not make the rule, but could equally be an exception that proves the rule. Indeed:

> The absence of negative outcomes… lends further weight to the view that solo DI mothers represent a specific subgroup of single-parent families (Weinraub et al., 2002), *and cannot be likened to single parent families resulting from separation, divorce or accidental pregnancy, who often show poorer outcomes for children and their mothers* (italics mine).[82]

Otherwise:

> Large-scale epidemiological studies of father-absent families consistently show that children raised by single mothers are more likely to show psychological problems and are less likely to perform well at school....
>
> The specific concerns centre around the effects of growing up in a fatherless family and are based on the research ... that shows negative outcomes in terms of cognitive, social and emotional development for children....

Not least:

> ...from the perspective of the child, it is not known what the psychological consequences will be of discovering that their biological father is an anonymous sperm donor whom they may never meet.

Society's experience with 'alternative family forms' suggested that "these families will not, on average, be able to reduplicate the investments and consolidation of which has been in the past the primary goal of marriage."[83]

In being a 'rights' issue, the 'best interests of children' (born or unborn) did not actually figure in the change to the 1990 Act. In the wake of the legislation, the number of lesbian couples given IVF rose nearly fivefold overall compared to 18% for heterosexual couples. By 2012, NICE, the NHS watchdog, issued draft guidelines stating that gay and lesbian couples should be offered IVF – if they had already tried to have a baby previously through a private clinic. After an appeal to the European Convention on Human Rights, NHS Trusts would have to meet the costs involved.

It is inevitable that some children will always be brought up by lone parents. But was it relevant to whether a policy should dispense with the need for a father as a condition for effectively all reproduction? Should the law not focus on the broader social impact that legal presumptions about parenthood and marriage have on the conduct of all parents if 'mother', 'father' or 'biological' parent(s) are rendered politically incorrect locutions'?

Having wiped fathers from the statute book, Evan Harris moved on to guide a motion though his party's conference in 2010 calling on both marriage and civil partnerships to be opened for both same and 'mixed-sex [sic]' couples.

Also in the wake there were moves towards the eradication of anything that might associate procreation with parents of different sexes or convey heterosexually oriented concepts. In 2012, the NHS in Scotland removed the word 'Dad' from a 220-page pregnancy handbook (*Ready, Steady Baby*) for fear of giving offence after receiving one complaint. The cost was £100,000 for the new 'inclusive' version using 'partner'. Did it matter that this might be undermining the significance of marriage, collapsing it into unions of convenience that might be a one night stand or an agreement to run a market stall? Did it matter that mothers and fathers are 'carers' or 'parent A and parent B' like interchangeable, anonymous donors at the IVF clinic?

With fathers now optional or surplus to child rearing, marriage as a parental alliance lost its foundational rationale. With law having done so much to reduce marriage to a flexible terminable agreement, same sex marriage seemed almost ineluctable.

Chapter Four

Deconstruction and Reconstruction

4.1 The New Orthodoxy

Whatever might eventually emerge about David Cameron's launch of equal or same-sex marriage, the ground was clearly well prepared by the cumulative dismemberment of the conjugal institution. "Everybody knows that marriage is no longer for life" says one columnist – joined, in the same edition, by another pronouncing "… as wedlock itself becomes a thing of the past…."[1] With its distinctive connections to permanence, exclusivity and procreation removed or diluted, the view of marriage as an affirmation of adult emotional intimacy had seemingly overpowered the understanding of a committed public bond. In this context, SSM was not "an outlandish deviation; it is the logical result of a popular contemporary view of marriage as a personal right of the individual, created for the individual, for purposes that the individual alone defines."[2] With spousal and inter-generational dependence and mutuality disdained by state and market and certainly not to be 'privileged' or recognised compared to other 'family forms', the result may have reduced the idea of marriage in the minds of many to "little more than an affectionate sexual relationship of tentative commitment and uncertain duration."[3] Given expectations of lavish parties on top of the penalties in the tax/benefit system, it might perhaps be better eschewed.

The new orthodoxy of marriage as necessarily just about couples is something upon which the most conciliatory revisionists and extreme transformers can agree. Hence, the unselfconscious statement from David Cameron's favourite think tank, Policy Exchange, that same sex unions simply meant that more will "participate in marriage" as, "in law [it] would *remain* a partnership between two people" (italics mine).[4] This is in line with that Massachusetts *Goodridge v. Department of Public Health* decision defining marriage in terms of a 'private', 'intimate', 'committed' and 'exclusive' union that is 'among life's momentous acts of self-definition.' It was 'incorrect' to claim that children had anything to do with it. Instead, the attachment of the partners to one another was the *sine qua non,* or so the state must now insist.[5]

The British government's consultation paper on same sex marriage in 2012 made no mention of creating a family, procreation, mothers and fathers, children, family ties or communities, except to refer to the needs and aspirations of the "transgender community".[6] With marriage just "about two people who love each other" and enabled to "express their love and happiness", children are not "significant in terms of the continuance of a group identity – national cultural or familial", only as personal add-ons like a dog or carpet.[7] Any idea that marriage serves Edmund Burke's alliance between the unborn, living and the dead is left well behind in amnesia concerning any historical, philosophical, moral or cultural legacy that relates to social being.

The 'couple paradigm' has been characterised as: "'me', 'me', 'me' marriage" – representing the "victory of marriage-as-narcissism… primarily about an individual being comfortable and happy, even if it is just temporary". No longer indivisible from the "process of having, educating, caring for and imbuing with goodness children who will go on to become the future guardians of society", marriage is just "about you and your lover … ensconced in a loving bubble…." or "vacuum … wrenched from any broader notion of social or generational responsibilities …merely to satisfy an individual's own needs."[8] Elsewhere, the critics of the 'me' model are cast as despotically inclined for seemingly believing that:

> …government has a paternalistic right and duty to impose misery and deprivation on those who do not elect to conform to a particular model of family life… and that individuals may not be trusted to decide for themselves what mode of living will give them fulfilment and satisfaction.[9]

But, if marriage is deprived of any social meaning, then equal access is "in certain measure self-defeating" since no reason remains to have it at all.[10] And, if there is nothing special about the original institution, why not include whatever permutation or participants anyone might fancy to merge into that melee of 'families of all shapes and sizes'? In the circumstances, it is surely contradictory to claim:

> The struggle for same-sex marriage rights is only one part of a larger effort to strengthen the security and stability of diverse households and families. LGBT communities have ample reason to recognize that families and relationships know no borders and will never slot narrowly into a single existing template.[11]

There is puzzlement here about why not everyone had kept up with this agenda, since civil rights, "alongside the … growing tolerance for diverse living arrangements, makes any rejection of same-sex marriage seem all the more in need of explanation and comprehension."[12] A reply might be 'why keep up with these trends?' Why assume "the permanence of some of the current drifts in demography, reproductive practices, and the pluralism of family forms"? Why assume that "since these social realities have already evolved, then same-sex marriage is all the more justified"? Did it not occur to anybody to question the "use of law to reinforce those forces in civil society intent on reconstructing marriage…"?[13]

4.2   Wanting What You Hate?

Why, if at all, and in what form, was marriage desired by the 'gay' constituency itself – and how has this been justified by arguments emerging before and during the installation process? What were the conceptions of the prize and on what terms, if any, have they thought that marriage applied to them? Had homosexuals "simply looked at the revolution heterosexuals had wrought and noticed that, with its new norms, marriage could work for them, too"?[14] Why would anybody even want the leftovers when marriage had been so diminished and in retreat? Opponents characterised SSM as an absurdity pushed by opportunists.[15] It was "not the urgent need of an oppressed minority but the desire for a definitive symbolic statement … a powerful social statement, the supreme capitulation of a reluctant straight population."[16] It goes "far beyond the original plea for tolerance and an end to legal persecution… [to] a demand for approval, the glorification of a lifestyle which is, by definition, childless."[17] Is it really just another scalp for the pole? Put less confrontationally, and on a reconciliatory note, equal marriage delivers complete dignified accreditation and full social status or membership of society, a strong sign or full endorsement for homosexuality as perfectly acceptable.

For heterosexuals, there has long been a relatively broad consensus about sexual fidelity, sharing resources, providing mutual support, and aspirations to lifelong duration.[18] Same sex marriage's exponents have been under little pressure to explain or clarify their demands. Post Section 28 guilt probably played a role when it came to backing away from asking searching questions, or accepting at face value justifications about equality, sharing in benefits or combating prejudice. Right up into the new century, gay activists invariably wanted nothing to do with marriage – unless it was destruction. The message was as Tatchell framed it: "innovate, don't assimilate" with the vision of:

> …a new sexual democracy, without homophobia, misogyny, racism and class privilege. Erotic shame and guilt would be banished. There would be sexual freedom and human rights for everyone – queer, bi and straight.[19]

Who wants to buttress and reproduce heterosexual beliefs, standards and roles, says Nancy Polikoff in 2003.[20] Even in 2012, lesbian feminists like Julie Bindel were true to tradition by still calling for marriage to be outlawed for everybody, as a necessary condition for the liberation of women from patriarchal oppression.[21]

If marriage was anathema to homosexuals, then seeking to be admitted to it looks akin to turkeys voting for Christmas. The great advantage of gay relationships purported to be how they can be tailored to individual requirements. People can make it up as they go along, without promising sexual exclusivity or to share their worldly goods if they do not want to. Instead of arguing for something that throttles the free libidinal impulses of humanity, 'gay' people should continue to argue for abolition of this and gender 'boundaries'. Who could "possibly disagree with equality"?

asks Peter Tatchell:

> I can! Call me ungrateful and pushy, but I don't like the way the lesbian and gay community has dumbed-down its aspirations to the flawed goal of equal rights. Whatever happened to the lofty ideals of gay liberation and sexual freedom? [22]

Andrew Sullivan, a leading gay intellectual, sympathises with this approach, there being:

> ...something baleful about the attempt of some gay conservatives to educate homosexuals and lesbians into an uncritical acceptance of a stifling model of heterosexual normality.[23]

Hence, 'no' is often the answer to whether those who have enjoyed unusual freedoms within their own communities, [are] ready to pledge the permanence and faithfulness that traditional marriage requests.[24] Equality within the system and its mores "involves conformity to their [heterosexual] rules" and is no recipe for liberation, but rather "capitulation!"

> ... the equal rights agenda is not about respecting difference, but obliterating it. ...equality is essentially a policy of social assimilation. As a condition of equal treatment, we homosexuals are expected to conform to the straight system, adopting its mores and aspirations. The end result is gay co-option and invisibilisation [*sic*].[25]

Or it is "the surrender of our unique, distinctive queer identity"; involving "the abandonment of any critical perspective on straight culture". Some may unthinkingly want their place in the heterosexual sun, while others who refuse to become facsimiles of straight morality stay marginalised and excluded. The:

> ...unwritten social contract at the heart of law reform is that lesbians and gays will behave respectably and comply with the heterosexual moral agenda. No more cruising, orgies or sadomasochism! In return, the 'good gays' are rewarded with equal treatment. Meanwhile, all the sex-repressive social structures, institutions and value systems remain intact, and the 'bad gays' remain sexual outlaws.[26]

Some homosexual groups detected a recent and "dramatic shift in the homosexual zeitgeist" away from the revolutionary impetus – something aided and abetted by increasing concessions and equality moves. If integration looks as if it might be replacing 'fighting the system', it is because some activists had moved:

> …from defining our needs on our terms, to meekly falling in with the prevailing heterosexual consensus. The dominant gay agenda is now equal rights and law reform, rather than gay emancipation and the transformation of society. That political retreat represents a massive loss of imagination, confidence, and ethical vision.[27]

Seen as abandoning the real struggle, those homosexuals arguing for inclusion are castigated by others for pretending that homosexuality is a trivial and largely meaningless difference within the general run of humanity – about as interesting or banal as left-handedness. As much or more than by persecution, 'gay' people are depicted as marginalised by this 'normalisation'.[28] Reflecting a "faith in the liberal-humanist and liberal-capitalist projects" this project amounts to "a desire to 'sit at the table' (rather than 'turn the tables')" along with opening up new niche consumer markets. While admitted to have been partly "a response to the perceived opportunities opened by a multiculturalist paradigm", it is condemned for allowing homosexuals to "maintain their identity" only to the "extent that they are prepared to subscribe to the dominant values of the society". The want "to obtain a 'piece of the pie' by appeal to a hegemonic order" instead of challenging "the structural roots of inequality".[29]

On the other hand, it is the explicit aim of destroying marriage which has alarmed critics outside any 'gay' nexus. This recalls the buildup to Section 28, as consternation spread at the ways in which homosexuality had been used as a weapon *against* the family and given a starring role in school children's liberation. Surprisingly, joining in here with conservative groups are some voices within the 'gay' rights camp objecting to calls to 'eliminate' marriage. They believe that such rhetoric threatens to "keep gay people marginalized for centuries, if not forever". Some also even question why revolutionaries of any persuasion feel obliged to identify themselves with homosexuality. They accuse abolitionists of giving credence to the

US Republicans like Rick Santorum and Michele Bachmann – who see homosexuals as "inherently subversive and revolutionary, longing for the basic institutions of the heterosexual world to be torn down". Consider those people marching with giant phalluses or exhibiting themselves in little posing pouches who "didn't choose marginality and exclusion." It:

> …would be a betrayal of them – not a fulfillment – to choose to stay there, angrily raging, when American society is on the brink of letting them into its core institutions, on the basis of equality, at long last.[30]

The conciliators have a point. By the end of the last century, explicit abolitionism was looking somewhat like a cultural insurgency led by tiny professional urban elites.

4.3   THE THIRD WAY: EXPROPRIATE, CHANGE, DISCARD

The view of many is that homosexuality may not be so much the conjugal family's nemesis, but rather a model for sexual and familial relations of a superior order. Whether they explicitly signed up to this agenda or not, it is a perspective shared by politicians and academics (to a greater or lesser extent) who support SSM. They too desire to overhaul or eliminate marriage as hitherto understood. These *transformers* repudiate the ostensibly conservative revisionist case if this means parity on straight terms, within a pre-existing framework of values and laws devised for heterosexuals and with the institution continuing much as before – unlikely as this might be.

This may not quite be grasped by those who think that, as we seem to have moved on from the 'smash the family' screams of the counter culture rebels, sexual minorities have little appetite for the 'outsider status' and have instead bought into a default of conventional monogamy. In reality, overhauling marriage on gay terms helps to keep homosexuals in the vanguard of a new sexual order, as the legacy of the counter culture meets up with 21st century diversity objectives and appeals to rectify injustices. As what might otherwise be a self-evident contradiction becomes an achievable goal, a real opportunity is perceived to move back to the future, with a "re-awakening of the radical Utopian vision that fired the lesbian and gay liberation movement of the early 1970s", something "lost when civil rights and law reform came to dominate lesbian and gay campaigning…."[31]

In a process of creative destruction, conferring the "legitimacy of marriage on homosexual relations will introduce an implicit revolt against the institution into its very heart." Sir Adrian Fulford, homosexual High Court Judge and judge on the United Nations International Criminal Circuit promised that: "Pink Law will not be an anomaly but rather the shape of things to come."[32] Michelangelo Signorile, a prominent US activist, urged lesbians and gay men to demand the right to marry as the most subversive action they can undertake so that they may radically alter an archaic institution or 'debunk a myth' and transform the notion of 'family'.[33] Put forthrightly by Masha Gessen, gay activist, at the Sydney Writer's Festival in May 2012, she declared – to loud applause – how it was "a no-brainer that [homosexuals] should have the right to marry, but I also think equally that it's a no-brainer that the institution of marriage should not exist. … (F)ighting for gay marriage generally involves lying about what we are going to do with marriage when we get there – because we lie that the institution of marriage is not going to change, and that is a lie" rather than "creating fictions about my life." There was little or no criticism of Gessen.

Andrew Sullivan in his *Virtually Normal* argues, like Peter Tatchell, that homosexual relationships are superior to heterosexual monogamous marriages since:

> …there is more likely to be greater understanding of the need for extramarital outlets between two men than between a man and a woman; and again, the lack of children gives gay couples greater freedom. Their failures entail fewer consequences for others.[34]

Extolling the "spirituality" of "anonymous sex", Sullivan thinks that using marriage to export this "openness" of same-sex unions and the "gay relationship's necessary honesty, its flexibility, and its equality could undoubtedly help strengthen and inform many heterosexual bonds".[35] Allies include Yale University's Jonathan Katz who insists that same sex marriage could topple sexual exclusivity as "one of the pillars of heterosexual marriage, and perhaps its key source of trauma".[36] Peter Tatchell lays the blame for modern health problems upon the "eroto-phobic and sex-negative nature of contemporary culture" and its supposedly destructive:

...puritanical attitudes ...evident in the censorship of sexual imagery, the inadequacy of sex education lessons, and the criminalisation of sex workers and consensual sadomasochistic relationships.

Homophobia "damages heterosexuals" because these are "denied the pleasure of relationships with half of humanity ... depriving themselves of some wonderful sexual and emotional opportunities".[37] (Among the curiosities of our age is the dogma – from a mash of Freud, Marcuse, Reich and Kinsey – that people are somehow unfulfilled or stunted without outlets for sexual 'release'.)

By "rejecting equal rights within the status quo" and remaining "true to the radical ideals of the gay liberation pioneers", open same-sex relationships will be the model for all relationships, promising "a much broader and more empowering vision of human rights and sexual liberation that will benefit people of all sexualities". Marriage as "the life-long union between a man and a woman" will move towards its demise as it becomes a transitional phase or gateway rather than a barrier to the free, promiscuous life. Therefore:

...our transcending of heterosexual mores is a positive and immensely liberating experience. ...queers tend to be more sexually adventurous with a wider repertoire of sexual behaviour, less bound by the strictures of traditional morality, and more experimental in terms of relationships. ...we've adapted much better to safer sex [*sic*]. ...the fact that homosexuals are different from heterosexuals is a real virtue that we should all be proud to shout about.[38]

Since Tatchell believes – following the tradition of Alfred Kinsey – how everybody is born with the potential "to be queer" he challenges any idea that "exclusive heterosexuality is somehow natural and eternal, and that lesbian and gay sexuality is inevitably destined to remain a minority sexual orientation". (Kinsey believed that without social constraints and hysteria, humans would be sexually 'active' from babyhood with both sexes and other species.) Instead:

In a society where there were no pressures or privileges associated with being straight, a lot more people would be queer or bisexual. ...

the struggle for lesbian and gay liberation is in everyone's interest. It is about the right of everyone to experience the joys of queer desire.[39]

Similarly, Professor Roger N. Lancaster looks forward to "more options, not fewer" as gay marriage promotes "a more benign view of variation" where it would be "a shame if gay marriage were to make the world a drabber, more conformist place" because homosexuals take on the inhibitions of married straights.[40]

These views are shared and promoted – albeit more calmly and persuasively – by prominent academics like Anthony Giddens. As Tony Blair's or New Labour's court sociologist, he wielded considerable influence on the characterization of its 'Third Way'. Along with feminists like Harriett Harman and Patricia Hewitt, they took the legacy of the counter culture to the heart of government. Bragging that his (*sic*) discipline of 'critical social theory' "outflanks Marx from the Left"[41] by dismissing its discredited state control of industry, he re-sold the substitution of sexual for economic oppression – both of the female by the male and in a general Neo-Freudian sense.

In Giddens' suave retro version of liberation, "marriage in the traditional sense is disappearing and the gays are the pioneers" of modernity, or the "prime everyday experimenters" and exponents of a "pure relationship".[42] This is one of sexual equality bound only by 'communication' and unconstrained by dependencies or anything beyond the 'project of self'. Completely unregulated by rules or external standards, it lasts only so long as the parties feel they are getting the right levels of satisfaction in what Jeffrey Weeks terms 'families of choice'.[43] With "living arrangements ... diverse, fluid, and unresolved, constantly chosen and rechosen"[44] Giddens' and Weeks' experimenters are re-affirmed as the elite troops of that emerging 'diversity' of 'family forms' that establishment researchers and pundits have proclaimed as the innovative successors of the conjugality that they have been eager to dispatch. Predictably, those 'going steady' or in friendships, sexual or otherwise, began to be characterised in academic literature as 'families of choice'. (Lifestyles News, Britain in 2008.)

The conjugal family is caricatured and condemned as a left-over of 'beleaguered tradition' or violent fundamentalism in contrast to the forthcoming 'transformation of intimacy' where couples inhabit a 'democracy of the emotions'.

...we know that family life in earlier times often had a quite pronounced dark side, including the physical and sexual abuse of children, and violence by husbands against wives.[45]

Does not Giddens know that babies and children are disproportionately abused and killed by stepfathers and – even more – by mothers' boyfriends? Does not Giddens know that the US Department of Justice's statistics show that married women have less than half the possibility of suffering domestic violence? Does not Giddens know that the British Crime Survey indicates that married women have the least risk of domestic violence? Does not Giddens know that in feminist Sweden lone mothers are the most vulnerable to threats and violence, with a five-fold risk compared to other women?[46] Does not Giddens know that Europe's Family Policy Institute (FPI) reports that while 11% of Spanish couples cohabit without marriage, they account for 58% of the most violent crimes between couples? For every protection order issued for married couples, there are ten for cohabiting couples. For every homicide in a marriage, there are 12 in unmarried unions. Spain's recent increase in such homicides is largely explained by how these have jumped 45% for cohabiters, while falling 15% for married couples.

For those seeking to change it, the new paradigm of marriage will not presumably have any "dark side" when marriage ceases to "be regarded as a special privileged institution" and is made to "catch up with the diverse, pluralistic society in which we live...."[47] Progress is the emergence of a 'decentred' or 'plastic' sexuality freed from any procreative needs and resulting obligations. Viewed as more progressive than sluggish heterosexuals, homosexuals with multiple partners, fleeting contacts and 'episodic gay sexuality' are admired for their disassociation from 'differential power' or oppressive 'gendered' sexuality. A post 1960s bathhouse model of sex opens up the possibility of the wholesale 'democratisation' of life, cutting the tap roots of heterosexual and parental power in exchange for self-actualisation and an 'equalised interpersonal domain'. With alternative sexualities, or swinging, polyamory and bondage/domination/sado-masochism (BDSM) – now a growth industry – we are reminded how much homosexuals have blazed the trail for all.

The aspiration of sex unbound by moral, social, religious or even personal ties or duties would constitute a precedent for human society. None is on record that has not regulated or placed limits on sexual behaviour in some shape or form, with marriage more about restraining lust than encouraging it. In fact, marriage's diminution, along with the promotion of self-gratification, has led to less happiness and more isolation and distress for both adults and children.

Again, if all relations are reduced to self-interest, why enact any marriage policy at all? The transformers are effectively one with abolitionists who reject marriage as a useless or unjustifiable fiction. For those seeking equality on these terms, marriage is superfluous. It cannot become a free association of persons and an area of free expression without becoming meaningless and imploding, as activists have understood. The warning resounds that if "society becomes increasingly focused on individual and immediate transitory desires ... the consequences of same-sex marriage may be severe indeed."[48]

4.4   Velvet Revolution

Privatisation sounds better than abolition. If "any sexual relationship (no matter how idiosyncratic and no matter how far removed from the continuation of life)" has the same value as traditional marriage..."[49] why has the state any reason to concern itself with its nature, advent or dissolution, or what its constitution and parameters might be? This might be a view shared with those heterosexuals who really see no need for marriage (or, indeed, children) and maintain that this is unwarranted 'state interference'. At least (it is said), let everybody create their own tailor-made partnerships or forms of association, choosing their rights from a menu, unbiased by any social or economic pressure to conform to any particular pattern.[50] With affection unconstrained and all responsibilities freely entered, maintained or discarded, public policy would be neutral between different expressions of individual choice.

> – then it can be argued that a society meets its obligations to promote and protect basic human needs and capabilities associated with sexual intimacy by simply giving individuals the necessary freedom to connect with potential sexual partners. ...a perfectly libertarian state, where any consensual sexual relationships are tolerated but where no relationship

is recognised or privileged over any other, would satisfy that minimum moral threshold.[51]

Seen through this "normative lens of the market sex is simply another good or service around which people can contract to bind themselves."[52] With nothing to embody in public institutions, here is freedom of choice without regard for the nature of the choices made or how these might be evaluated independently of a person's wants. After all, prenuptial contracts allow parties to define their own rights and responsibilities and lump sum exchanges provide divorcing parties with a clean break to marry anew.

Since to remake marriage as a personal contract is to abolish it, so homosexual columnist Matthew Parris suggests that the word be completely removed from legal language in exchange for 'civil union' – with 'registering' or 'declaring', not weddings. The "rights and duties marriage entails are no longer shared between the State and all its citizens" anyway, given how Muslims and Catholics have different understandings. Any residual matrimony would reside with the Church, Synagogue and Mosque. Otherwise, the state might provide contracts specific to individual requirements – a true liberation "from the need to conform to the notion of 'marriage'". Britain's 85 sharia courts are already issuing divorce settlements, adjudicating domestic violence and deciding access to children, or enforcing sexual inequalities with ministerial approval.

Otherwise, it is imagined that citizens could choose from something like conventional 'marriage' contract to ones between dependants, friends, relatives or lovers. Wrong to privilege certain kinds of intimate relations over others, these 'partnerships' or 'co-dependencies' must presumably be available to threesomes, foursomes, communes or any other group(s). Relationships of convenience need not have a sexual component or intimacy at all, or any meaning or purpose apart from "enforceable understandings about property, eviction or inheritance". [53] Someone might well ask why couldn't "business partners declare their relationship a marriage and save on the insurance premiums?"[54] Parris speaks of how "some of these agreements might be (as now) deemed to apply even when not specifically sought" – which threatens to impose something which nobody chose and whose form is indeterminate.[55] Marriage may have gone, but it leaves behind a cornucopia for lawyers – and a highway open to the state.

Fluid partnerships certainly fit with the demand of the National Coalition of Gay Organizations, back in 1972, for the "repeal of all legislative provisions that restrict the sex or number of persons entering into a marriage; and the extension of legal benefits to all persons who cohabit regardless of sex or numbers. Group marriage could comprise any combination of genders."[56] There are boasts that an 'open', 'progressive' model is a significant improvement on traditional marriage, and constructivist views feed liberationist notions that everyone should move beyond binary distinctions to inhabit a fluid bisexuality. This was supported by leaders of the women's liberation movement like Barbara Ehrenreich and Gloria Steinem, the founding editor and publisher of *Ms* Magazine and signatory to the manifesto *Beyond Same-Sex Marriage: A New Strategic Vision For All Our Families and Relationships*.[57] The *Future of Marriage* by Jessie Bernard was influential in the 1970s, with its 'future of options' for 'new forms of relationships'. These could include communes and polygamy, group marriages, weekend marriages, non-sexual marriages, no or limited commitment marriages, 'swinging' and more. Proponents of such diversity may claim never to have:

> ...understood the distinction of 'primary' partner. Does that imply we have secondary and tertiary partners, too? Can my primary partner be my sister or child or best friend, or does it have to be someone I am having sex with? I have two friends who have lived together for 5 year and raised a daughter. Are they not partners because they don't have sex? [58]

Martha Ertman, US law professor, wants polyamatory organised on the model of limited liability companies. Judith Stacey – a prominent New York professor and gay rights champion who testified before Congress against the Defense of Marriage Act – wants marriage to have "varied, creative, and adaptive contours...."[59] She hopes that same sex marriage will promote a "pluralist expansion of the meaning, practice and politics of family life" where "some might dare to question the dyadic limitations of Western marriage and seek some of the benefits of extended family life through small group marriages."[60]

Using the same formula that familiarised the public with homosexual relationships and, substituting 'poly' for 'gay, Hollywood is giving polygamy a makeover with dramas like *Big Love*. Intimate relationships between three or more people – "is quite normal already, it's just not out of the closet yet", say the stars of a US reality TV show *Polyamory: Married and Dating* (2013–14). Living as a threesome with a child, they are "spreading the gospel of polyamory, hoping to speed up societal acceptance of this kind of set-up" as a "new paradigm" as ABC's spokesman explained. Rights to multiple concurrent relationships were already showcased in 'progressive' mainstream publications like *Newsweek* (28th July 2010: 'Only you and you and you'). Making headway in Europe, Germany's popular weekly magazine, *Focus* (May 2010) pondered "How Shall I Love – and If I Shall, How Many? Why emotions, sex, and our relationships are going to change." By August 2011, polyamatory had made it to British ITV. We meet three women who all share the same man. They consent to this, so what's the problem? More, they each have other 'partners' and these 'partners' have other 'partners'. There is an *Independent* write up of three lesbians in an open 'poly' (February 2012) and talk of the advantages for children of being brought up in a group, as it was for the communes of the 1970s. This seen as a 'back to the future' drawing on those early socialist fantasies of communal matri-centred child-rearing. A *Guardian* writer exclaims: "What's wrong with polygamy? ... a child brought up by three loving parents would have some quite big economic advantages, and humans have cooperated in child-rearing since the year dot." Therefore, "…if three, or four, or 17 people want to marry each other simultaneously and equally, why should they not be granted the same status as two people…?"[61]

The lawsuits are already under way abroad, not least for the right to include a third party who was used as a sperm donor or surrogate mother to produce a child. In the USA, the organisation Beyond Same-Sex Marriage has more than 300 LGBT and allied scholars, activists (including Ivy League professors) calling for the legal recognition of sexual relationships involving more than two partners. University of Calgary's Elizabeth Brake recently suggested 'minimal marriage,' where individuals have legal relationships with more than one person, reciprocally or asymmetrically – choosing the sex and number, the type of relationship and which rights and responsibilities to exchange with each other.[62] If any parties wanted to make adultery a wrong their contract would specify this. In the *Independent*

Terence Blacker condemned lifelong commitment as an "absurd illusion" as "marriage rarely lasts for life". He does not explain what "rarely" means.[63] Is he thinking of one or five per cent, or the reality which is in fact sixty per cent or thereabouts? On the basis of such assertions, are policies apt to be made. Temporary contracts could dispense with divorce and can always be renewed if both parties like how things are going. Two years after Mexico City legalised 'gay' marriage, these were next in the queue.

If people would still be free to contract according to a Christian, Muslim or any other system, does each impose its definition and conduct of marriage on the parties involved? Can Catholicism impose a no-divorce rule and Islam polygamy – with state backing? Would there not be accusations of discrimination made against religious bodies that do not 'marry' any combination of people, or lawyers who refuse to draw up certain kinds of contracts? This might illustrate how, once marriage becomes detached from complementarity and procreativity, it unravels, with little or nothing to stop it dispersing into a variety of relationship contracts, linking any number of individuals in any conceivable combination.

4.5   'ME ME' MARRIAGE

The parties to proposed contracts of convenience inhabit a highly individualistic free market of human relations devoid of inter-generational ties and responsibilities. The family as once the clearest example of an institution based on a transcendent bond gives way to autonomous individuals with random living arrangements.[64] Since marriage's significance and existence depended upon explicit public recognition so, aside from any remaining religious injunctions, the ability to make any normative judgments about this or its substitute(s) must wither and die. Emotions are inconstant anyway, and inherently fragile emotional or romantic attachments or individual projects would make less and less sense. If you did not specifically contract to look after a sick 'partner', presumably you immediately divorce if they become ill, or if they do not bring in the amount of money they agreed they can be dispensed with.

All this suits those who – and whether or not ostensibly 'postmodern' – deny that there are any objective conditions that a relationship must meet to make it distinctive of a certain kind of union. Instead, it is whatever anyone says it is and therefore nothing in particular. As people try living together (or not) any way that takes their fancy, absent is any notion that the quality of the choices made might be evaluated independently of a person's wants, and thus according to some moral base.

> The individual agent is thought to be the source of all moral value and for him or her to be constrained by convention, which may perhaps lack an immediate justification, is regarded as an unconscionable loss of liberty. Individuals are encouraged by opinion leaders to be 'autonomous' and 'authentic' and to resist the demands for conformity. …a regrettable concomitant of this liberation has been the near abandonment of the notion of personal responsibility for action, which was a strong feature of *traditional* liberalism.[65]

It is difficult to see how freedom itself can arise if people are removed from all those unchosen aspects of themselves which are preconditions for human autonomy. Under a privatised system, people would lack any reference points for beliefs and behaviour which exist only insofar as they are externalised in a common life. People can no more make it up as they go along than infants locked in a cellar will spontaneously speak French or Mandarin. If families and relationships "know no borders and will never slot narrowly into a single existing template", there is no template.[66] Admittedly, what often lurk in the background are those naturalistic notions about instinctual forms which (helpfully for the optimistically naïve) obviate the need for culture or consciousness – where, for example, people 'bond' like ducks.

The reality is that human beings must discriminate or draw lines and boundaries all the time. Otherwise, human life would be reduced to Kipling's cat that 'walks by night, and everything to him is the same.' The meaning of an individual action is found "not in the private desire which prompted it, but in the public custom which gives it form", where the obligations of marriage are not contracted between partners, but imposed by the institution, so that when a man and a woman marry, they enter something "not of their own devising".[67] Monogamy requires a culture that recognises this in formal institutions, which are created to embody and carry on systems of meaning and provide guideposts for decision making. Experienced as existing outside individual consciousness, these make marriage more durable than cohabitation or relationships that have no reference beyond the here and now. Indeed, if marriage is just a "legal construct with totally malleable contours" how could the law ever get it wrong?

> No one deliberates or acts in a vacuum. We all take cues (including cues as to what marriage is and what it requires of us) from cultural norms, which are shaped in part by the law. Indeed, revisionists themselves implicitly concede this point. Why else would they be dissatisfied with civil unions for same sex couples.[68]

The view that the law should be neutral is logically impossible anyway.

Criticising supporters of (heterosexual) marriage as "judgmental", Labour leader Ed Miliband claimed that "what matters most is the strength of your commitment and whether you provide a good and loving home to your children"; something that "comes in different forms."[69] Where does Miliband think people get notions of commitment from, or make choices other than within a specific, socially embedded tradition? What are "different forms" of commitment? Why is commitment found in some circumstances more than others? Who sets the example to help teach further generations what commitment is and is not? Those who believe that the absence of regulation will make personal relations loving and happy fail to answer the question of how people might live together in the absence of anything that shapes and sustains a common life. Ironically, even Parris is credited with acknowledging that:

> No man is an island.... There are ultimately no "private" acts. Everything we think, everything we say and do, however privately, shapes and influences us, our families and friends, and so touches the world outside. It is just fatuous to pretend that if a great many men are unashamedly making love to other men, however privately, that is without impact on the whole of society....[70]

The more that *ad hoc* unions are made up by participants on a case by case basis, the less is people's understanding of just what kind of relationships, if any, they are to form and sustain, as the essentially public nature of marriage is obliterated. Once monogamy or commitment is defined out of marriage, people are no longer educated in their meanings – precisely what transformers are aiming for.

4.6 WHERE ARE THE CHILDREN?

All the suggested 'individually tailored relationships' and variants of 'coupledom' dispense with any mutual assumption about reproduction.[71] Missing is all recognition of how generational obligations "are independent of individual preferences: they have a past and a future beyond our control. …they provide a stake in the future that is beyond individuality…."[72] Yet, when generative connections become incidental or forsaken, any imperatives to care or connect to anyone or anything outside our impulses and beyond our lives dissolve. With adult needs prioritised, no norms create conditions for the children seemingly left exiled from kinship in ways previously unknown to human beings. As David Cooper (*Death of the Family*) sought back in 1971:

> Nothing is to be left to the family. Mothers, fathers, brothers, sisters, sons and daughters, husbands and wives have all predeceased us. They are not there as people to be left anything of oneself or left anywhere in oneself…. The age of relatives is over because the relative invades the absolute centre of ourselves.[73]

Children's interests are not served by the vagaries of private choice and convenience. Andrew Sullivan admits that the lack of children in same sex relationships effectively frees the partners from responsibilities. Is this model fit for parents? When the sexual alliance is separated from the parental alliance, children are severed from their uncontested claim on their parents' (especially their father's) care and protection. Cast aside is the persistent core value of family systems throughout the world, and the root of kin altruism – that the people who give life to the child are the ones to care for it and will, on average, invest most in its well-being.[74]

Autonomy might be foremost, but what is often forgotten is that only those societies which reproduce survive. Even libertarian bachelor boys have to rely on other people's offspring to keep their world going. Free marketeers are fond of insisting how children are just another consumer good, and no business of those who do not acquire them. However, children can never recompense their parents for giving them life and rearing them,[75] let alone pay interest on the investment, and nor are the childless ever going to pay back those who provide the means for sustaining society and everything they derive from it. As John Locke insisted, a different logic applies to the domains of market and to 'conjugal society' because of their differences in nature and purpose. Children are not parties to a contract. Instead, the raising and education of children imposes a sacred obligation or "a charge so incumbent on parents for their children's good, that nothing can absolve them from taking care of it." The market is premised upon the equality of all competent adults to exercise property rights, while the family has to accept the reality of inequality and protect the most vulnerable of humanity.[76] The market runs on self-interest and self-preservation. This is contrary to the guiding principles of duty and altruism in the realm of family.

Children require their parents out of necessity, even if the parents themselves go on shopping around for a better deal or new excitements and adventures. John Stuart Mill observed how matters of divorce were usually discussed "as if the interest of children was everything, and that of grown persons nothing" and how it often seems unreasonable and even oppressive that parties to a marriage contract should be bound by conditions external to their wills. But protests about limits to freedom are checked by considerations of how calling someone into existence puts others under an obligation. Claims to personal liberty may be strong but, if children are to develop into free beings themselves, they need a lot of help. If this is not forthcoming, it is "... a moral crime, both against the unfortunate offspring and against society."[77] Made victims of the exercise of arbitrary adult power:

> ...children lose something that is fundamental to their development – the family structure. The family is a scaffolding upon which children mount successive developmental stages ... It supports their psychological, physical and emotional ascent into maturity ...Whatever its shortcomings, children perceive the family as the entity that provides the support and protection that they need.[78]

Market and family coincide in requiring autonomy from outside interference to function effectively, unless it is to correct specific abuses. The invocation of political powers in these pre-state domains carries risks, except insofar as it is to protect life, liberty and property and ensure that an impartial arbiter oversees the activities of equals. Ironically, it is the belief that nobody has any business imposing any particular vision of moral order that threatens to destroy freedom's domains.[79] Libertarians appear to be oblivious to how marital dispersal or de-regulation might sabotage the limited government they seek. If child welfare is an issue, the state is the more obliged to use its power to identify who or what a child's parents are or take over its care, shifting this away from the civil society that preceded it. There is a tie up here with leftist beliefs, where the renunciation of any integration of sexual behaviour, procreation and care by natural parents, supposedly enables us to focus on our 'collective responsibility' for children and other dependants. The move is away from notions that the needs of children are a private concern of the parents or, where men are concerned, that fathers have to be 'brought into' families in any way at all. For feminist legal theorist Martha Albertson Fineman, men who wish to be involved with children have to negotiate their way into the 'care-giving dyad', where the stand-alone mother involves anyone else as she sees fit.

Mundanely, if *all* parents, in and out of individually tailored 'partnership contracts', are treated as singles supported by the welfare system, how much does this cost and will it provide a subsistence base or a living standard commensurate with that of the childless? Would there be a distinction with others still holding a marriage certificate (if extant) – which entails that the welfare system count their earnings into allocations for their family (as at present)? Otherwise, the effective abolition of marriage obviates any possible recognition of mutual support in the tax system or elsewhere. With no general obligation to share resources or any duty of one to any other, this also ordains the abolition of pension rights and exemptions from inheritance taxes – otherwise matters would become impossibly complex, cumbersome and expensive. Many perks from employers to staff were traditionally made because some employees bore the cost of families. Where firms have extended such rights (e.g. travel permits) to civil partners and cohabitants, they have then been pressured to give child allocations for friends so as not to be 'discriminatory', so they end the privilege.

4.7   Contracting Children?

Whether compatible or not with complete and universal state funding of breeding females, the purely 'affectional' couple concept of marriage might point towards an 'affectional' conception of parenthood. Where adults acquire obligations to children separated from their own intimate lives, any notion that the people who made the baby are its parents moves aside to accommodate the diversity of personal choice. Those who think up the baby – not bear or sire it – are the parents. "The mind is more important than the body, especially to people with PhDs."[80] In his world of adult hedonism, Anthony Giddens envisages that parents – two, three, four or more – could make contracts and negotiate parental authority with children.

Does it follow that 'parent' or child can terminate a contract, and would this be on agreed or imposed terms or a matter of unilateral choice, like no-fault divorce? How any of this would fit with adult union agreements is presumably a matter for lawyers. Parenting contracts or not, how can adult relationships with their choices, changes and conflicts remain separable from the child's security and welfare? Giddens acknowledges that children need protection and care and does not refute the research on child rearing outcomes, but this does not disturb his case. Responsibility can always be handed to the state to pick up the pieces.

The sunny interpretation has it that what this portends is a "democratization of personal life" as freedom of expression and choice proceed hand in hand with democracy even "in the global political order at the most extensive level."[81] This amounts to compliance with international law, whose functionaries provide for children. What still goes unrecognised is that, when the ideology of choice and liberation from constraints gains strength, a free society cannot be sustained by atomised individuals. Therefore, public controls become ever more trivially authoritarian and intrusive as with Clem Henricson's proposals for a more "significant role for the state in supporting and regulating family relationships" or defining "the role of parents vis-à-vis their children", within the "continual promotion of a socially liberal perspective…."[82]

Fluid sexual relationships or a core 'family' unit of mother and offspring do not only present no barriers to state intrusion. Little is left to create the moral sentiments of allegiance, service and responsibility basic to the common good since marriage severed from continuity, and focused on self-satisfaction, ceases to have its customary role in building society's infrastructure or bridges of social connectedness. Those "people who claim to be above such attachments, and who argue that nations and religion are outdated, may be social capital free riders, living off the trust built up by those institutions they disdain."[83] This might seem irrelevant now that anybody can grasp their 'human rights'. But amidst the debris of dislocation and atomisation, only the enforcement of regulations and coercion keeps down disorder as a "controlling state centralism reaching into every aspect of personal life" tries to "secure the mandate of health, safety, or other ethically neutral goods".[84] We may be reaching this point as elites see no entity or social order that they value and wish to conserve.[85]

4.8   A BETTER FUTURE?

Worries about the fate of children under arrangements for adults disconnected from procreation have been overridden by claims that better child rearing or 'parenting' is going to take over. The 'good practice guide' for social workers about recruiting gay and lesbian adopters for British Association for Adoption and Fostering (BAAF) claims that "gay men and women who choose to create families" will "have the advantage of redefining and reinventing their own meaning of family and parenting". Lesbian activist Masha Gessen explains:

> I have three kids who have five parents, more or less, and I don't see why they shouldn't have five parents legally... I met my new partner, and she had just had a baby, and that baby's biological father is my brother, and my daughter's biological father is a man who lives in Russia, and my adopted son also considers him his father. So the five parents break down into two groups of three... I would like to live in a legal system that is capable of reflecting that reality, and I don't think that's compatible with the institution of marriage....[86]

These who exist outside of the traditional family have "the unique opportunity to break out of preconceived gender roles" and to be "a new kind of [unspecified and unexplained] father or mother to a child"[87] which can replace the conjugal family that BAAF's spokespeople insist was created for colonisation.

Bodies dealing with the education and training of adoption practitioners might be expected to be aware of the evidence that marriage is good for children. Instead, it is put down as a "myth" that children do best in married couple families and a "fact" that "children thrive in many different types of families" because there are "increasingly more diverse types of families." The confident assertion is how "evidence" reaches "the same, unequivocal conclusions ... the children of lesbian and gay parents grow up as successfully as the children of heterosexual parents." This is next to the admission: "There is a need for a study on ...outcomes for children... [compared] with those of children adopted by heterosexual parents. ...no such study has yet been undertaken."[88] Instead, there are plenty of extravagant claims. Constantly repeated is Judith Stacey's statement on family structure before the US Senate:

> ...the research on children raised by lesbian and gay parents demonstrates that these children *do as well if not better than children raised by heterosexual parents*. Specifically, the research demonstrates that children of same-sex couples are as emotionally healthy and socially adjusted and at least as educationally and socially successful as children raised by heterosexual parents. [Italics mine] [89]

If, in conditions of diminished kin altruism, some can raise children as efficiently or even to standards superior to those of married biological heterosexual parents, then they are able to do something that heterosexuals in step-parenting, cohabiting and lone adult contexts have been unable to do – replicate and even surpass the optimal childrearing environment of married, biological-parent homes.[90] However, while 'gay' parenting studies are regarded as definitive affirmations by policy makers, lawyers, social scientists, journalists and others, reviewers examining their scientific credentials have had no hesitation in dismissing them as largely politically motivated fiction.

We conclude that the methods used in these studies are so flawed that these studies prove nothing. Therefore, they should not be used [in legal or other instances]...to make any arguments about "homosexual vs. heterosexual parenting. Their claims have no basis. [91]

Several hundred studies reviewed for the Attorney General of Canada all contained at least one "fatal flaw" and not a single one "was conducted according to general accepted standards of scientific research."[92] Previously, another overview had spoken of a universal lack of scientific standards in studies that should never have passed peer review. Some studies "had to disregard their own results in order to conclude that homosexuals were fit parents"[93] – something recently confirmed.[94]

What we need to know with any investigation is that researchers have sampled those who represent the broader group about which they are going to make generalisations, something particularly problematic in this area.[95] Even Judith Stacy acknowledged the absence of "studies of child development based on random, representative samples" of gay parents.[96] Instead, small convenience samples, often recruited through gay organisations, venues and press and disproportionately involving well off, educated lesbians, might be compared to single heterosexual mothers – if controls exist at all. Sometimes the respondents may not be parents – just fantasising about being one.[97] To problems with volunteers and missing comparison groups, we must add the lack of controls for confounding factors, together with the self-reported data or retrospective reports that create unrepeatable results.

Studies often focus on matters like 'the value of children to fathers', 'parenting behaviours' or child outcomes like 'self-esteem' or 'sex-roles'.[98] A leading US advocate for homosexual parenting insists how research must describe the strengths of "lesbian families" since they provide "a model of justice, especially in terms of the division of labor at home".[99] Homosexual families have often been described as healthier than others because they have the advantage of being free from constraining gender roles. It "is noteworthy that …outcomes of societal-level concern are absent" – like criminality, drug taking, education, labour force participation, childbearing and so forth.[100] Many effects are not optimally observable until at least mid-late adolescence or early adulthood, when differences often start impacting on later relationships – as with parental divorce.

An exception was an Australian comparative analysis of 58 children each living with heterosexual married parents, heterosexual cohabiting couples and homosexual couples matched according to socially significant criteria. The sample is small, but did not rely on parental reports and examined children's developmental outcomes. Results were that the children of married couples were more likely to do better academically and socially than those of cohabiting and homosexual couples.[101] For excessive drinking, drug use, truancy, and criminal offences, the adult children (18+) with homosexual parents reported higher rates than those of heterosexuals. They were far more likely to report being homosexual. It is a repeated finding that children reared in homosexual households are far more likely to engage in early sexual behaviour and adopt a homo/bi-sexual lifestyle. One review of nine studies put this at seven fold compared to children from heterosexual households.[101a]

This study has been sidelined or critiqued for using teacher reports (these included standard tests and assessments) – even by those whose own studies may lack controls. Its results are echoed in recent work using the New Family Structures Study (NFSS), a nationally-representative, large probability sample which compared how 2988 young adults (aged 18–39) from a variety of different family backgrounds fared on 40 different social, emotional, and relational outcomes.[102] A considerable advance on previous studies, data was collected by an independent, high ranking survey firm supported by the National Science Foundation.[103] The backgrounds under scrutiny covered an intact, married biological family from 0 to 18; adopted before age 2; parents divorced later or had joint custody; lived with unmarried biological parents until age 18; step family where parent married again; lone parent, where the biological parents were either never married or divorced and where the resident parent did not marry (or remarry) before the respondent turned 18, and other combinations which included deceased parent(s). The respondents were asked about whether their mother or father ever had a same-sex relationship. The presence of children in same sex households matched national estimates. What came out was just how unrepresentative typical convenience samples have been – with their stereotypic upper-middle class, well-educated and prosperous lesbians 'out' in the 'community'. These might be more of an ideal than a common reality on the ground. Recent comparisons of children adopted by homosexual and heterosexual couples which show similar outcomes (only a year later for 130 four to eight year olds) refer to carefully placed children.[104]

After a multitude of controls (including having been bullied as a youth, and the 'gay friendliness' of the respondent's current state of residence), those who reported that their mother had had a lesbian relationship did very slightly worse than others from lone parent and stepfamilies and a lot worse than those from intact, biological families (on 25 out of the 40 factors from education to employment to depression to drug use). As elsewhere, adopted children came closest to those growing up with two biological parents. There was a high rate of instability and turmoil with same sex parents (mothers left home and children went into foster care in greater numbers), which might explain much of the results, although this study was concerned with comparisons not causation. (Again, only 61% of children of lesbians reported themselves to be 'entirely heterosexual'.) This underlines how non-intact families are, on average, poorer quality child rearing environments, regardless of the sexual preferences of parents. We do not have a fabulous "new kind of father or mother to a child"[105] but, in this imperfect world, mundane, messy turmoil. Is this the reality behind claims like those of Masha Gessen?

Changes do not get easier with repeated transitions; instead, multiple changes cumulatively disadvantage children.[106] Other work attempting to isolate the extent to which children's academic achievement may be associated with their current family structure, changes and prior family structure came to much the same conclusions. This seven-wave panel study collected data from more than 20,000 nursery children in 1998 and followed them to 12 years. The 158 living with same-sex (overwhelmingly lesbian) couples during at least one wave scored lower than their peers from married, two-biological parent families. (The worst scores were for children with cohabiting and single parents.) Again, this was indicative of family disruption and transition. The study provided no information about children living with lone homosexual parents or those in more complex family structures, because size limits the kinds of analyses that can be made. It is unlikely that the results would be better.[107] Further work with the same sample duplicates the findings.[108]

When social scientists began studying divorce, remarriage and lone parenthood, many hoped to disprove the deficits for children that had been identified in early studies. Was divorce not a new beginning where, if mother was happy, the children would be better adjusted and contented than with parents who did not get on? Problems could be attributed to the 'conflict' or dissatisfactions back in the old home. Thirty or more years of rigorous research has shown clear links between negative outcomes and childhood experience of family disruption.[109]

Since poor outcomes owe so much to turbulence, there is the suggestion that this is explicable in terms of processes uniquely problematic for homosexuals – stigma induced stress, lack of social support and legal security. Otherwise, we are looking at results from "the era of fake heterosexual marriages". Where some subjects reported "both a mother and a father having a same-sex relationship" these must have been "bisexual swingers" or "closet cases who covered for each other".[110] There is a view that today's and tomorrow's children of same sex parents are more likely to be 'planned' than yesterday's – where most came from a parent's previous heterosexual union rather than in-vitro fertilization or a surrogate. It is not unreasonable to expect that SSM may help some children by providing greater stability and, at the same time, lessen 'sham' marriages which break up. Since same sex parents have to be far more selective about reproduction, the children may turn out better. We are reminded that many children of heterosexuals are 'unplanned' – 50% is routinely quoted. However, opposite sex relations are open to reproduction and most of heterosexuals' 'unplanned' children will be more or less expected and, whether or not, will be accepted. Children of same sex parents are 'planned' because they cannot reproduce together and have to use at least one biological parent from outside.

There may be a refusal to recognise that 'gay' families can be as (or more) chaotic and as 'diverse' as others, or even more prone to disruption, given not just social stigma or pressure but the volatile nature of sexual attractions and identifications. It is unlikely that there will *only* be those who, grasping their 'gay' identity early in life, steadfastly move on into secure 'gay' families with no deviations on the way. This is akin to a widely scorned 'heterosexist' model anyway. Full or 'true' causation can perhaps never be completely determined because we cannot randomly assign children to various family structures at birth.[111] Same-sex families are still primarily created through opposite sex relationships and, given the fluidity of sexual behaviour, this will continue.

From a contrary perspective, some maintain that "apart from the adoption of children in need" non-biological parents "do not ameliorate social evils but share in them. In many instances, they exacerbate them" because their access to children is "parasitic upon the demise of conjugal society...."[112] with husbands and wives divorcing to join same sex lovers and men and women offering their sexual organs, sperm and eggs without intending to take any parental responsibilities. Irrespective of how much of this judgment is valid, the "social evils" relate to the issues that are inescapably involved in prioritising the satisfaction of couples.

Chapter Five

DIMENSIONS OF EQUALITY

5.1   EQUAL IN WHAT?

The different views on the prospects for marriage's future are intertwined with the justifications or imperatives for including same sex partners. Approaching the issue in the context of equality, there seems to be no basis for treating relationships differently, so the freedom to marry whom one loves must be a fundamental right. The simple *revisionist* view or interpretation limits itself to the recognition of the union of two people (whether same or opposite sex) who commit to caring for each other. This sunny take is what Government and its proxies have been anxious to transmit:

> It seems pretty clear that most gay people have no desire to change the nature of marriage, instead they wish to 'join' or be a part of the institution, because of the respect that they have ... Nor is it clear how giving a small minority the same ability to get married to that enjoyed by the rest of society would weaken marriage.[1]

Equality lends itself to 'containment'. A mere cosmetic or "incremental change ... rather than a revolutionary one"[2] adds a new group to the married category while keeping intact the essential structure. Here are Kevin and Gary rather than Kathy and Jim who want to seal their love and take care of each other throughout the vicissitudes of life. The only difference is 'orientation'. Otherwise, they are equivalent in their humanity and similarly situated with respect to marriage.[3] At this level of abstraction, it is a matter of extending marriage's societal and symbolic benefits to address an injustice towards a minority. This leaves the institution and the understanding of its nature unchanged, apart from it ceasing to be exclusively heterosexual.

Others construe this as well-meaning naivety – complementing a saccharine view of rights as expanding individual fulfilment. This is not something that tends to come from gay activists for, even where not hoping for marriage's impending demise, these tend not to deny that the abandonment of the conjugal understanding of marriage will have transformative institutional and social effects. It certainly implies:

> ...that the Jewish and Christian understanding of marriage and family life is thoroughly misguided ...that humankind itself has been misguided – wrong – to recognise something different, special, or sacred about the sexual union of husband (male) and wife (female). ...that marriage has nothing to do with the different complementary nature of men and women. ...that marriage is an arbitrary social construct that can be and should be pried apart from its cultural, biological, and religious underpinnings and redefined by anyone laying claim to it.[4]

What on the surface may appear to be just a matter of extending a facility to a hitherto excluded group, is contentious if the institution in question is inherently inapplicable to those seeking entry. Then it is a case of not receiving a benefit because of the failure to meet the requirements. The demand might be that: "Fair treatment dictates that people should not be denied access to a public institution on account of their sexuality"[5] but, if a specific 'sexuality' is pertinent to membership some may not meet the requirements. It depends on what respect and to what end people are supposed to be equal. Racial, sexual or other differences may be relevant when it comes to medicine, but irrelevant when it comes to having the vote or a car licence and, for a handicapped parking space or membership of a learned or professional body, other criteria for admission apply. Otherwise, equal treatment for low and high ability children predicates that exams must make no distinctions, and equal treatment for nationals and migrants means that border controls should be abolished. Since equality does not mandate that things which are substantively different must be treated as if they were the same, revisionists who maintain that "the law must be applied equally to all except where objective differences justify differentiation"[6] are shooting themselves in the foot.

Not least, equal marriage is an attempt to apply gender interchangeability precisely where gender difference demands that biological reality (motherhood) be reconciled to social necessity (fatherhood).

Infertility – from choice, accident or age – might suggest that it is arbitrary for marriage to require a man and a woman. How is same sex union distinct from any other kind of sterile union if a woman without a uterus is no more open to procreation than a man? The reproductive organs of an infertile man or woman – and all women are infertile much of the time – are not 'reproductive' any more than other parts of the anatomy.

> No wedding certificate anywhere in the world is granted on the condition that the marriage is a procreative one and it would be regarded as absurd if an infertile couple was not allowed to marry. Many heterosexual marriages, for medical reasons or for reasons of choice, do not result in children being born....[7]

Thus, goes the argument, having two sexes has been an arbitrary marriage requirement, rather than a qualification rooted in biology as this meets culture. If only opposite sex marriage is allowed, then this should mandate fertility testing.

Even when procreation is unobtainable, are not "other goods (mutuality, love, and the like) attainable"?[8] If heterosexual spouses know they are infertile and have sex, it is for pleasure and to express their love – the same reasons that 'gay' couples have sex. The thinking is that all non-procreative sexual acts use bodies for mutual pleasure, and contracepted or infertile heterosexual acts are of the same character as homosexual activities. Otherwise, must the state discourage contraceptives or heterosexual premarital sex? It all seems to follow that there are:

> ... no grounds for supposing that the goods shared by infertile and elderly couples cannot be shared by gays in committed relationships. The inclusive path would acknowledge all of this while preserving the reasonable natural-law claim that sexual activity should be channelled into committed and loving relationships, whether heterosexual or homosexual.[9]

Another version of this argument has it that there is no reason to oppose equal marriage since assisted reproductive technology voids marriage's relationship to family making.

However, had marriage no intrinsic connection to children, it would not have arisen in the first place. If children come from anywhere, it is from a male and a female and this, not instances of infertility, set the norm. That some heterosexual couples are childless, for whatever reason(s), does not mean that heterosexual and homosexual couples are equally sterile (or fertile). Sometimes infertility is corrected or people change their minds. Homosexual relations are inherently, not accidentally, sterile, so there is no choice whether or not to reproduce.

If infertility legitimates a radically new understanding since some spouses do not reproduce, this would seemingly argue for removing all incest prohibitions. After all, consanguinity has no relevance where reproduction cannot arise. An attempted amendment in the House of Lords sought to make the differences between marriage and civil partnership more pronounced by opening the latter to family members. Whilst initially successful, the government rejected the amendment on the basis that the collection of rights and responsibilities provided by the Act would not be appropriate for family members generally. Not least, two sisters in a civil partnership for tax reasons would have to go through a process like divorce in order subsequently to marry.

Arguments for precisely this move have it that, if there are worries about passing on genetic diseases, then all prospective parents should be genetically screened.[10] A bit about eugenics being popular with the Nazis is thrown in as this case is made against incest prohibitions. The reality is that there is a high chance of close relatives having handicapped children, whilst for strangers this is low and usually unpredictable.

The similarities between SSM and consensual incest have been deployed in the legal case of Columbia University professor David Epstein, when on trial for alleged sexual involvement with his adult daughter.[11] By 2005, Patrick Stübing had been convicted several times for incest with his sister. His case reached the German constitutional court which upheld the law (as did the European Court in Strasbourg), although its vice-president Winfried Hassemer forcefully dissented. With a *Guardian* writer asserting how: "the big debate on incest has not even begun" so:

In time, the law against incest will come to be seen as the infringement of human rights that it is. As it is unlikely…that incest will suddenly become a mass sport if the law is changed, the concern about it is just the usual control-freakery about all matters sexual.[12]

Anything seems to be justified if there is an instance in history or even in literature:

Consensual incest has been portrayed sympathetically in popular fiction for centuries from 17th century plays like 'Tis pity she's a whore' to Jerry Springer.[13]

Pharaohs married their sisters and, if it was good for Pharaoh, then it's good enough for us.[14] It is suggested that Egyptians were "more relaxed" and progressive about such matters. Actually, sibling marriage was not a practice among ordinary ancient Egyptians. Pharaohs did it because they were thought to be deities on earth, and acting out foundation myths, and, more mundanely, sought to keep inheritance within the immediate royal family. At the same time, they acquired extra wives in alliances with foreign rulers. Rather than having been "relaxed", ancient Egyptians were bound by tradition to a degree alien to *Guardian* writers.

What has been applied to same sex unions is the 'prohibited degrees of relationship' provision even if there can be no issue and no consummation. Is this meant to limit the avoidance of inheritance tax? Otherwise, a father might marry his son and pass on his estate without death duties.[15] The incongruities abound, like the preposterous transfer of one of the more arcane aspects of marriage law to same sex partners, where a civil union is voidable if at the time of its formation the respondent was pregnant by someone other than the applicant![16]

These are not the only problems the disarmingly simple equality premise runs into. Marriage not only stabilises a union which presupposes the creation of children, its consummation has been by the generative act that reflects the complementarity of male and female. Ever a condition for 'proper' marriage, no other legal status has been dependent upon a sexual act. This might be one of those "non-existent practical" grounds that Douglas Murray thinks are used to oppose equal marriage.[17]

If two people unite in marriage, then (among other things) they unite organically or in the physical dimension of their being. Suppose they pledge to play tennis exclusively only with each other, until death do them part. Are they married? No. Substitute any other non-sexual activity and they still are not married. Moreover:

> People's bodies can touch and interact in all sorts of ways, so why does only sexual union make bodies in any significant sense "one flesh"? It follows that for two individuals to unite organically, and thus bodily, their bodies must be coordinated for some biological purpose of the whole.

Individuals are naturally incomplete with respect only to:

> ... sexual reproduction. In coitus ... a man and a woman's bodies coordinate by way of their sexual organs for the common biological purpose of reproduction. They perform the first step of the complex reproductive process ... they are biologically united, and do not merely rub together ... And this union occurs even when conception ... does not occur ... organic bodily unity is achieved when a man and woman coordinate to perform ... the generative act; ...[this] free and loving expression of the spouses' permanent and exclusive commitment ... is also a marital act.[18]

No matter what else same sex relationships may be, none of the wide variety of sexual activities suffice as the mark of bodily union. When consummation is abandoned as indicative of the completion or confirmation of a marriage and its absence removed as grounds for annulment, equality is not achieved. Any such clause was already omitted from civil partnerships legislation because those framing it could not identify any homosexual act that might count as consummation. This has helped single heterosexual people of the same gender to gain rights to tenancies, rights of residence or business assets simply by contracting a civil union.

Much the same applies to adultery or 'sexual unfaithfulness' as an 'unreasonable' behaviour that can justify ending a marriage. There is no equivalent for same sex unions, whether a general one of 'sexual infidelity' or specific sexual practices with a third party, so it is left hovering as a matter for 'individual dissolution proceedings'. The Women and Equality

Unit, back in 2003, stated: "Adultery has a specific meaning within the context of heterosexual relationships and it would not be possible nor desirable to read this across to same sex civil partnerships".[19] Faithfulness or sexual exclusivity is a defining characteristic of marriage and connected to the procreative role, which logically has no application to people of the same sex. If homosexuals have a child, this *has* to involve a third party. As with abandoning consummation, the "only appropriate and balanced way to deal with this would be to scrap the act of adultery as a basis for divorce altogether."[20] Otherwise, are not heterosexuals being discriminated against for having to remain faithful to each other? Equality is achieved by abandoning conjugality. We are left with the irony that trying to incorporate same sex couples changes the nature of the institution: "same sex marriage is therefore in a certain sense self-defeating, for in seeking equality with something unlike yourself the thing that you join is no longer what you joined."[21]

While fidelity is expected of heterosexual unions, even if it is not always achieved, is sexual exclusivity compatible with homosexual experience and expectations anyway? For many protagonists in this debate, commitment is clearly confining. It is difficult enough anyway to provide principled grounds for the norms of fidelity, monogamy and permanence that might be compatible with the rejection of the traditional conception of opposite sex marriage. When terms like 'committed', 'faithful' and 'stable' are used for same sex relationships, this might suggest sexual exclusivity. In practice, 'monogamy' is more likely to mean being in a close emotional but *not sexually exclusive* relationship. Sexual exclusivity has been a minority view in the 'gay' movement, even in its so-called Christian manifestation. Demands for exclusivity might even "compromise our [gay] capacity for relating... [making] serial commitments, and serial faithfulness, a more realistic aspiration".[22] Significantly, while there are penalties for perjury in connection with entering civil partnership or marriage, no criminal offence equivalent to bigamy exists. If concurrent unions are acceptable in one sphere but not the other, questions of inequality again arise.

5.2   THE RACE ANALOGY

Analogies made with anti-miscegenation when it comes to qualifying for marriage deserve close consideration, relying as they do not simply on assumptions that barriers are unjust or discriminatory, but that sexual identity is as fixed and determinant as race. Civil partnerships "only served to reinforce a sense of alienation" on a par with "the days of apartheid when black people were told they could still ride on the bus, they just had to sit at the back."[23] Actually, proponents of segregated public facilities did not argue that it was physically impossible for blacks to sit in the front of buses any more than opponents of interracial marriage did not deny that unions of black and a white people were possible. The aim was to prevent these being realised. Crystal Dixon was fired from the University of Toledo after she wrote to the *Toledo Free Press* (sic) disagreeing that gay rights were equivalent to black civil rights struggles.

> As a Black woman, I take great umbrage at the notion that those choosing the homosexual lifestyle are 'civil rights victims.' ...I cannot wake up tomorrow and not be a black woman. I am genetically and biologically a black woman and very pleased to be so as my Creator intended.[24]

People make choices about what they do with their genitals, not about the colour of their skin. Many individuals exist on the borderline when it comes to sexuality, but everybody remains a human being of a certain race.

The accepted wisdom certainly has it that sexual orientation involves an inborn and absolute identity that admits of no challenge or change. The advertisements on buses, school walls and public buildings proclaiming how "Some People are Gay: Get over it!" reinforce the message that sexual orientation is no more disputable or changeable than height, eye colour or other endowments to which environmental variables and individual choice make little or no contribution. Furthermore, what we are talking about is something which encompasses a person's entire being. Notions of fixed orientation establish boundaries and wards off suggestions of a slippery slope or doors opening onto a plethora of other dispositions or, indeed, that homosexuality can be a transient phase or quirky exception to the heterosexual baseline. It is curious how in academia environmental determinism rules – think of the opprobrium that descends on anybody claiming that intelligence is at all genetic – but 'orientation' is different. A meeting in the Commons in January 2013 to discuss matters relating to 'orientation' had a 'gay' professor asserting that it was homophobic to raise the issue and inconceivable in a tolerant society. Claims are made that:

> ...there is an extensive amount of empirical, objective research into this matter and it is refreshingly clear in this regard. Sexual orientation is an enduring, fundamental part of a person's psychological make-up and is remarkably resistant to attempts to alter it. In fact, evidence suggests that attempts to change a person's sexuality ... are not just ineffective but dangerous. [25]

"Dangerous"? While I do not venture into areas of 'reparative' therapies or 'gay cures' any more than 'gay' causes or origins, this is at odds with the faith in psychiatric interventions for all manner of conditions and propensities (which undergo 'spontaneous remission' and probably at a higher rate than they are 'treated' or 'cured').

It is curious that, alongside this essentialist viewpoint, is another which posits how people can take up sexual identities and change them almost at will, as when Peter Tatchell boldly asserts: "It is a choice, and we should be glad it's that way and celebrate it for ourselves."[26] Similarly, people may transgender either way, back and forth, man to woman, woman to man. And, indeed, there is mounting enthusiasm over reports that people are having more same sex encounters or relationships.[27] There is apparently quite a fashion trend where:

> Female celebrities are falling over themselves to, if not explicitly identify as bi, then admit they've had sexual relationships with women in the past. And the more I quiz my straight female friends, the more they admit to having had a sexual experience with another woman at some point, having never mentioned it before.
>
> As far as I'm concerned, people feeling less need to rigidly define their sexual preferences can only be a good thing. ...what was I doing when everyone else got the obligatory lesbian experience memo?[28]

The reality of the volatility and flexibility of sexual attraction and behaviour puts question marks over any rigid concept of 'orientation' as something of the same order as race or sex. If it means defining people through sex play, then this is strongly influenced by culture, social trends and fashions – and may help account for the considerable discordance often found between the sex of partners and ascriptions of sexual identity.[29]

However, even where we find concessions to fluidity, it still tends to be insisted that once adopted or tasted, 'orientation' – or a same sex one anyway – is not meant to be up for question. Grasping at certainty here may help to avoid some of the dilemmas of postmodern strictures about imaginative constructs or 'labels' which 'society' forces people to adopt and define themselves according to social and linguistic contexts. It also ensures that laws designed for classes of people with immutable, non-behavioural distinguishing characteristics are extended on the understanding that sexual orientation is as inherent and uncontrollable as skin colour.

Again, while it may be strongly believed that having an 'orientation' is important to qualifying for marriage, logically this is irrelevant. Disabilities may be 'natural' or special obligations imperative and, like an inability to find a mate, these circumstances – not prejudice or the state – may prevent some people from getting married. If we discovered "that no sexual desire had a genetic basis that would not be an argument against marriage in general."[30] If a desire for multiple partners has a genetic basis, is that an argument for polygamy? It is easily argued that humans, particularly male humans, are naturally somewhat polygamous, but monogamous marriage imposes restrictions on this behaviour or 'orientation'. Eric Anderson, first openly US gay high school coach, argues as much. The reasoning is that since many men experience difficulty remaining faithful, the result of this disconnect between society's expectation of fidelity and men's inability to stay monogamous is heartache and disillusionment, and the sooner we let go of the monogamy ideal, the happier they will be.[31]

Unavoidably, and whether this is fixed or fluid, an endowment or a choice, sexual orientation is a self-attribution or subjective evaluation, not an objective allocation. Despite categorisations of 'gay or straight', there are correlated or interconnected dimensions, including attraction, behaviour, fantasies, relationships, lifestyle preferences and self-identification – which need not go together. Some researchers seek to shift away from paradigms that impose narrow definitions or identity labels, moving towards broader and more variable attributes as well as different dimensions (e.g. 'sexual' or 'emotional'). Contemporary ideas of 'sexual orientation' are historically recent and belong to the modern West,[32] even if over the centuries, physicians and alchemists may have advanced notions of innate same sexual affinities.[33] The Hungarian writer Karl-Maria Kertbeny is credited with having coined the word 'homosexual' in 1869 as he began to describe scientifically the phenomenon which he himself possessed. In turn, the German lawyer Karl Heinrich Ulrichs advanced a hereditary explanation for his condition as a third sex where a man's body is inhabited by a woman's soul. He advocated the de-criminalisation of this inborn condition in favour of medical treatment as well as tougher laws against sex with prepubescent boys (he was himself molested).

While the Western male homosexual model may be comparatively recent, a distinction might still be made between a pre-World War II pattern and that which reached its full expression with the counter-culture of the 1960/70s.[34] In a progression from pathology to alternative lifestyle, being 'gay' emerged "associated with a particular historical moment and social (and often political) self-identification."[35] Words like homosexual now seemed offensive for being 'heterosexist' and/or clinical (suggesting something amiss) although they were prominent in 1930s subcultures. In contrast, "'gay' is a magical word [which] has a creative power of its own ...the key indicator for today's liberated homosexual", signifying those who are not just attracted to the same sex, but "*celebrate* this attraction."[36] There is the process of 'coming out' like an initiation into full tribal membership, with a self-conscious place in a 'gay' community.[37] With the elevation of promiscuity, few groups changed their sexual behaviour so rapidly in the aftermath of cultural upheaval and the removal of penalties for sodomy. Uniquely, confrontation was sought with the conjugal family. By the 1980s, the culture of sexual extremism led to the experience of HIV/AIDs and rising rates of other sexual diseases. The sexual transition of the 1960s undoubtedly facilitated widespread exposure to anal sex for cohorts who came of age in that period, together with a wide variety of activities virtually unknown in the earlier Western phase.[38] Questions arise as to whether and by how much the hyper-sexualised lifestyle applauded as *the* authentic 'gay-way' was minority driven. A distorted picture may have then contributed to a generation adopting promiscuity as basic to identity and liberation – as for rights organisations today.[39]

Inseparable from the insistence on solid orientation is the belief that there is a significant minority as easily quantifiable as it is identifiable.[40] Even in the 21st century, lobby groups and media will not let go of Alfred Kinsey's 1948 claim that 10% of males are "more or less exclusively homosexual" even if he talked about "4 percent of the white males".[41] Kinsey put most in the middle of his spectrum as bisexual, with none exclusively heterosexual; estimating that 38% of men and 17% of women had homosexual experience and 13% and 7% were homosexual for at least three years. He based his 'statistically common behaviour' on volunteer samples with high proportions of prisoners and sex offenders. He added thoughts to acts and translated early play into life-long patterns. His figures have never been replicated.

Nineteen US or Canadian random household samples of over 18 year olds were identified in a project for the Office of National Statistics (ONS) in 2008.[42] The proportions self-identifying as lesbian/gay/bisexual (LGB) ranged from 0.9% to 4.9%. Official US figures put exclusive homosexuals at 0.7% and 5.5% of men as ever having had homosexual intercourse,[43] and in a poll of adolescents, 0.5% described themselves as predominantly homosexual.[44] A 2010/11 report by the ONS put Britain's combined homo/bi-sexuals at 1.5% or almost 750,000 according to the Integrated Household Survey (the biggest pool of UK social data after the Census, with a response rate of 96%).[45] One in 200 chose 'other' and 3% 'don't know' or refused to answer. Even if all those missing or evasive were secretly homosexual this would not make Kinsey numbers. The younger age profile of homosexuals compared with the rest of the population might reflect greater toleration, publicity and more experimentation and uptake.

As Kinsey's notions have informed educational curricula and policy making, much public money has been spent on the basis of figures which have turned out to be miscalculations or lies. Predictions about HIV/AIDs in the 1980s had to be drastically reduced for the US after being grossly overestimated on advice from pressure groups using his estimations. Two decades on, British ministers introducing partnership legislation endorsed Stonewall's downsized Kinsey figures of 5% –7%, implying a homosexual population of 3.5 million to underscore how they were acting on behalf of a significant minority. Over representation in big cities, arts and entertainment might suggest that homosexuals are more prevalent than they actually are.

Disappointed pressure groups put low figures down to embarrassment or fear. Legend has it that there is a "hidden population" of missing millions hiding in shame, until "it becomes less risky to identify oneself as LGB for the purposes of research."[46] This is despite interviewers becoming increasingly discrete as sexual orientation has become a routine part of data collection – along with films increasingly showing explicit gay and lesbian sex. A UK household survey (by computer) which asked about sexual identity, attraction and gender of sexual partners on sliding scales, with a multi-stage, complex design using alternative nomenclatures found that 0.8% identified as 'entirely homosexual'.[47]

One examination of sexual orientation identity, stability and change over a 10-year period drew on data from the National Survey of Midlife Development in the United States (average age 47 years).[48] At Wave 2, 63.6% of homosexual and 64.7% of bisexual women, as well as 9.52% and 47.1% of homo/bi-sexual men reported a different sexual identity. Similar results are available from five waves of longitudinal data from New Zealand, where there were massive changes in identity labels and movement in and out of same sex behaviour and attractions.[49] Similarly, polls show significant proportions or even majorities of those characterised or self-identifying as 'gay' having had sexual relations with the opposite sex,[50] although the converse is far lower for heterosexuals.[51] Even a poll commissioned for the gay US magazine *Advocate* of nearly 3,000 homosexuals (male and female) found that, over a lifetime, nearly 60% also had opposite sex partners.[52] Similarly, a British probability survey (6399 women, aged 16 to 44 years) conducted from 1999 to 2001, reported that while 4.9% had ever had same-sex partners and 2.8% in the past 5 years, 85% of these also reported male partners.[53] The overwhelming majority of self-described lesbians began sex early and had considerably higher numbers of male partners than heterosexual controls in the survey.[54]

Thus the argument arises over whether bisexuality represents sexual fluidity, a temporary state of denial or transition to homosexuality or, as Alfred Kinsey advocated, a third or 'balanced' sexual ordination for 'normal' uninhibited people. There may be over-classification if a same sex episode, passing attraction, thought or feeling can label people with fixed orientations. Considering all this, it is understandable how "estimating a single number for the prevalence of homosexuality" is "a futile exercise because it presupposes assumptions that are patently false: that homosexuality is a uniform attribute across individuals, that it is stable over time, and that it can be easily measured."[55]

All this is confused by the elevation of more subdivisions or add-ons into identities, where LGBs (gay, lesbian, bisexual) grows to LGBT (plus transsexuals) then to LGBTQ (plus queer or questioners). As other sexual proclivities like polyamory (multiple concurrent sex partners) are emerging as 'orientations', this might appear to add weight to the argument that human rights decree that all orientations should be provided for. There are Zoos (those in consensual sexual relationships with animals) laying claim to an 'orientation' present since birth. Cody Beck, a zoophile is thrilled how, since he came 'out', activists' efforts have broadened minds about what qualifies as socially acceptable sex, although he is disappointed by the gay rights rejection of zoophilia as a legitimate orientation.[56]

The least that low solidity and high fluidity might suggest is the necessity for easy transit between same and opposite sex unions, where those who feel they have married with the 'wrong' orientation can opt out into another, more compatible union or, as more argue, into group marriage.

5.3   ALL YOU NEED IS LOVE

Recognising love for what it is has a direct, popular emotional appeal. Does not marriage's value arise "from the human needs and capabilities that it seeks to promote and protect; needs and capabilities that merit moral respect regardless and independently of gender"?[57] Many positive human values, such as devotion and intimacy are indeed shown by those outside heterosexual monogamous relationships. The focus on complementarity and generativity may ignore the range of emotional and other aspirations that go into marriage, and so devalue it. We might also be reminded that: "Since the need to be cared for by others and the capability to care for others often accompany sexual intimacy, there is more at stake for individuals than simply having opportunities for sexual satisfaction.[58] Emotional and physical intimacy are not easily separable and it is here that marriage "encourages us to construct our lives around the love for and commitment to another human being in order to meet the needs and provide for the well-being of ourselves and others". Homosexuals argue that any failure to fully support SSM is a failure to recognise their "full humanity", which tells them that: "their needs and capabilities associated with physical and emotional intimacy are less worthy and less valuable simply because they involve someone else of the same gender".[59]

This insufficiently explains why satisfying or enjoyable friendships outside the conjugal bond need legal recognition, with or without the giving and receiving of sexual pleasure. Law has not concerned itself with friendship and nor has love involved the state. If any people choose to live together because of care needs or companionship, why should their relationships not be similarly recognised? In the legislative campaign for civil partnerships, and then 'gay' marriage, a constant has been the story of the "grieving partners ... unable to stay in their shared home or to inherit the possessions they have shared for years when one partner dies suddenly..."[60] or even visit their hospital bed. However, no-one I know has ever been prevented from visiting sick or dying friends or acquaintances in hospitals or care homes. If any such discrimination applies, it is something shared, for example, with the friend or neighbour looking after a disabled person. For every hardship endured by homosexuals, there are probably far more in relationships without sexual connotations experiencing the same problems. Civil partnership law (which does not specify sexual behaviour) allows two homosexuals a waiver of inheritance tax, but not two sisters. In 2006 two elderly sisters who lived together took the Government to the European court of Human Rights in an attempt to get the same inheritance tax rights as homosexual couples. They claimed to have saved the Government thousands by caring for their elderly sick relation until death. When civil partnerships were being introduced, it was estimated (2001 census) that there were almost 60 times as many (over 4.6m) house sharers to less than 80,000 people living as a same sex couple. As it stands, tenancies are transferable to cohabitees of any orientation.

Is there any particular social contribution, public concern or common good at stake if flatmates are lovers – or not? Friendship is founded in common pursuits, background, interests, conversation, and is valued for itself. This might be impoverished where "emotional, psychological, and dispositional intimacy seems inappropriate in non-sexual friendships."[61]

Again, it is children who particularly relate marriage to matters beyond the private concerns of its participants. Why should the state have an interest in any home sharers' personal lives, other than to ensure that they do not suffer disadvantages when it comes to matters like tenancies? Rights can be secured by legal arrangements (like power of attorney or wills), which anyone is or should be free to make and whether as romantic partners, widowed sisters, or celibate monks. The benefits do not involve legal redefinitions, and there is no need to dilute the status of marriage. Instead of all the present incentives to live apart imposed by the tax/benefit system, perhaps people should be encouraged to live together to spare the immense strain upon housing, environment, health and social services represented by the increase in one adult households.[62]

5.4   BACK TO THE FUTURE?

Equal or same sex marriage purportedly *restores* a historical right or practice. Notions that, in times past, marriage was not as restrictive about sexual combinations as we might have been led to believe are unlikely to be separable from assumptions about fixed 'orientation'. Nobody is obliged to repeat anything that happened in history. Here we have another of those contradictions we find so much in this area of dispute, where appeals to historical precedent occur in conjunction with the disparagement of conjugal marriage as 'Stone Age' or 'medieval'.

Throughout history, a society's customs and laws have not explicitly forbidden marriage between two (or more) people of the same sex because, like cross species marriage, this would seem as or more inherently absurd and purposeless as the emperor Caligula making his horse a senator. Independently of whether or not same sex sexual behaviour has been practised, tolerated, scorned or encouraged, effectively institutionalised or outlawed and persecuted, it was inconsequential and irrelevant to marriage. Even in societies that have permitted polygamy, the union of man and woman is central, not that between two or more women or two or more men.

Homosexual academics like James Boswell claimed to have provided evidence of same sex commitment ceremonies in early Roman Catholic and Eastern Orthodox communities.[63] Many have been impressed and enthusiastic and his 'findings' are still cited in the 21st century.[64] Conscious of the gay rights movement, scholars were initially slow to come forward. Once they did, they quickly found major fallacies in his reasoning and major errors in his research.[65] This might be a prime example of the advocacy scholarship which has become such an unfortunate trend in academia. Using questionable material to re-write history distorts facts to reach false conclusions and promote political agendas, whether feminist, Afrocentric, atheist or 'gay'.

Boswell based his arguments on highly subjective readings of accounts of *adelphoiesis* or sealing ceremonies, used in church liturgies to confirm loyal brotherhood, helping to construct his case by using equivalents for the words used that have modern homosexual connotations which the originals lacked. For example: translating *adelphos* (brother) as denoting a homosexual lover. Ancient rituals to affirm adoption or friendship are still present in Eastern Christianity. They are completely different from marriage ceremonies, and are from times when the church imposed penalties for sodomy which the early fathers described as disgustingly obscene and contrary to nature.[66]

There are similar misinterpretations of poetic or literary texts dealing with erotic love which conventionally used the masculine pronoun. Again, literature is not evidence. Boswell's work furthered a genre where all companionship mentioned in scripture or literature is given homoerotic interpretations – whether Jesus and St John, SS. Peter and Paul, Sergius and Bacchus, and so forth. Again, this ignores the Christian stress on the brotherhood of believers and the Fatherhood of God. It negates how the obligatory altruism marking human familial relations is transferred to non-kin relations, with origins in generational bonds and kinship, not male on male sex.

The search for antecedents of SSM reaches giddy heights in Professor of anthropology Roger N. Lancaster's claim that same sex friendships or sexually exclusive institutions or associations, particularly where entrance is marked by "officiating authority, amount to something very much like 'marriage'". These include: "orders of monastic nuns, certain priesthoods, any number of warrior castes and... groups of women who lived collectively on the Chinese Kwantung delta in the nineteenth century." Moreover, reproduction is "always a *social* understanding" with "little that is 'natural' or 'self-evident about it". In the beginning, Gilgamesh was provided with a male friend, rather than Adam with Eve and Aristotle believed reproduction involved transferring a homunculus. Is Lancaster trying to say that two men can procreate as man and woman if we have the right "social understanding"? The pinnacle of Lancaster's absurdity is reached in his claim that "same sex relationships were the very models of ideal heterosexual marriages."[67] Not far from this are Peter Tatchell's assertions that, since the 1949 Marriage Act did not stipulate male and female, a ban on same sex marriage originated in the 1970s, when Lancaster's "coercive heterosexuality" targeted gays for exclusion.[68] As Roger Sandall observes, it is the symbolic power of fictionalised pasts that counts. However false, newly concocted myths are justified so long as the cause is just.

If brotherhood ceremonies or monastic vows were never intended to sanction homosexual relations, neither were feudal oaths. Promises to serve, obey and love your lord were made in times of great social dislocation and weak or absent central authority. People had to rely on each other for protection and made alliances that imitated the absolute loyalty expected of kin. This is despite an *Observer* reviewer's claim that warlords embrace on a pact in Shakespeare's *Coriolanus* out of 'homoerotic attraction'.[69] It was not coincidental that the extended family also increased in importance in hazardous times.[70] In early Germanic and Frankish societies kinship was a major organising principle which, upon Christianisation, was extended through ritual to godparents – a spiritual kinship by sponsorship which specifically forbade sexual relations.[71]

Formalised adult same sex relations would contravene expectations of children to continue the family line, contribute to production and, in many societies, attend to ancestral rites. Non-generative relations could never possess the same value as (potentially) procreative, cross-kin and multi-generational alliances – to share risks and recruit support from a network of relatives. They might even be a mockery of marriage. In one of Juvenal's *Satires*, a cross dresser sits on the bridegroom's lap in a "parody both exhilarating and monstrous, to which nature refuses the fruits of procreation".[72] In pagan and Christian Rome, marriage was a 'sacred and enduring union' contracted for 'marital affection' and the 'propagation of offspring' (*consortium omnis vitae*).[73]

Great lovers from antiquity are often held up as models of homoerotic relationships although, if they were around today, many would be in jail.[74] This includes Nero, who castrated a boy to marry, and the idealised North American Indians who raised young men to be 'passives' and 'sexual resources' for the tribe. Emperors and high-ranking officials may have had young male lovers or sexual activity with boys. These were often slaves in societies where women were sequestered, high status adolescent males were regularly chaperoned (with good reason), and effeminacy despised, as in Ancient Greece. Even where cultures incorporated homosexual relationships, these never involved aspirations to have or transform marriage. Indeed, some 'queer' studies specialists maintain how it is "certainly arguable" that historically "the space for close, affectionate and intimate relationships between men, which were none the less regarded as heterosexual, was in many ways greater then it is at the moment." In this context, sodomy was unacceptably threatening and confusing, particularly when it involved those in power, not least because it represented a disruptive "incursion of desire into fields (friendship, policies, bonds between men) which are explicitly founded on its repudiation". Furthermore, the practice of same sex relations historically and across cultures is frequently misunderstood. There have been those with same sex attractions or who indulged in same sex behaviour, whether as a phase in maturation or a supplement to heterosexual relations (without the danger of pregnancy) – particularly when women were unavailable. Using boys for sex fits into what can appear as 'homophobic' cultures, because homosexuality was not seen, or approved, as another lifestyle.[75] Describing Mombasa in the 1980s, "homosexual relations ... are almost without exception between a younger, poorer partner [a paid *shoga*] and an older, richer one, whether their connection is for a brief act of prostitution or a more lengthy relationship."[76] The older one "may have been a *shoga* himself ... but is likely to be successfully married to a woman as well as maintaining an interest in boys." Most boys with homosexual experience moved to heterosexual relations before marriage.

This situation is similar in the ancient Greek and Roman context where men chased women and boys.[77] Since both were receptive, "pederasty was not so different from heterosexuality" and thus "paradoxically acceptable". Far from a 'homo/hetero' distinction, ancient belief was that "a boy was 'other' in relation to a man [and] because of his temperament... analogous to that of a female." Thus:

For a boy under the age of puberty and thus lacking semen and …
erotic sensations, it was not a serious matter to be courted … Being
sexually inept, they risk nothing.[78]

A historian presenting a TV programme on Roman art rhapsodises over
a pot with scenes of (bearded) adult males sodomising (beardless) boys. It
is uncertain if he is aware of this reality or ignores it in his jolly account.
Children are now taken to see such objects as part of 'gay history' events
– while modern society purports to despise paedophilia. In such times "…
the phallic component is uppermost in the appeal… in one poem, Meleger
delights in the vision of five boys ministering to a single" man.[79]

Sexual relationships between boys and men may only have been approved
in Athenian aristocratic circles, where there was an emphasis on the social
and intellectual advantage these might provide, where men had pedagogic
responsibilities towards boys they seduced. At lower social levels, this was
more likely to be perceived as debased – with youths and women of free
birth kept away from adult male venues. With ethics dominated by matters
like the corruption of youth, there was a fine line to walk when chasing
boys, since sexual acts perpetrated upon them could compromise male
development. Ruining their malleable incipient sexuality was offensive
– just as a man behaved badly if he seduced another's wife or daughter.
Puberty produced a gender change as a boy became a man. Any attempt to
"obstruct this metamorphosis and therefore prolong the natural femininity
of childhood… would mean going against nature"[80] – hence the extreme
caution about having sex with those navigating adolescence and entering
manhood.

Adolescents… acquire a sensibility that makes them vulnerable. …
because they respond, they can also be changed by the sexual act. They
learn what, how and where to feel, they train their bodies and acquire
habits … they run the risk of becoming effeminate – which also means
remaining infantile.[81]

There might be attempts to extend childhood with continued penetration.
A constant of pederastic attraction is how the soft childish and feminine

body is more exciting as it becomes sexually sensitive and, once arousal to the particular type of stimulus occurs, it can form a pattern for the recipient. In contrast to an asexual boy, an adult male playing the sexually receptive partner was regarded as an object of ridicule. The:

> ...adult *cinaedus* fights the physiological virilisation of his body by wriggling his bottom, cross-dressing and, above all, removing body hair. It is a struggle against time and against the loss of childhood's femininity. ... If he prefers to remain that welcoming body, as if a boy, or a woman, the transformation has not succeeded: he has turned out badly..., a man who desires another man.[82]

5.5   GAY APES

Adding to the tribal and historical pedigree given for SSM, a 'gay' animal theme is being increasingly employed and expanded. Here: "every species, from beetles to shrews to chimpanzees, has a consistent minority who prefer their own sex"[83] and their behaviour is interpreted as a precursor to or even equated with SSM. Once it was abhorrent to emulate 'brute beasts'. Now animals are meant to provide us with demonstrations of how all manner of practices and predilections are normal, widespread and therefore validate and predicate social and legal change. Popular broadcaster Stephen Fry speaking for Out4Marriage in October 2012 attacked critics with claims that, while 260 species had 'gay' tendencies, only humans were homophobic. Two male penguins seemed so devoted to each other that zookeepers gave them an egg to hatch. They were "dubbed 'gay' and elevated to the status of the Elton and David of the animal kingdom" – just as in Toronto others made it to children's books like *And Tango makes three* along with 'gay' classic *King & King*.[84] When they mated with females there were complaints that this was 'homophobic' as "if some fundamental human right was being broken".[85]

In similar vein, Brett Mills, head of media studies in the University of East Anglia, criticised the BBC and David Attenborough as homozoophobic for failing to highlight the homosexuality 'pretty much everywhere' among animals and skewing the audience's view of what was 'natural'.[86] In *The Life Of Birds* (1998), male sandpipers circled one another in an 'aggressive' manner and in *The Life Of Mammals* (2003) male chimps embraced in 'friendly affection' – when all might have been homosexual. Accounts of animals pairing, mating and raising offspring are accused of suggesting that heterosexuality or 'family' rearing is normative or necessary, and ignoring options like promiscuity and single parenting. Other 'natural' examples add to claims that homosexuals make superior parents because such birds 'outperform' heterosexuals with better nests and parenting – raising questions of where they get the young from to 'parent', or are they practising?

Contradictions abound. Why is 'better' parenting endorsed for 'homosexual' creatures, if all 'options' are equally good? Interestingly, when Friedrich Engels insisted that early or primitive human society was one of unrestricted sexual freedom where every woman belonged to every man and every man to every woman, he was emphatic how this was not to be contradicted by cases of birds that mate for long periods: "examples of faithful monogamy among birds prove nothing about man for the simple reason that men are not descended from birds".[87]

Actually, there are also faithfully monogamous (Azara's owl) monkeys where males are closely invested in the care of their (biological) young – but seemingly neglected as role models for humanity.

If animals do not find or are kept from mates, they may instinctively mount or engage in nesting behaviour with other males. (It is commonplace that human prisoners resort to sodomy.) Sexual activity amongst animals is seasonal. There is a surge in hormonal levels during a 'mating season' when males become very aggressive and will mount almost anything until finding a female. Male penguins copulate with dead bodies and engage in coercive sex with chicks that leads to death. What 'orientation' is the dog humping a table or trouser legs? A chimpanzee (Nim) trained to use human dialogue (by Herbert Terrace of Columbia University) is filmed trying to copulate with a pet cat. Many species are cannibalistic. Some eat their own young. It is usual for males who replace another in the pride (lions) or troupe (apes) to kill offspring of the previous male(s) before re-impregnating the females. This has similarities to the behaviour shown in the disproportionate level of infant and child killings perpetrated by unrelated human males, particularly where they have not made a commitment to the mother and any children she might have had with other men.

Animals cannot conceptualize sexual categories, have no rules, legal structures or institutions and their behaviour does not constitute a moral code. (Documentaries have been criticised for invading animals' 'rights' to 'privacy' when they can have no such concepts and unselfconsciously defecate, masturbate and mate.) Accusations are not unjustified that, as with Boswell, there are those out to topple the ethical code of Christian civilisation. Atheists like to claim that animal behaviour is the basis for social and moral order. Here we find A. C. Grayling insisting that the empathy shown by apes is a "more than sufficient evolutionary source of human morality. What else could underlie bonding, mutual awareness of needs, sharing and co-operation…?" Complaining about the "limitations of sexuality that have been forced upon us" Grayling muses how animals not only "share an emotional life not too distant from humans" but one "free of the perversities and limitations of sexuality that have been forced upon us…" by religion (i.e. Christianity).[88] He does not appear to recognise how human beings create understandings which exist independently of their individual manifestations, where it is in the nature of morality that this provides public reference points. Individuals need to find themselves reflected in the social order, in order to recognise externally the value of what they do. To Grayling even a state or nation is "highly artificial" and thus "arrant nonsense".[89] Are people to roam around the whole world like troupes of baboons with no direction to anything, incomprehensibly clashing when not randomly mating? As explained:

> We have reason … to create the maximal self, which mediates in all our dealings. The maximal self does not exist in the state of nature, but only in society, and is sustained by customs, habits and beliefs that are easily destroyed and which we destroy at our peril.[90]

An instance in nature can be found to justify anything, as Engels and (now) Raymond Tallis remind us. This might be seen as projecting your own images onto your chosen creature – where "an anthromorphizing gaze can be cast with equal fondness on creepy crawlies."[91] As a further dig at those who read "strict monogamy" from nature, Engels observed how: "the palm must go to the tapeworm, which has a complete set of male and female sexual organs in each of its 50 to 200 proglottides or sections, and spends its whole life copulating in all its sections with itself."[92]

There is the pervasive feminist insistence that while women might bear babies, they have no more inclination to look after them once produced than do males or passing strangers, since maternal care is purportedly socially imposed. Presumably, spawning fishes would be the models. The fact that all mammalian females care for the infants they produce becomes irrelevant in this instance.

5.6 A MATTER OF BOUNDARIES

Clearly, same sex or equal marriage is far more complex than just a cosmetic change or matter of sharing existing rights with a few more people. Not least, inherent contradictions prevent this being assimilated to the template of the conjugal union. Where marriage is available to those of the same sex, it is not about procreation. Where consummation and fidelity are irrelevant, it is not about sex. Practically, what initially happens is that the question of 'how is equality achievable for same-sex marriage' becomes 'how is conjugality made compatible with same sex union?' To avoid discrimination, and enforce uniformity where there is none, the latter must provide the shape of things to come. When not addressing the matter in terms of misrepresentation, advocates for redefining marriage increasingly acknowledge that (for them) the desirable effect will be the radical transformation of the institution. Rather than just expanding the pool of eligible people allowed to enter an established and unchanged institution, the nature of the prize being distributed is, unavoidably, altered in the process. The departure from the traditional conception of complementary and generative union negates marriage's constitutive norms, stripping men and women of any institution that belongs to them. They are deprived of the distinctive union across the sexes which reflects their unique capacity and responsibility for creating and rearing children. Aristotle's verdict would be that 'The worst sort of inequality is to try to make unequal things equal.'

The alternative is separate forms of union, designed for different types of relationships – which might suggest for some people that marriage and civil partnerships were a fair compromise providing two separately tailored institutions to serve two different relationships. Making distinctions in law is not inherently unjust but simply recognises differences. Civil partnership provides financial security combined with openness. It gives equal rights while avoiding sexual complementarity – there being no consummation to seal and no adultery to end unions. As 'long-term' not 'life-long', these offer flexibility, and partners do not have to speak prescribed words or make vows in the presence of witnesses. Is it equal if heterosexuals are both denied anything exclusively of their own, yet disallowed civil partnerships? MPs and gay rights campaigner Peter Tatchell have called for this discrimination to end, so that actual or prospective parents may (presumably) have lighter, non-exclusive relationships.

Ever hovering is the matter of boundaries, or rather, their absence. Same sex unions have little or no form or parameters – apart from agreement between consenting adults. If exclusivity is replaced by open relationships, moral distinctions between traditional (monogamous) marriage and polyamory die. When measures once instituted to recognise committed, complementary and generative relationships are given to others who do not fulfil the original criteria, the process becomes arbitrary. The principles that justify the legal recognition of same sex unions also justify recognition of other unions, sexual or not. Otherwise, is there not inequality? If marriage is a union of any two persons, yet equates with loving whomever we choose, this is not a truly neutral policy. Theresa May, as Home Secretary, declared that:

> I believe if two people care or each other, if they love each other, if they want to commit to each other and spend the rest of their lives together then they should be able to get married and marriage should be for everyone, and that's why I'm coming Out4Marriage.

She was joined by Desmond Swayne, the Prime Minister's parliamentary aide, arguing for Christian blessings for same sex couples: "I believe that the promises of the Gospel are unconfined: they're for everyone, and the sacraments that follow from that should be available to everyone."[93] Again, there is no consideration of consequences beyond the first post. Similarly, Deputy Prime Minister Nick Clegg proclaimed how nothing was:

> ...more fundamental than the belief that people should be able to love whomever they choose: that we should let one another be, free from discrimination and able to enjoy the full equality that is each of our right.[94]

Love whomever they chose? Is it not bigoted or discriminatory to deny the right to any combination of people to enjoy this beneficence? If "unnecessary interference by the State" must go, this is at odds with assertions that "equal marriage will almost [*sic*] be the final destination or the ultimate goal, rather than the beginning of a slippery slope"? [95] After all, we are still:

> ...by the revisionists' logic ...discriminating against those seeking open, temporary, polygynous, polyandrous, polyamorous, incestuous, or bestial unions. After all, people can find themselves experiencing sexual and romantic desire for multiple partners (concurrent or serial), or closely blood-related partners, or nonhuman partners. They are (presumably) free not to act on these sexual desires, but this is true also of people attracted to persons of the same sex. [96]

Drawing on the reasoning of J. S. Mill, if the "State's role should be limited to only prohibiting something in law if there is evidence that the prohibition prevents harm to others," [97] where is "harm" in permitting three to marry?

Calls for recognition of multiple relationships are heard from rights exponents asking for the repeal of restrictions on the sex or the numbers of persons entering a marriage or allowed to adopt, with extensions to polyamorists or plural loves ('triads' or 'truples' with 'open' relationships). Everywhere same sex marriage passes into law, the pressure for multiple and/or temporary unions mounts up. A BBC documentary (*Monogamy and the Rules of Love*, August 2013) featuring a number of people in polygamous relationships affirmed that monogamy was out of fashion. Polyamorous relationships could become the norm, since there was little room for sexual fidelity in a "society where choice is everything". Its presenter suggested that the "taboo" surrounding intimate multi-partner relationships could disappear within the next ten years and, as: "No-one asks us to only love one of our children. Why shouldn't it be any different with romantic love?" [98] An actress asserts how monogamy was "an odd state... for women". Better to have "three relationships over the three stages of your life ...your young life, your middle life, and your late life". After all, "[m]arried couples have always abandoned each other, run off and divorced, even when the stigma was high". [99] Anyone expecting any consideration of the possible effects on children was bound to be disappointed.

The mounting scorn for monogamy is furthered by the escalation of adulatory features showcasing homosexual relationships in group contexts. In "the wake of a survey revealing that women are increasingly open to same-sex experiences" an actress enthuses over her lesbian lover ensconced along with her son and his father: "Whomever I love, however I love them, whether they sleep in my bed or not, or whether I do homework with them or share a child with them, 'love is love'. And I love my modern family" – paraded as "a more honest family".[100] This voluntary "honest family" arrangement is elsewhere attributed to the modern delusion that people can keep all their options open all the time, avoiding any constraints or demands as long as they [and the children] don't make any demands or 'impose their values' on others". [101] Allan Bloom's verdict that this "absoluteness of desire uninhibited by thoughts of virtue is what is found in the state of nature" might looks like the realisation of Engel's dream of primeval society's group marriage or A.C. Grayling's moral directions from the planet of the apes. To Bloom, this:

...represents the turn in philosophy away from trying to tame or perfect desire by virtue, and toward finding out what one's desire is and living according to it. This is largely accomplished by criticizing virtue, which covers and corrupts desire. Our desire becomes a kind of oracle we consult; it is now the last word, while in the past it was the questionable and dangerous part of us.[102]

It is insufficient to reply that societies that have legalised same sex marriage have taken no steps to legalise polygamy or polyamory. All this may seem far-fetched, but then so was 'gay marriage' when sodomy was decriminalised in 1967. While the UK Government said that it has no intention of allowing polygamous marriages as part of SSM legislation, it has not explained in any detail its reasons for taking that position. Given the track record of courts interpreting the Human Rights Act, the prospect is not absurd. Law is captive to changing fashions, particularly given an understanding of justice which requires meeting personal and interest group demands.

Legalisation is recent anywhere, but where same sex union is allowed or awaits implementation, other sexual minorities emerge with the same demands on the same basis: 'This is me, I am not hurting anyone, and I am discriminated against on the basis of my sexuality'. Polyamorous supporters in New Zealand called for legal recognition just weeks after same-sex marriage was legalised and Australia's Green Party is campaigning for poly marriage. In the Netherlands in 2005, a *ménage a trios* between two bisexual women and a man was given legal sanction because the law did not seemingly forbid more than two parties to the arrangement (heterosexuals were given civil partnerships when homosexuals were allowed to marry). By 2013, the politician who masterminded the gay marriage campaign was optimistic about group marriage which was already being openly discussed. As a judge in San Paulo (2011) ruled that a couple could convert their civil union (recognised since 2004) into marriage, three people were allowed to enter. In 2001, the Law Commission of Canada submitted its 'Beyond Conjugality' report to Parliament, which proposed allowing the registration of any personal relationship in lieu of marriage, and the arrival of same sex marriage in 2005 gave a significant boost to the drive to legalise polygamy. With schools encouraged to display ('Love has no gender') posters with threesomes,[103] a Canadian Polyamory Advocacy Association now campaigns for polyamorous relationships to be put on the same legal footing as others. Polyamorists are said to comprise 0.5% of the population and engage in relationships which embrace groups of heterosexual, homosexual, bisexual and transgendered people. The US polyamory movement is prominent on legal and academic circuits. It has its own flagship magazines and organisations and hopes to use gay marriage as the door to legalised polyamory. Before same sex marriage was on the Scottish statute book, Ian Stewart insisted that people should be free to marry more than one partner "without interference" as a "matter of equality". He said, "Polyandrous and polygamous marriage will not devalue or undermine the validity of homosexual or heterosexual marriage in any way whatsoever."[104]

Faced with the problems of proliferation as much as merging irreconcilables, then perhaps the best answer really is to set people free to "create their own families in the way most suitable to them."[105] After all, why should the state have any right to recognise or impose one form of relationship over another? Is it not more honest simply to surrender to marriage's outright abolition? As we appear to be left just with a means to self-fulfilment, some people might be led to conclude that "perhaps the proper response is to ...achieve equality of relationships by indifference to all."[106]

Chapter Six

MARRIAGE RENAISSANCE?

6.1   SAVING MARRIAGE?

Notwithstanding the possibility that disintegrative trends might be accelerated by the redefinition of marriage, arguments were quickly assembled to support David Cameron's seemingly sudden rush to legislation. Unusually, marriage was characterised as having "been one of the bedrocks of civilisation, helping to bind individuals and communities together" and it was suggested that there "is no comparable social institution for this positive role in society."[1]

Far from SSM fundamentally altering the institution, transforming its social role and meaning, and undermining its structuring norms of monogamy and exclusivity, it was being suggested that it would be the institution's saviour. The Home Secretary Theresa May promised that: "homosexuals will be missionaries to the wider society and make marriage stronger."[2] Jumping aboard and taking the helm, they would reverse marriage's fortunes. By doing what no government had done they will rescue what heterosexuals have spoilt – a cheap solution, if it would work.

Thus, conjugal deconstructionists were matched by a conservative version of the 'transformer' take where, instead of being marriage's undertaker, same sex union is *the solution* with which to revive a decrepit and dying institution.[3] This was broader than claims for same sex unions being beacons for spicier relationships and the more equal distribution of household labour.

6.2 PRIORITY POPULATION?

In addition to affording leadership opportunities, there is the prospect of marriage as the remedy for homosexuals' own tribulations – something debate has avoided if it involves acknowledging the possible drawbacks of this lifestyle. Also avoided has been the way this conservative perspective imagines that homosexuals will benefit from marriage, as this relates to control and order, in line with the understandings of Durkheim. Health concerns have, of course, been a leading rationale for LGBT friendly interventions and initiatives throughout health provision, policing, law, media and, most prominently, education. These interventions seek to address the purported lack of social approval for same sex relationships – extending to public events, promotional campaigns and drives against those who dissent throughout public life. Indeed, claims about the health consequences of not embracing and furthering the interests of this group have had little parallel elsewhere, both in terms of harms inflicted and crying out for redress and the rapid and overwhelmingly uncritical acceptance and implementation of the exponents' suggestions. Along with other affirmations, it is part of an ever more welcoming environment. Boasting about his proposals, David Cameron pointedly used the narrative of the persecuted gay pupil:

> …there will be young boys in schools today who are gay, who are worried about being bullied, who are worried about what society thinks of them, who can see that the highest Parliament in the land has said that their love is worth the same as anybody else's love and … and they will stand a bit taller today.[4]

From the moment SSM was mooted, accusations of the harms a discriminatory environment visited upon homosexuals extended to terrible tales of mass suicides of youngsters, attributed to a lack of recognition. (One MP asserted in a public meeting that he knew of a group of teenagers who committed suicide due to homophobia. I repeatedly asked for any evidence or reference, and none has been forthcoming.) Another MP, who accused Church leaders for criticising SSM plans, moved seamlessly into assertions that "there are still kids being bullied in school. There is still a situation where we have no Premier League football players who feel able to come out."[5]

Conservative advocates' argument for SSM's wider social benefits shifted from social problems to the advantages of marriage for adults and then on to the welfare of homosexuals "excluded from an institution that will benefit them". Homosexual tribulations are then "the first argument in favour of equal marriage..." even if they are "a small minority of the population". The speculation is that the "pacifying effect of marriage" on young straight men "could also have equal benefits for young gay men" – despite the absence of suggestions for reversing the increasing opt out from marriage by "young straight men".[6] No assertive pressure groups champion what might as much or more be regarded as a downgraded and marginalised section of society. If anything, an "unthinking and automatic rubbishing of men ... is now so part of our culture that it is hardly even noticed."[7] Why must reducing health disparities in LGB populations be "an important public health priority" when the adverse consequences for the general population of dismantling marriage have been ignored? Should not justice demand equal priority? Is there not a legitimate interest in children growing up in the most favourable or optimum conditions, rather than spawned randomly?

Marriage's benefits for adults have been recognised even less than those for children. Since the average age at first marriage is increasing, and growing numbers remain unmarried, the relations between marital status, morbidity and mortality should merit serious attention. Higher marriage and employment rates (which are often coterminous for men, particularly low or semi-skilled men) would probably reduce their suicide rate. Men may not derive much satisfaction from their work, but it is validated through responsibilities towards others – that can enrich even the most menial tasks. More live-in, working, married fathers would benefit themselves, public safety, public finances, mothers and children. This is the best bargain society can have. Otherwise, what we have is little short of a crisis in development, with few growth points for young men, especially at the lower socioeconomic reaches of society. If the "importance of social institutions and social incentives in guiding behaviour is traditionally an important part of centre right philosophy",[8] this hardly applies more than here. How do conservative revisionists envisage SSM will be the force for revival as the newcomers salvage virtues from the old order to carry into a reformed model, if the conjugal family is abandoned territory? It is then useful to know about the fortunes of marriage in respect of both minorities and majority populations where same sex or equal unions have been recognised around the world.

6.3   WELCOME TO THE PARTY

It might certainly appear as if heterosexuals have neglected to look after marriage when the damage done by their infidelity, divorce rates, casual cohabitation and unwed births is considered.[9] Is not individual indulgence at the grass roots the real threat to marriage? Self-denial has given way to self-interest, regardless of the long term harm done to self and others. Having 'smashed the family' themselves, this indictment puts heterosexuals in no position to accuse others with wanting to wreck it when all they have sought is incorporation:

> ...[n]othing could be easier in the face of heterosexual promiscuity, premarital sex, teenage pregnancy, and skyrocketing divorce rates than to fasten our attention on a long-despised class of people who bear few children. ...on reflection, such attitudes embody a double standard of permissiveness towards straights and censoriousness towards gays who engage in acts that are essentially the same.[10]

After all, the notion is put about through every form of communication that sex is a recreational activity which has little to do with making babies.

This fails to take into account how marriage has been systematically dismantled. Decay owes itself not simply to a lack of morals or corruption on the ground, but the rise and entrenchment of anti-family doctrine and its practical consequences.[11] It is perhaps more than a little unfair to lay all the blame on those who have taken up the suggestions or gone with the incentives that have been set before them in terms of the funding of the stand-alone mother, the progressive dilution of the marriage contract, fiscal discrimination, linguistic deletion, endless denigration, dispersal of marital rights and the defenestration of fathers in law and public policy.

Even so, it might still follow at the very least that SSM will not contribute to disintegrative trends, doing very well as these are without it. Even better:

> At a time when many heterosexuals are spurning the idea of marriage, here is a section of society positively lobbying for the right to respect and continue the institution. Perhaps gay marriage will encourage more

straight people back on to the marital path.[12]

This was not without support from pro-marriage homosexuals like Jonathan Rauch who are eager to reverse marital decline and reintegrate sexual behaviour into marriage, so that its 'civilizing domesticating' features might be shared by all.[13] Far from subverting traditional norms, this force for revival promised to "strengthen ...valuable notions of commitment, fidelity and responsibility..."[14] A win – win situation? David Cameron's Work and Pensions Secretary Iain Duncan Smith quickly accepted that same sex marriage was the way forward to a better society. This conservative endorsement of SSM prompted the Marxist response that: "the key issue is the broader role that marriage plays in supporting the politics of state austerity and the rolling back of the welfare state." The expansion of the "legal family" was purely to "encourage lesbians and gay men to take on care burdens and financial dependency...."[15]

However, if "marriage equality ... is a social good and a small minority of the population should not be excluded" how does the *non sequitur* follow that since: "the most significant driver of social instability and poverty – [is] family breakdown... Backing [same sex] marriage... would encourage strong and stable families, and tackle the social breakdown that fuels poverty."[16] The "small minority" is more likely than the general run of people to be childless, higher income men. There is that continual oscillation between arguing that there are benefits for all and no harms from SSM – which are not the same. The precedent of same sex adoption was not encouraging. Supposedly, this would lead to a rise in adoption's dismally low rates as lots of eager would-be gay parents rushed forward, but rates remained low or even fell. The numbers of heterosexual, especially Christian, married couples who were put off by the antipathy shown towards them in the same sex adoption debates might even have exceeded those recruited through gay adoption campaigns.

Above all, how was "backing marriage" to tackle "social breakdown" reconcilable with understanding this just as a "partnership between two people" which enshrines the severance of paternity from nuptiality?[17] The contradiction was present in the Prime Minister endorsing the Big Society while accepting marriage as a contract with no reference beyond two adults' emotions and sexual choices – or a state registry of friendship. What went unanswered is the argument that if marriage is "detached from the natural, complementary teleology of the sexes, [and]…becomes nothing beyond what each of us makes of it", this may deplete any prospective benefits. Perhaps this was unseen.[18] Again, the perception of only one generational couple relationships might testify to how removing the basis for a norm erodes knowledge as much as adherence to that norm. Not least, the inward orientation of coupledom in any form is at odds with how marriage in its traditional context invokes the social pressures which strengthen adherence to standards basic to the common good.[19]

For benefits to impact upon social problems there must be a significant rise in the general marriage rate. The only suggestion as to how equal sex marriage could possibly accomplish this is that it will be for the best in the best of all possible worlds because, (writers for the think-tank Policy Exchange quote from the *New York Times*):

> Gay people are able to celebrate their differences with straight people, without rejecting the rest of society ... gay people are not united by race, creed, political ideas or income. Their parents and siblings are likely to be straight. Gay people are not a community apart, they are an integral part of society. The impact ... is not limited to those gay people who want to marry, but sends a signal to all that they are "invited to the party".[20]

Is this telling us that there will be a surge of heterosexuals into marriage because, as a minority of a "small minority" marries, the population is caught up in a vast spontaneous public acclamation? Aside from being characteristic of the way that policies are so often driven by emotional sloganeering or 'spin', there is affinity with vacuous revolutionary declarations where 'people will rise up', 'there will be a new dawn', etc. What is "the rest of society" supposed to make of a possible invitation to a gay wedding celebration? At the same time (and in a completely contradictory vein), businesses are reassured that the impact on pension rights is going to be very small, since:

> There is no evidence that there will be a large surge of gay people getting married after equal marriage is introduced and even a moderate surge would only be equivalent of a small increase in heterosexual marriage.[21]

Apart from a party invite, what else? Suppositions about prospective benefits might be offset against what limited evidence we have from around the world about rates of uptake and endurance, as well as the fortunes of marriage and families generally, where equality or access to recognised unions for same sex partners has been available. A big limitation here relates to how same sex or equal marriage has only recently been legalised in a handful of countries.

6.4   OPPORTUNITY EMBRACED?

[*An expanded version of this appeared in Morgan, P, What Happens to Marriage and Families where the Law recognises "Same-Sex marriage"? 2013, SPUC.*]

A decade ago now, it was asserted that any notion that giving marital rights to gay couples will "undermine heterosexual marriage is based on the consistent misuse and misinterpretation of data".[22] Since then, it is suggested that marriage rates have remained high or even grown in countries that have enacted (what vacillates between) 'partnerships' and 'marriage'. Constant is not the same as rising. We should at least expect some upward trend, if only because homosexuals rush to be wed.

Any pursuit of a marriage revival, whether for minorities or the majority, would have to confront the processes propelling what has come to be known as the second demographic transition of the Western world. Increasing rates of relationship instability, informal cohabitation and unwed births have weakened the conjugal family as the primary child rearing environment.

The Nordic countries are leaders. Not far behind are France, Belgium, Great Britain, and Germany, along with the USA and Canada. To a greater or lesser degree, moral and cultural controls have disappeared and religious influence has faded. Privileges once reserved for marriage are often available to individuals regardless of relationship status. Male provision for families might be sidelined or frowned upon: mothers expected to be employed and self-sufficient; young children in day care, and spousal benefits or exemptions eroded or non-existent. Southern European countries like Italy and Greece have tighter family patterns and lower rates of cohabitation, family dissolution, and out-of-wedlock births. There is a general movement towards the Nordic pattern facilitated by secularisation, increasing sexualisation, easier marital dissolution and the influence of European institutions.

The disintegrative process is somewhat held in check by the tendency for parents to marry after a couple of births, pointing to the persistence of norms and family pressures that relate child rearing to spousal commitment. As out-of-wedlock childbearing pushes beyond 50%, a stalling process is evident as this enters the toughest area of cultural resistance, particularly in the higher echelons of society. Once that marker is breached, the tendency to marry at the second birth dissipates. While mass cohabitation is initially more of a prelude to marriage or separation, it then extends into a substitute for marriage. People conform to suggestion and example and, as married parenthood moves towards a minority phenomenon, it loses the critical mass needed to be a socially normative force.

In the Nordic countries, civil unions or 'registered partnerships' have been available for the longest time – Denmark from 1989; Norway from 1993 and Sweden from 1995. Norway moved to 'gender-neutral' marriage in 2008 and Sweden in 2009 imposed it virtually overnight without consultation. Since marriage, particularly in Sweden, has long had little or no recognition or status, the two have been treated for all intents and purposes as virtually identical. Initial exceptions later withdrawn were that there were no rights to marry in a state church, adopt children or access reproductive technologies. The Netherlands first introduced same sex marriage in 2001, followed by Belgium in 2003. Both countries created civil partnerships a few years earlier. Dispensing with civil unions as a prelude, Spain and Canada moved directly to marriage in 2005. France introduced PACS or civil contracts in 1999 which gave some rights to cohabiting couples, regardless of gender. In 2004, as a mayor conducted a same sex marriage ceremony and a court nullified the union, France then moved towards equal marriage. Since 1997, when Hawaii became the first state in the USA to allow reciprocal-beneficiary registration for same-sex couples, 19 states and the District of Columbia have granted some form of legal recognition to same sex relationships. The variants include marriage, civil unions, domestic partnerships, and reciprocal-beneficiary relationships. Most prominently, there have been civil unions in Vermont (2000), domestic partnerships in California (1999) and marriage in Massachusetts (2004).

Where civil partnerships have been on offer, the uptake has been minimal. Danish experience is that a cumulative total of 2168 partnerships were registered in the years 1990–1998, encompassing 1.7% of the homosexual population.[23] For a slightly longer period of 1989–2001, 3,463 people in a cohort followed over time married a partner of their own sex compared to 882,302 who married someone of the opposite sex: a ratio of approximately one to 250,000.[24]

The prediction for the UK in the White Paper of 2003 of 62,000 civil partnerships being formed in the first five years turned out to be exaggerated.[25] According to the 2001 Census, same sex households had been overestimated by more than 850%, with fewer than 40,000 in England and Wales.[26] The Government then admitted that very few homosexuals would wish to enter into a civil partnership. According to its 'high take-up scenario' 96.7% of all homosexuals in the UK would still not register a civil partnership.[27] By 2011, approximately 53,417 civil partnerships had been formed since December 2005. Numbers fell from 16,106 in 2006 to 8728 in 2007, falling 47% to 6281 in 2009, with a rise to 6795 in 2011 – representing less than one person per 1,000 unmarried adults aged over 16 in England and Wales. (Before SSM became a reality in England and Wales, the ONS seemed set to make the numbers difficult to know. Like the designation of all and any relationship as a 'partnership' in research, it set out to amalgamate the figures for 'opposite-sex' and SSM until protests halted the move.) See Appendix, Fig. 1 – number of civil partnerships in the UK by quarter of occurrence, 2005/2011.

The Netherlands saw 2%–6% of homosexuals entering in the first five years, much the same as Belgium.[28] By 2010, one in three Dutch homosexual couples living together had their relationships officially registered, with nearly 11,000 married and more than 6,000 in registered partnerships. Survey data suggest that 2.8% and 1.4% of Dutch men and women are gay or lesbian – indicating that the homosexual population is approximately two thirds of a million – a high estimate. Claims are that same sex marriage is declining in popularity. The 2,500 couples who married in 2001, the year it was legalised, dropped to 1,800 in 2002, 1,384 in 2010 and 1,355 in 2011 – a 52 fold difference from the heterosexual marriage total of 70,217. By 2009 less than 2% of marriages involved same-sex couples. The number registering partnerships varies between 400 and 600 per year.

Researchers remark how their "first observation is that the incidence of same-sex marriage in Norway and Sweden is not particularly impressive."[29] Figures have been low and suggest that 1% to 5% of the homosexual population contract a civil partnership or marriage. Trends indicate that the numbers tend to decrease after an initial burst and with little or no difference between partnership and marriage rates. For the 1,293 partnerships contracted in Norway in 1993–2001, 196,000 heterosexual marriages were entered; indicating a ratio of around 7 new same-sex unions to 1,000 marriages. For almost 20% of registered partnerships over the 1990s, one partner was previously married. In least 16% of the cases, one was a parent, although not particularly likely to be living with their children.[30]

In Sweden, there were 1,526 partnerships during the period 1995–2002, compared with 280,000 heterosexual marriages registered – or 5 to 1,000. The vast majority of early partnerships involved men, after which the sex gap narrowed. Suggestions are that 1% to 5% of the homosexual population contracts a civil partnership or marriage.

In the first four years when same sex marriage became available in Massachusetts, the average was about 3,000 per year, including those from out of State. Overall, same sex households have increased in the USA, from 358,000 same-sex (married or unmarried) households in 2000 to 646,000 plus in the 2010 census (roughly 131,729 married and 514,735 unmarried) and account for 0.6% of all households.[31] The period in which same-sex marriage has been available in Canada varied from province to province (all maintain their own statistics) until national legislation took effect in July 2005. Depending on the province, it seems that between 0.15% and 14% of homosexuals have entered marriages. Again, the rate tails off over time.

Overall, there has been little or no difference in take-up between same sex marriage and registered partnerships. In places that have one or both *and* significant numbers of homosexuals, there has been no enduring groundswell. Experience with same sex partnership/marriage tends to bear out activists' claims that the existence of the 'right' is all, and participation more or less irrelevant. After all, 'equality' is not a numerical proposition. This is perhaps overlooked by some who believe they speak for reticent homosexuals desperate to share in a heterosexual privilege.

When same sex couples marry they are more likely than their heterosexual equivalents to change their minds later. Publicly professed legal partnerships do not seem to prevent more frequent dissolution compared to levels for married heterosexuals.[32] Longitudinal Swedish and Norwegian data on 2,819 same sex and 222,000 opposite-sex marriages included information on characteristics such as age, geographic background, as well as experience of previous opposite-sex marriage, parenthood and education. Compared to heterosexual unions, breakdown rates are 1.50 for men and 2.67 for women in Norway. Within five years 20% of male and 30% of female unions were terminated, compared to 13% for heterosexuals. It is similar in Sweden, where male unions are 50% more likely to end than heterosexual marriages and the risk for females is nearly double that for men. Comparisons of childless unions leave this unchanged as do controls for various demographic and socioeconomic variables. The instability of same sex unions has been labelled 'dynamism' to indicate superiority in contrast to the 'inertia' of marital stability – attributable to their lack of 'clear power structures' which oppress opposite sex relationships.

In the Netherlands, two thirds of same sex 'divorces' up to 2010 were by females.[33] Whether in Sweden, Norway or Massachusetts, this follows the heterosexual pattern where more females than males instigate divorce. Previously, a study compared same-sex cohabiters, different sex cohabiters and opposite sex married couples in the Netherlands between 1989 and 1999 (after which same sex partners could move into marriages). The dissolution rate for same-sex cohabitation was 12 times higher than the rate for different-sex marriage and three times higher than the rate for opposite sex cohabitation.[34] Dissolutions seem to be increasing for UK civil partnerships, with a 28.7% rise between 2010 and 2011 (compared with 5% for divorce). Again, female dissolutions are double those of male, with the rate rising as formation declines, with 6.1% of female partnerships dissolved in 2012 compared to 3.2% for male. See Appendix Fig. 2 (Number of civil partnership dissolutions in the UK, by quarter, 2007/11).

The high dissolution levels seen for same sex unions might indicate unfamiliarity with the norms of official unions. Equally, the symbolic meaning for those who have just acquired a right or now feel able to freely enter publicly available unions should predict lower separation rates. Since only the most eager and committed couples move in together, this highly selective group's relationships might even have been expected to be more likely to remain intact than those of more heterogeneous opposite sex couples.[35]

The message from the pooled data on relationship history for subjects in their 30s from the two British cohort studies of 1958 and 1970 is of continuity, rather than a break with the situation before official unions became available.[36] Same-sex couples accounted for 1% of all couples (similar to Sweden's 0.7). 40% were preceded by another union, compared to 29% of different sex cohabitations and 5% of marriages. The probability of a union lasting five years was .88 for marriage, .67 for opposite sex cohabitation and .37 for same sex cohabitation. Matters like socio-economic status and age explained next to none of the differences. Same sex dissolution levels were probably underestimated as short term unions were likely to be under reported. Should homosexuals supposedly have more trouble being open about their relationships because of stigma, then this does not match with the consistency of breakdown.

Dissolution rates tend to increase for marriage and cohabitation if the heterosexual partners had not grown up in a two parent married family, the explanation being that intact unions provide more positive role models and attitudes toward marriage. Curiously, this does not seem to apply to homosexuals. Danish information on the childhood correlates of first marriages in the national cohort of 2 million 18–49 year olds confirms how heterosexuals with unknown fathers, or who experience parental divorce or early termination of residence with both parents, are around a fifth less likely to marry than peers who grew up in intact marriages with known fathers during their first 18 years.[37] Conversely, all measures of parental relationship instability were positively linked to same sex marriage. Men who experienced early parental divorce were 39% more likely to marry homosexually, and for those who ceased to live with both parents before 18 years this was 55% to 76% higher. The trend was less pronounced for women, but still elevated where there had been maternal death, short parental marriage, or long duration of living with father only. Women who lost their mothers aged 12–17 years opted for SSM almost twice as often as non-orphaned women.

Maternal and paternal ages are also significantly and inversely associated with heterosexual marriage, but reversed for homosexual men (not women). Men with 35+ year-old mothers had 34% higher SSM rates than men with younger mothers. For each yearly increase in maternal age the likelihood increased. Men and women with siblings also had significantly higher heterosexual marriage rates and lower SSM rates compared with only children. Both men and women who grew up as the youngest child in a sibship were also more likely to marry homosexually than peers with younger siblings. While this might seem to support suggestions that late position in a male sibship has an important connection to homosexuality, there was no indication that older brothers were particularly common. But we are not dealing with a representative sample and there is no information about religious, economic, and educational variables. Men in SSM could be the exception to a rule that many older brothers are a formative factor for homosexuality.

There are further features of formal Scandinavian unions that warrant mention. One is high death rates – seen in the early years of same sex unions in Denmark, [38] plus the way that partners have been, on average, considerably older than corresponding opposite-sex spouses in Norway and Sweden.[39] Matters of inheritance rather than home building may be uppermost for same sex partners more than they are for heterosexuals.

High rates of non-national partners also suggest that many same sex unions serve immigration purposes, particularly for men. In Sweden, 45% of male partnerships included a non-citizen and 43% in Norway. Sweden is one of the most globalised countries. In the last few decades, the potential marriage market has increased dramatically, with increasing numbers of migrants, along with Swedes who travel, work or study abroad, and the rise of the internet.[40] It is part of a wider process, where over 20% of Norwegian marriages in mid-decade were between spouses with and without an immigrant background.[41] The probability of marrying spouses from outside the European Union has doubled for native Swedish women and quadrupled for men in less than 20 years and many will not have met in Sweden. Same sex unions with a foreign partner are particularly likely to dissolve, with nearly a half rapidly folding up. This suggests unions of convenience made (or bought and sold?) for resident rights and citizenship.

This has not been considered in the UK, but it is possible, particularly given the low number of homosexuals interested in unions for themselves. Nothing in law says you have to be homosexual to marry another man, and no consummation is required. Advertise abroad for a husband, charge him, divorce him and repeat.

6.5 HETEROSEXUAL CELEBRANTS?

Removing any incentives to get and stay married has had unsurprising effects on Scandinavian marriage rates. Swedish rates started their dramatic fall by the end of the 1960s (registering the lowest in recorded history in 1997) accompanied, as we have seen, by rising cohabitation, unwed births and single person households.[42] Sweden and Norway are the kind of places where we might expect to find that same sex unions have rescued marriage, whether or not welcomed by elites. Indeed, oscillations in Scandinavian marriage rates post-1990 have led to claims that same sex partnership/marriage has helped to revitalise the institution. If societies with such low marriage rates can see a boost from same sex marriage, why not elsewhere?

This has been forcefully put (mainly in reference to Norway) by US advocates William N. Eskridge and Darren R. Spedale.[43] They accept the data showing a close correlation between legal and economic changes and lower marriage, high divorce and unwed birth rates. Throughout the 1980s, Norwegian marital households with children plummeted, falling 18% from 1989 to1993 as cohabiting ones with children rose 70%. Contrary to doomsters' predictions that same sex partnerships and marriage would cause acceleration, whether temporarily or long term, the claim is that there was no further plunge. While there is still a continuous rise in cohabitation with children and a decline in marriage both absolutely and comparatively in the 1990s, same sex unions were "no stake through the heart of marriage". Instead, they were responsible for how "the trend slowed down a little bit after 1993."[44] Tabloids and media suggested that marriage was made 'fashionable' for young people due to royal rather than 'gay' weddings.

Demographers described both perspectives as 'misguided'.[45] In times of recession and unemployment, marriage may be suspended until financial circumstances improve, particular if this is closely connected to the desire to start a family. This happens anywhere, but societies with very low formal unions rates present further problems for analysis. There is greater volatility and a liability to be affected by predictions and one-off events as well as economic conditions. If any slowing of disintegrative trends is going on at all, there are a plethora of explanations besides SSM, which are bound to be more complex than simplistic mono-causal hunches. As suggested, the third phase of marital decline tends to stall around the 50% rate of unwed births due to attachment to traditional norms in more resistant sections of society. Small rises in the number of Norwegian marriages over recent years appear to relate to increases in those of marriageable age (including immigrants), along with catch-up by those marrying late in life (often with children born out of wedlock), and more divorcees available for remarriage (rather than a rise in their marriage frequency). People marry late and divorce frequently, and they increasingly cohabit for long periods. For young people, marriage rates are still falling heavily up to the mid-30s and, even here, there has been a further tip downwards in recent years. At the same time, divorce has generally remained high. While the period 1995 to 1999 saw divorce rates slowing somewhat in Norway by 2000–2001, the numbers were back at those projected in 1994. See Appendix Fig 4.

A case has also been made for Belgium having a slightly upward marriage trend. Like Scandinavian experience, this is difficult to reconcile with the marriage rate per 1,000 population dropping from 6.5 in 1990 to 4.4 in 2000 and 4.0 in 2009.[46] Again, the waters are muddied by immigration, where entrants from the Muslim world have a higher marriage rate than the home population. Belgium's divorce rate is amongst the highest in the European Union. The crude rate per 1,000 inhabitants stood at 3.0 in 2009 – higher than Denmark's 2.7 and Sweden's 2.5. The UK rate was 2.2.

Slightly more marriages and lulls in rising divorce levels in countries with generally low marriage rates do not mean that two parent married families are undergoing a revival. This has more to with the institution's overall decline than any renaissance.

Norway's out-of-wedlock birthrate rose from 39% to 50% between 1990 and 2000 and, together with Swedish rates, the tendency to marry with the second child weakened in both countries. Denmark saw a levelling off during the 1990s at around 45%, which seems to relate to a slight increase in fertility among older couples more likely to marry after multiple births. At the same time, there was a 25% increase in cohabitation and unmarried parenthood among mainly younger couples. About 60% of first born children in Denmark now have unmarried parents. Belgium's unwed birth rate stood at 45.7% in 2009. This is a steep rise from 4.1% in 1980 and 11.6% in 1990, compared with the UK's 11.5% in 1980, 27.9% in 1990 and 46.3% in 2009.

Family dissolution rates differ from divorce rates when so many people rear children outside marriage. The evidence indicates that throughout

Scandinavia and Europe cohabiting couples with children break up at three or more times the rate of married parents. Rising cohabitation and out-of-wedlock births are true proxies for family dissolution.

In the Netherlands, marriage is also in decline among heterosexuals, with higher rates of divorce and out of wedlock childbearing. Marriage had a mini-renaissance in the late 80s and early 90s, although it only ensured stability for a few years as the long term trend was still downhill. Dropping quite steeply from 88,000 plus in 2000, marriage is at its lowest since WWII (with 70,000 plus in 2010).[47]

The slight upward move in 2002 may be partly accounted for by same sex marriages and registered partnerships, which offer a lighter relationship for heterosexuals as well as homosexuals. Nearly one in three women entering a partnership are over 40 years old, compared to the more than one in five who get married. As from 2001 heterosexual couples could convert their marriages into partnerships which can be annulled without a court order. Using this process of 'flash divorce', some 30,000 couples separated in this way up to 2009, almost completely compensating for the decrease in formal divorces from 2001. At the same time, the rights of married couples and registered partners were extended to unregistered cohabiters.[48]

Four in ten Dutch babies are now born to unwed mothers. The rise has been particularly rapid, from 24.9% in 2000 to 43.3 % in 2009, compared with 11.4% in 1990 and only 4.1% in 1980. In the decade ending in 2009, the share of unmarried parents among people in their thirties went from 8% to 28%. Provinces containing cities (like Amsterdam and Rotterdam) have the highest proportion of babies born to single mothers. However, the level of single lone mothers seen for the UK and US is still not matched, and if the mother has a subsequent child, she is likely to marry. This suggests a remaining connection between marriage and family building, as might the way in which two-thirds of cohabiting couples aspire to marry some time.[49]

Nevertheless, this is happening in what has been a generally family centred country which has tended more to resemble Italy than Scandinavian or Anglophone nations. This is the case whether we look at low proportions of children aged three and under attending day care, youngsters eating meals with their family, the influence of local citizens on education and fiscal support for families. However, recent years have seen moves away from domestic interdependence and mutual support towards the independent partner pattern. Until 2001 the Netherlands had a personal transferable tax allowance. As happened with the child tax allowance in the UK in the 1970s, this was abolished in return for a cash payment (which could be drawn as a lump sum once a year) payable to the non-earning partner. Predictably, once a tax allowance becomes a 'benefit', the cry goes up that many receivers do not 'need it'. And, as the 'de-gendered' pattern of work and child rearing – matching 'de-gendered' marriage – has become a political aspiration, why pay a 'housewives' premium' or a 'kitchen sink subsidy'? Hence, the allowance began to be scaled back in 2009 with a view to it ending completely in 2024.[50] Younger women, especially those with children living at home, have already seen it reduced by up to 33%.

Spain has seen a pronounced acceleration in its marriage decline. This started to abate a little by 2009, perhaps due to more same sex unions being formalised in advance of a centre right government terminating the arrangement (it did not). The annual number of marriages fell by over 14,600 over the first three years (2005-2007) in which same sex couples were able to marry. For the next three years (2008-10), the annual fall was 34,000. The descent is quite precipitous, since Spanish marriage rates (per thousand population) had been reasonably steady compared to some other countries, at 5.9 in 1980: 5.7 in 1990 and 5.4 in 2000 before the plunge to 3.8 in 2009.[51] This includes the more than 18,000 same-sex couples who got married between 2005 and the end of 2010 (when 2.1% of marriages were between people of the same sex). The State Federation of Lesbians, Gays, Transsexuals and bisexuals (ELGBT) believes the number is higher, since not all marriages have been recorded.

At the same time as Spain's socialist government introduced same sex marriage it also brought in legislation known as the 'express divorce' to make the process easier and faster. The legal change eliminated the need for physical separation before legal proceedings could begin. In the following year (2006), 126,952 divorces were registered, a 74.3% increase on the previous year. The sharpest rise was seen in divorces between those who had been married for less than a year – up 330.6%. As with divorce liberalisation elsewhere, the argument is made that the 2005 law is not responsible for the number of break-ups, it only made it easier for people to divorce who would previously have separated.[52]

There are two patterns here, with same sex unions both an effect and a cause of the evisceration of marriage, especially its separation from parenthood. In countries like Sweden that have long pursued policies antithetical to conjugality, cohabitation and out-of-wedlock birth rates were rising and marriage rates were falling long before the enactment of same sex partnership/marriage. This is then part of the end game which locks in and reinforces existing trends toward the separation of marriage and parenthood.

Compared with Scandinavia, where concerted anti-marriage policy well antedates same sex unions, marriage in more traditionally family centred societies like Spain and the Netherlands did not approximate to the definition of "a form of voluntary cohabitation between independent persons" (as in Sweden).[53] Here the introduction of equal marriage is the tipping point which initiates or is party to marriage's rapid dismemberment in the context of a general libertarianism. Making civil partnerships available to heterosexuals and distributing the privileges of marriage to uncommitted relationships is associated with the casualisation and trivialisation of unions, driving home the message that marriage is outdated, and that virtually any living arrangement is acceptable.

So far, SSM hardly looks like a force for revival which is somehow going to slow or reverse marriage's decline. There is a vacuum anyway when it comes to suggesting how this could possibly be. This is not to say that it is a reason for marital decline anywhere, just that it is doing nothing to counter it.

Chapter Seven

REMEDIAL PROPERTIES?

7.1 HEALTHIER FUTURES?

The supposed 'health inducing' properties for sexual minorities that have arisen in so many debates over SSM involve two competing (but not necessarily incompatible) discourses. What the efficacy of marriage might be when it comes to reversing minority adversities deserves more examination than it has received, as do other attempts to make the world more accepting and approving of alternative sexualities. The implications for others beyond the immediate beneficiaries should not be ignored.

The medical submission to the Government's consultation on Equal Marriage from an LGB group within the Royal College of Psychiatrists (chaired by Prof. Michael King) was certain that marriage's generally beneficial effect upon health would apply to that of homosexuals too. Common sense might suggest that benefits could be amplified even beyond those for heterosexuals. As the writers for Policy Exchange outlined, there might be practical gains if the health costs of the afflictions of sexual minorities were reduced, with one in ten 'gay' men in London HIV positive and one in twenty nationwide. Taxation funds the lifetime costs for infected individuals to the tune of around £280,000 to £360,000 each, with annual costs £858m (2010)[1] indicative of how massive resources have gone into providing care and finding remedies, without parallel elsewhere.[2] A study credited to Stonewall and quoted from a *Guardian* article claimed that, over the past year, 3% of homosexual and 5% of bisexual men had attempted suicide, compared to 0.4% of all men.[3] This included the 6% aged between

16 and 24, together with another 15% who harmed themselves. This catalogued a multitude of other tribulations of homo/bi-sexual men, to make the point that their needs, especially concerning mental health and drug use, were being overlooked by the NHS. What Policy Exchange writers added was how:

> ...many parts of the gay 'scene' are still dominated by heavy drinking, drug abuse and short-term relationships – both of which can be detrimental to long term physical and mental health. Websites such as 'Gaydar' and phone apps such as 'Grindr' offer the kind of on-demand sex that is still seen as a key part of the gay 'scene' in 2012. ... short-term behaviour and levels of risk taking ... still forms a far bigger part of gay life than it does of heterosexual life.[4]

Indeed, promiscuity and extraordinary unhealthy sexual practices are often represented as distinguishing features of a wonderfully rich gay life. Some are prepared to call for "less insistence on gay solidarity all the time" and admit that:

> The gay scene is incredibly sexualised. Kids come out into this sexualised world where there is lots of booze and lots of drugs, there's nothing that's just healthy, gentle and relaxed. It's empowering to have lots of sex, but only if that's what you actually want, if it's you making the choice.[5]

Since such problems might seem particularly likely to be soluble by marital norms, so boldly:

> ...it could be argued that what many on the right [sic] describe as the "homosexual lifestyle" (actually only the lifestyle of a minority of gay people) is partially because gay people have been deprived by society of the ability to marry, and the order and social support that marriage brings. ... the social institution of marriage and the social acceptance and social incentives offered by it can only be beneficial to gay people.[6]

Does it follow? The optimism about the beneficial impact of SSM on male promiscuity has been compared to claims that legal abortion would end child abuse, for every child will be a wanted child. Would benefits be transferable anyway? It might be cheerfully believed that marriage's redefinition means a convergence in heterosexual and homosexual behaviour, with long standing conjugal norms carried over or transplanted into same sex unions, to the end of greater well-being. But which way are we supposed to be going when David Cameron's propagandists insisted that their married homosexuals would revive commitment, fidelity and responsibility for heterosexuals? Others hope that, as the abolition of the conjugal conception of marriage ends norms like fidelity, SSM will oust monogamy, a process now increasingly pushed by 'cutting edge' media touting open relationships and threesomes. It will hardly make people more likely to abide by marital norms if any appreciation of the basis for these norms evaporates. Those who extol the virtues of anonymous sex believe that the 'openness of same sex unions' could enhance the relationships of heterosexuals, raising questions about how transitory and disruptive relations are supposed to improve anyone's welfare. As there is no logical stop to who and how many marriage is meant to embrace when it is broken from conjugality, would its benefits also apply to more than two parties? The *ménage a trois* in the Netherlands was, after all, defended by a Minister for Justice as fulfilling 'a useful ordering function'.

Notions of SSM enhancing social order and control run headlong into the yearning for a free sexual utopia, with the liberated life a world away from suggestions that same sex unions mean calmer times and better health. If marriage faces further dissolution, there is little or nothing to transfer. It is here that conservative advocates are reticent if it means engaging with those who want marriage because they hate heterosexual monogamy so much. Perhaps wishing to be distanced from this familiar liberation agenda, it is conceded that "promiscuity, teen pregnancy, and other matters are reasonable causes of public concern" and how equality "does not require that we scrap the whole [*sic*] of traditional morality".[7]

Peter Tatchell might well cry how "Queer politics is against assimilation" and how "We don't need a marriage certificate to validate our partnerships…"[8] Not wanting to comply with heterosexual norms, or to conform to rules and expectations relevant to a man and a woman, is by no means the only reason why the argument from social order (which might be construed as a rather patronising take on gay fortunes) enters turbulent waters. The Durkheimian position that people need moral regulation and social control to manage their own needs and aspirations is at odds with the attribution of problems to the ways that dominant culture, social structures, and norms fail to reflect minority group sexualities. Hence it is questionable that "legislative and financial protections for same-sex couples will lessen the likelihood of suicide as an outcome of sexual non-normativity." What is deplored is the movement of the "1970s liberationist ideals" away from "both the destabilisation of heteronormativity and the introduction of a range of sexual and familial arrangements" in exchange for "the protection of same-sex relationships that are modeled on heterosexual marriage". Instead, it is suggested that what should still be sought is "broad cultural change that might open new possibilities for youth sexual identity development or critiquing [*sic*] the very notion of normativity that is central to youth suicide ideation – both of which were goals of 1970s Gay Liberation political organizing". Only then will we have a political approach which might foster "an environment of protection for younger non-heterosexual persons".[9] In the meantime, LGBT people as "a high risk group" need protecting from damaging heterosexist society and referral to gay organisations "before late adolescence or even young adulthood when the emotional damage may already have occurred."[10]

Some reconciliation between different viewpoints is possible if SSM has health inducing properties because its mere existence or availability – whether anyone partakes or not and whether anyone's behaviour is changed or not – represents a big reduction in 'homophobia' and discrimination *per se*. This makes marriage, abolishing stigma, stamping out bullying, outlawing discrimination, and 'celebrating' diversity to create a world welcoming to homosexuals, prophylactic enterprises as much as equality drives. As society says that homosexual relationships are wholly accepted and a public good, then this, not "mimicking heterosexual norms", will be decisive and there will be a decline in discrimination and general hostility will decline through "trickle-down acceptance".[11] This does not preclude how the presence of a significant other could encourage earlier help seeking and mollify distress, as well as provide care and support. Professor Michael King argued for equal marriage as a public health strategy because it 'will further' or 'could' reduce discrimination against LGBTs (RCPsych. College responds to Equal Civil Marriage consultation, June 2012). It was possible to maintain that those who asserted how the welfare of children might be harmed by SSM contributed to 'minority stress'.

Revisionists, transformationists and abolitionists may all subscribe to this perspective. A third dimension to the argument for health benefits only really applies to the USA. This refers to practical matters such as partner health insurance benefits. Marriage is a strong predictor of private and employer-based health insurance and the American Medical Association recognises that exclusion from marriage might contribute to health care disparities. However, *all* unmarried couples are two to three times more likely to be uninsured than the married, and the health care deficits of homosexuals have been overstated. Women generally are significantly less likely to have coverage. Health care access among men in same-sex relationships is equivalent to or greater than for men in opposite-sex relationships, and both are similar in their odds of having unmet medical needs owing to costs. Perhaps the focus on men with HIV compared to the general US population has suggested otherwise but, given their greater access to Medicaid and low-cost health programmes, their position cannot be generalised.[12]

If the question arises why heterosexuals have to make the vow to get the benefits, the answer could be given that marriage has always been part of the landscape they inhabit and, married or not, they may generally have lower rates of mental and other afflictions compared to homosexuals. But for homosexuals to demand the universal accreditation of marriage in order to boost their welfare, irrespective of whether they use it, has suggested an uncertainty and fragility which was absent from the original bold liberationist stance – something that has led critics to categorise such demands in terms of a 'needy politics of identity'.

Admittedly, there was some earlier speculation that civil partnerships might bestow health advantages via extra stability.[13] It was said that, since these took place with a social ritual and had important legal, social, and financial implications, along with the prospect of a shared future, these would confer similar benefits to heterosexual marriage. However, 'inferior' civil partnerships were soon excluded as insufficient or ineffective as preventatives compared with the existence of 'proper' marriage.[14]

7.2   ADVERSITIES TO OVERCOME

Since, under the control model, participation is necessary if SSM is going to have any remedial effect, behaviour is very much at issue here, and Policy Exchange ventured where others fear to tread. Most alarming is the recent spiralling growth in sexually transmitted infections (STIs) driven by young heterosexual women and men who have sex with men (MSM), with anal sex and multiple sexual partners altering the demographics and nature of sexual disease.[15] By 2010, there were more than 30,000 MSM living with HIV.[16] New diagnoses among MSM increased overall by 70% from 2001 to 2010 (1,810 to 3,080). It doubled among young men as other categories declined.[17] A quarter to a third more are estimated to remain undiagnosed. As the primary means of transmission (of 24 categories) homosexual behaviour drives HIV/AIDS in the Western world.[18]

Old fashioned syphilis grew twelve-fold in less than ten years, with the UK's rate higher than at any time since 1950, an increase greatest for those aged 16–19.[19] MSM account for three-quarters, mostly in the 'gay' centres of Manchester, London and Brighton. As gonorrhoea rose 25% overall (in England 2010/2011), cases among MSM rose by 61% to represent 50% of all diagnoses, with the risk of contracting this as well as syphilis fifty times greater than for heterosexuals. There are also the rises for MSM in chlamydia, genital herpes and warts, together with the anal and oral cancers related to sexual activity which have doubled since the mid-1990s. A variety of parasitic and other intestinal infections often endemic in the tropics are becoming sexual diseases, with nearly all cases of lymphogranuloma venereum in MSM often accompanying HIV and other STIs.[20] A significant proportion of MSM are carrying the virus HHV-8, spread in saliva from faecal contact, and anal cancer is likely if this combines with HIV.[21] Ingestion of faeces in oral-faecal (scat) or oral-anal (analingus) contact can also give rise to hepatitis A and a variety of other infections – as might other faeces play. Fisting or 'hand-balling' can perforate the intestines, lead to hepatitis C transmission, bowel rupture and emergency colostomies.[22] There are instructions aplenty for such activities.

A significant and growing proportion of disease affects younger age groups,[23] along with suggestions that a large proportion who develop AIDS in the third decade of life became infected as teens, often by older men.[24]

This means some lads are being infected while still at school and under the age of consent.

With powerful anti-viral drugs available, a complete cure purportedly well on the way and the life expectancy of those receiving treatment approaching that of the general population, HIV may be thought not to be a major issue, and safe sex boring and old fashioned.[25] This may contribute to late diagnosis. In turn, the self-reports of ill health and distress by homo/bi-sexual and homosexually experienced heterosexual men may reflect an ongoing burden of HIV and other STIs.[27] Indications are that the HIV positive are significantly more likely to make a suicide plan, even if they had not already attempted this.[28]

There is also easier access to drugs and the use of internet sites to find venues for barebacking (unprotected anal sex) and group sex. Coinciding with the surge in disease is the sharp rise in hard drug use with "users bingeing for days at a time without sleep, and indulging in high risk sexual practices as they smoke, snort, or inject..."[29] Substance abuse by homosexuals was put at nearly threefold the rate for heterosexuals in a recent meta-analysis.[30] This is predominantly to facilitate sex, often with multiple partners.[31] The use of amyl nitrate (poppers) to relax the anal sphincter and produce euphoria is fifty-eight times greater than for men generally.[32] The effects raise the likelihood of infection transmitting damage.[33–35]

High levels of drug use are associated with a myriad of acute and chronic consequences, including depression and suicide as well as heart disease, psychosis, cognitive deficits, anxiety and violence. Visits to emergency departments and admissions for treatment have dramatically increased in the past decade or more.[36] A history of women having sex with women (WSW) also marks higher levels of intravenous drug and alcohol use and increased risks of adverse sexual, reproductive, and general health outcomes compared to exclusively heterosexual women.[37] This reflects how the incidence of risky behaviour increases with bisexuality, providing the best environment for transmitting STIs from male to female.[38] Since health, psychosocial problems and addictions are particularly interrelated for homo/bisexuals, these are referred to as a *syndemic*.[39]

Consistent across reports about men who have sex with men (MSM) are high rates of victimisation or coercion and abuse, sexual and otherwise, running at around two to threefold that for heterosexuals.[40] Some studies show a lower level of discordance with heterosexual levels of physical abuse – except very severe violence (which is greater in homosexual relations).[41] In a large representative sample (men engaged in same sex behaviour since 14 and self-labelling as homo/bi-sexual), 40% had experienced abuse or violence in the previous five years from boyfriends, with those under 40 years worst affected.[42] A *Guardian* writer mentioned a Stonewall study of men attending NHS facilities which reported how domestic abuse was a serious problem.[43] It was alleged that health services were paying insufficient attention due to homophobia blocking "interventions and strategies on multiple levels, including community, organisational and societal".[44] A half of those surveyed experienced at least one incident since the age of 16, compared with 17% of all men.

Some deplore the "silence about gay/lesbian battering", given that "same-sex relationship violence is a significant problem for a sizable part of the gay/lesbian/bisexual/transgendered community."[45] Abusive relationships may be under-reported if speculation is correct that women feel easier reporting victimisation by men. Other suggestions are that victims fear that acknowledging violence "may feed societal homophobia and contribute to prejudice about gay or lesbian relationships".[46] However, attitudes to domestic violence have also long been hostage to feminist ideology insisting that the 'patriarchal, nuclear family' is inherently a dangerous place where 'wife beating' is part of socially sanctioned male dominance over women. Because feminism emphasises the gender-specific female victim and male perpetrator and is unable to address why most married men are not violent, there is difficulty explaining violence in the context of non-heterosexual or even non-institutionalised heterosexual relationships.

Intimate partner violence and victimisation are difficult to address when there is a high turnover of relationships, casual sexual encounters and mutual assault. This is illustrated by a well conducted Vancouver study where, as often with male homosexual samples, the subjects tended to be in higher educational and income brackets (and over a quarter were HIV positive).[47] The pattern of violence did not clearly differentiate between victims and perpetrators since, as with a large proportion of incidents and in relationships as a whole, both partners were violent. In the vast majority of cases, violence was an escalation of ongoing conflict. As elsewhere, perpetrators and recipients described being ignored, sidelined or thwarted

– trapped in conflicts or provoked by emotional abuse.[48] One partner might be more involved than the other, but frustrated and angry because the other prefers something open and casual. The negotiation of a mutually agreeable arrangement might be especially important to male same-sex relationships. This is easier said than done. People may imagine that they are above the little green-eyed monster, but brief and 'open' relationships lend themselves to suspicion, jealousy and assault.[49]

If the tendency for multiple sexual partners and transient relationships plays no small role in an additive interplay, a recent Sigma survey reported that 63.6% of homosexual men in England had more than one sexual partner in the previous year.[50] Previous reports were that around a quarter had between 10 and 100 partners in the last five years, compared to 5.3% of heterosexuals. The percentage reporting over 100 partners was one hundred times greater.[51] In the (non-random, but minimally biased) sample of MSM for a Center for Diseases Control project in 15 US metropolitan areas, those who did not report a main partner in the previous 12 months had an estimated 6.5 casual partners, and those who did had 2.4.[52] Those reporting an 'exchange-sex' (for money or other benefits) partner had an estimated median number of 8.6 casuals versus 3.1 for those without. One of the largest surveys ever carried out is *Private Lives: A Report on the health and well being of GLBTI* [I is added for 'intersex'] *Australians.* Interviewing almost 5,500 individuals between 16 and 92, it found that 37% of the men had known their most recent sex partner for less than 24 hours and a quarter of all respondents expected sex at least once daily.[53] Only 5% of males and 10% of females had any interest in formalising any relationship(s).

With 'gay' authors insisting how "among gay men a long-lasting *monogamous* relationship is almost unknown",[54] Sigma recorded a median length of 21 months.[55] While about 60% of homosexual men had a regular partner in any year, less than half were 'closed' – defined as not having had sex with a third party in the preceding month![56] Couples who stay together for a long time may be like roommates or companionable flat sharers who find exciting new encounters outside the relationship.[57] Being committed to one man in any given year generally meant having sex with several others.[58] Relationships that last more than five years invariably incorporate external sexual activity,[59] which may help account for how the majority of HIV transmissions come from steady or primary partners.[60] All this makes for difficulties when it comes to estimating the durability of different relationships in different contexts. There may be concurrent relationships rather than casual sexual partners and it might not be clear whether singles have a 'main partner'.[61] The incidence of 'butch' masculinity is predictive of the most permissive relations.[62] The (usually) young men who might "start with a vision of monogamy" are dismissed by gay sociologist Barry Adam for:

> ...coming with a heterosexual script in their head and are applying it to relationships with men ...What they don't see is that the gay community has their own order and own ways that seem to work better.[63]

This still might not stop relationship difficulties and breakups being significant motivators of depression, suicidal ideation or suicide attempts.[64] It is hardly surprising that some researchers have linked suicide attempts (up to a half or more) to the distress involved in ending intimate relationships.[65]

Elsewhere there is condemnation of those who are felt unjustifiably to categorise all homosexuals as uncommitted and irresponsible on the basis of the behaviour of what might be a minority. An argument by 'stereotype', it demonstrates the moral failure of critics' arguments.[66] In turn, this objection is spurned as a "rose coloured view", leaving us asking the question "what is the true, real, actual nature" if "promiscuity or infidelity are [not] particularity distinctive qualities" of same sex relationships? Are these not "beyond serious dispute", as "defining characteristics ... out of the gay community itself"?[67]

7.3 Crying out for Commitment?

Anonymous, exploitative or voyeuristic sex requires little or nothing in the way of emotional involvement or communication, let alone relationship, where what we see might seem to cry out for that 'commitment device' to introduce stabilising heterosexual criteria, particularly fidelity.

Argument is made that sexual encounters are necessarily brief due to a lack of recognition, making relationships less enduring and more conflicted. Marriage as a 'commitment device' might discourage promiscuity and 'partner' turnover, encouraging instead stable, long term relationships which provide spousal oversight and regulation in the context of mutual care. Would this not reduce levels of risk taking, lessen the chances of contracting STIs, lower drug, alcohol problems and conflict as well as the translation of despair into suicidality and this into suicide? After all, same sex partners report more autonomy, fewer barriers to leaving and hence more frequent dissolution compared to married heterosexuals where lower levels of intimacy, equality, and constructive problem solving also increase dissolution rates.[71]

Research with twins and sibling pairs (to screen out genetic contributions or selection effects) certainly suggests how 'externalising symptoms' are the most controllable by marriage, compared to 'internalised' mental conditions and physical health.[68] Elsewhere it is suggested that as, at similar socioeconomic levels, same-sex cohabitants have not dissimilar health deficits as opposite sex non-married groups, committed monogamy is equally a key to health for both heterosexuals and homosexuals.[69] This might be illustrated by the psychological and behavioural impact of different relationships on the health of homo/bisexual men. The sample is 819 who self-identified as single (503); monogamous (182) or in open (71) or monogamish (63) relationships[70] where there is agreement that sexual activity with casual partners only happens when both men are present and involved ('threeways' and group sex). The monogamous reported the least amount of substance use compared to singles or men in open relationships, followed by those in monogamish relationships and the same applied to psychological and sexual health.

The processes maintaining relationships include those which attract people as well as stop them leaving. These involve laws, joint investments and emotional and social rewards.[72] Same sex couples, like many opposite sex cohabiting couples, may see less reward and more alternatives, where the absence of legal union makes it difficult to distinguish between casual dates and relationships with long-term futures. They do not have to fret about divorce costs, pension losses, insurance and inheritance rights. Homosexuals might have even fewer worries about what relatives might think, and there are unlikely to be children to consider or religious qualms. Lower costs might also be related to the existence of networks which provide more alternatives than heterosexuals have access to – an advantage attributed to "antigay stigma"[73] (Others claim that there is a lack of such support because of anti-gay stigma).

Acting as a bridge to parents, SSM might now "go some way towards tackling the sense of alienation felt by many gay people" where what is already known to affect invitations to family-of-origin rituals is the visibility of a couple's relationship.[74] This is described as key to "creating a livable and comfortable gay culture, with gay people as insiders rather than outsiders"; providing "role models to young people in their families, their communities and in wider society" which show how their lives do not have to be so different to those of their heterosexual peers. Increased societal and family backing might reduce the tendency to have multiple partners and enable couples to resolve difficulties rather than separate. When society becomes more accepting of the value of same-sex relationships, this will enable prospective partners to meet at work and other settings like heterosexuals do. The contention is that all this promises to have "a profoundly beneficial impact ... and help to normalise the aspiration that young people have of growing up and finding a stable, committed relationship".[75]

This is resonant with activist Andrew Sullivan's claims about giving "gay children" [sic] some "rubric by which life could be explained... in terms of their future life stories, their potential loves, their eventual chance at some kind of constructive happiness."[76] In turn, if there are poorer outcomes for children of 'gay' parents then these might even be "an artefact of the social stigma and marginalization that often faced gay and lesbian couples during the time (extending back to the 1970s) when many young adults came of age." In turn, all is "consistent with recent studies of gay and lesbian couples in countries such as the Netherlands and Sweden" with high instability patterns among same sex couples.[77] (These countries have same sex marriage and the studies involved official unions.[78])

7.4 OBJECTION

Much of this is contentious. The alternative status or esteem explanation for adversity to that of risky behaviour or lifestyle is particularly related to matters like psychiatric health deficits and suicidality levels. These are easier to attribute to homophobia in various forms, although, as we have seen, this explanation can be stretched to explain how a 'gay' man may, for instance, express himself through compulsive behaviour because oppressive culture damages his very being.[79] So much is concluded from a meta-analysis of 18 studies from 1994 to 2006. This tested the association between sexual orientation and teen substance use. It found that LGB youth reported higher rates of all varieties, including cocaine, methamphetamines and injection drugs (or, on average, 190% higher than for heterosexual youth and 340% for bisexuals) compared to heterosexuals.[80] The leading researcher explained how causal mechanisms, protective factors and explanations, as well as substance use outcomes, were largely unknown and there was little control for confounding variables. Notwithstanding, it was decided that "[h]omophobia, discrimination and victimization are largely what are responsible for these substance use disparities in young gay people" and how "[h]istory shows that when marginalized groups are oppressed and do not have equal opportunities and equal rights, they suffer. Our results show that gay youth are clearly no exception."[81]

Similarly, while an influential and extensive Australian report claimed how "same sex attraction is a healthy and natural part of the development of many adolescents" it accepted that "ample evidence to date [is] that same sex attracted young people engage in more behaviour that is risky to health and experience more dramatic health deficits than their heterosexual peers". This is a proxy for how: "homophobia has many negative impacts on the physical and mental health of these young people";[82] ranging from using "a range of legal and illegal drugs at a higher rate than heterosexual youth … to use marijuana weekly, party drugs monthly and to have ever used heroin", to self-harm and attempt suicide. The percentage injecting drugs might have generally dropped, but that for those with homosexual lifestyles remained double the rate of heterosexuals, along with a dramatic rise in STIs.[83] While reference is made to lifestyle choices and participating in gay recreational culture, it is decided that drug use is "to escape the isolation and pain of homophobia as it manifests itself in negative self-talk and in abuse from others...." This demonstrates "the importance of intervening early to reduce homophobia and to prevent the long-term over use [sic] of a range of drugs" with more gay affirmative policies.

Insisting how it is "unlikely our society would tolerate such a response [like homophobia] to any other naturally occurring phenomena", the Australian report catalogues the 'enlightened' campaigns now actively engaged in combating this menace. With schools under an obligation to teach about the nature and history of homophobia, there is "a responsibility to provide a safe space for the 10% [*sic*] of the student population who are same sex attracted to receive a fully rounded education". Only "Christianity remains a last bastion of resistance to what is regarded in legal and health arenas as a normal part of human sexuality".

There may be an unwillingness to accept that any behaviour is itself dysfunctional on the basis that society only considers something problematic because it deviates from straights' repressive patterns of courtship and romance. Even those advocating responsibility in the face of HIV/AIDs have been oft times labelled 'homophobic bigots'. However, this ignores how high levels of sexually transmitted disease and injury, drug taking, abuse and conflict may take their toll and contribute to serious mental as much as physical health consequences, regardless of social acceptance.

Explanations in terms of popular homophobia may have made violence and other health problems easier to acknowledge when these can be blamed on heterosexist norms. As much as "sexism creates opportunity for heterosexual men to batter women, homophobia creates opportunities for people in same-sex relationships to batter their partners". This leads homosexuals to replicate heterosexuality's "discourses" or dynamics of power and control in their relations.[84] Furthermore, "gender-role socializations and heterosexism create and enforce stigmas and obstacles for validation and reporting of this abuse".[85] Homophobia accounts for 'outing' threats being used for control, or where one partner tells another that s/he does not understand homosexual relations or sexual practices, that s/he will lose custody of children, or how the police, the justice system or the social services will not help. The victim may feel guilty about reporting an abuser with HIV because this may seem to betray the 'gay community'.[86]

It has been pointed out how it might be mistaken to assume that men in same-sex relationships perceive violence to be as problematic or detrimental to the degree that heterosexuals may do. There are other reasons besides fear or anxiety about society's 'homophobia' why those experiencing (particularly low level) violence and/or mutual abuse may be hesitant about adopting the 'victim' label and seeking help. It may not simply be a heterosexist or homophobic 'misconception' that violence might be 'mutual' or 'equal' – when, for example, courts make joint restraining orders.[87]

Going further are those claims that, if it were not for the surrounding environment failing fully to endorse and support homosexual identity, there would not be the kind of investment in relationships the dissolution of which causes so much grief.[88] As having someone to care is especially important in a hostile or 'homophobic' world, this makes breakups particularly hurtful. However, would there be less loss, or would the effect of loss be inconsequential, if homophobia disappeared? Would breaking up be easier to do? Are not unhappiness, conflict and distress almost intrinsic to concurrent and sequential relationships where one is either being rejected or doing the rejecting – for anybody?[89]

7.5   CONVERGING STANDARDS?

We may ask what is the effectiveness, so far as is known, of formal unions, when it comes to helping the participants enjoy a less troubled and more comfortable existence. Furthermore, to consider the esteem as well as the social control hypothesis, investigation needs to widen to matters of improvement (or not) in the well-being of sexual minorities where there is not just SSM, but genuinely more 'gay friendly' social environments. Are homosexuals in formal unions similar in monogamy to married heterosexual couples? Or does behaviour bear out criticisms about projecting or imposing heterosexual norms onto those with different expectations and standards? Proper understanding will require longitudinal cohort studies. Some surmise that male same sex relationships (particularly) may simply be less enduring because of something related to being male. This is not just about subcultures which encourage multiple partners and dangerous behaviour. It is about how commitment to women and children domesticates men. Women and (for the most part) children would be missing from homosexual relations, along with an absence of inner constraint, and the perceived outward interdiction of male-male relations:

> The two partners recognize each other's needs immediately, observe those proprieties that are necessary to conceal their mutual desire, accomplish their union, and separate, all the while entertaining towards each other an outlook of indifference, contempt or at best ... curiosity... The possibility of such an encounter is ...enhanced by the sense that no barrier divides one from the sex of the other, that his desire is immediately known and as ready for fulfillment as one's own.

This, combined with the natural predatoriness of the male, constitute the danger inherent in male homosexuality.[90]

Free roaming desire seeks not its complement but "the simulacrum, of the present feeling" by "narcissistically contemplating in the other an excitement that is the mirror of my own."[91]

Is this reflected in the Vermont study which compared same sex partners in and outside civil unions and heterosexually married siblings? Those conducting the study contacted all who had had civil unions during the first year of the legislation where, of the pool of 2,269 couples (some had died or moved), 42% were willing to participate.[92] They were asked to provide information for a married, heterosexual sibling and spouse and for a homosexual couple in their friendship circle not in a civil union. Of the 400 sets sent out to the first couples willing to provide contacts, 97% returned at least one questionnaire. While few lesbians or heterosexuals (15.2% for married men) had had sex outside their relationship, non-monogamy was reported by over a half of homosexual men in both types of union. A half of men in civil unions had an agreement that extra-relational sex was permissible, compared with 5% or fewer lesbian and heterosexual couples. Moreover, homosexuals often had extra-relational sex regardless, and both types of couples reported far more arguing about this than married heterosexual men (never). Since homosexual men may put great store by impersonal or anonymous sex ('tricking'), it might suggest that this is irrelevant for relationships and fewer than 10% reported any *meaningful* affair. This did not avoid the high rates of conflict and did not presage the sidelining of agreements over whether or not casual sex should be indulged. The implications were not discussed in the Vermont study as it moved on to demonstrate how homosexual couples are champions of equality for their distribution of household tasks.

Elsewhere, suggestions are made that "sanctioned outside sex is a sustainable and satisfying possibility" where:

If a couple is willing to be forthright and to problem-solve as needed, non-monogamy isn't by nature de-stabilizing. In fact, the results of this study would suggest the opposite – many study couples said non-monogamy enabled them to stay together.[93]

Most relationships became more and more 'open' over time. However, the Vermont study recruited only those (from the 'gay community') who had been in a 'long term committed relationship' for eight years or more, and practised "'outside sex' or an agreement for such". They might be like Dan Savage, homosexual, legally married and with an adopted son. This has not prevented him and his partner having had nine extra-marital partners between them, on the understanding that monogamy is not for men.[94] Such 'survivors' tell us nothing about how common such relationships are or about those who fell by the wayside.

None of this suggests much embrace of heterosexual norms. There is the reminder how heterosexual relations involve the:

> ...opening of the self to the mystery of another gender, thereby taking responsibility for an experience which one does not wholly understand, is a feature of sexual maturity, and one of the fundamental motives tending toward commitment. ... Only in a [mutual] vow is the trust created which protects the participants from the threat of betrayal.... For the homosexual, who knows intimately in himself the generality he finds in the other, there may be a diminished sense of risk. The move out of the self may be less adventurous, the help of the other less required.[95]

That there is both more at stake and more vulnerability in heterosexual unions is attributed by sociobiologists to "the reflection in consciousness of the procreative urge" which "subjects our individual choices to the imperious needs of our genes. (And there too lies the partial truth of the intentional Catholic doctrine.)"[96] The nature as much as the stability of relationships depends on factors besides the social and legal recognition that provide a framework within which these can be built and maintained.[97] If sexual minorities may not put the same value on faithfulness as heterosexuals, that might have nothing to do with social exclusion. They may not see a need to make much investment in relationships to start with, and may be pursuing different goals.

There was a test of speculations that 'gay' men might earn a 'marriage premium' like heterosexuals do,[98] especially considering their high income and educational levels. This even postulated that, if some homosexual couples were not in official partnerships because of non-availability in some places, should there not be *more* commitment than there is with heterosexual cohabitants who have deliberately opted to forgo marriage? A US study found that cohabiting gay men did not earn more than 'unpartnered' gay men or cohabiting or otherwise unmarried heterosexual men.[99] A conjecture was that this is because employers are basically homophobic and discriminate in favour of married men because this signals heterosexuality! This assumption has no basis in the evidence on the workings of the 'marriage premium'. To the extent that there is a differential it may be, rather, because homosexual men are unlikely ever to support a family and, in not being responsible to someone who expects precisely this, they have less incentive to focus on human capital accumulation and productivity. In any event, the male 'marriage premium' is scarcely something politicians and policy makers would want to encourage.

All so far might be summed up in a lesbian's book that conservative enthusiasts cited for the impact of same sex marriage on Dutch homosexuals, or how this made them feel more committed and responsible for their partners.[100] The sample was thirteen lesbian and six 'gay' couples. One male couple promised monogamy, the rest (married or not) were not in sexually exclusive relationships. Since most homosexuals would rather not marry, Vera Bergkamp, head of a Dutch gay rights organisation, pinpointed the three main reasons for the "lack of nuptial enthusiasm among gay couples": less pressure from family and friends; the absence of desire for children, and a more individualist, less family-orientated mindset.[101] These reasons relate to marriage's role as sustainer and creator of inter-generational and social bonds that extend beyond two adults' comfort or wants. The message:

> When I talk to my gay and lesbian students and other young queer people, there is no doubt that they are in favor of marriage equality. It's a no-brainer: why shouldn't there be equality under the law? But very few of them actually seem interested in getting married, now or later. That's true of both gay men and lesbians... Such ambivalence stands in sharp contrast to my heterosexual students, many of whom expect to get hitched sometime in the near future and some of whom have even made plans to do so after graduation.[102]

When the same sex Vermont couples ranked the three main changes represented by being in a recognised union in order of priority, these were: the legal status of their relationship (63.0%); desire for society to know about lesbian or gay relationships (54.3%); and, thirdly, love and commitment for each other (53.7%).[103] In the run up to same sex marriage, a 'gay' journalist asked:

> Why is no one pointing out what an offensive parody of a precious institution gay marriage would be? ...it isn't just the biological incapacity for procreation; relationships between men are predicated on an entirely different set of needs, assumptions and compromises than those of straight couples.[104]

Therefore: "homosexual marriage would place government in the dishonest position of propagating a false picture of the reality of homosexuals' lives"[105] if it is imagined that male/female patterns are desired, let alone replicable, for homosexuals.

7.6   MORE ACCEPTANCE: BETTER HEALTH?

As we move from the conduct of relationships to health outcomes so, conveniently, Danish death certificates have recorded registered domestic partnership status (RDP). Early reports found a somewhat elevated all-cause mortality risk in the first decade.[106] This may be due to the way individuals who are severely ill may more likely register to ensure a smooth transmission of assets. Mortality risk then fell for men who contracted partnerships after 1995 as efficient HIV/AIDS therapies became available, although female mortality remained a third higher than in the general population.[107] Another study, using data from 1994–1997, found tentative evidence of a link between RDP status and risk for suicide mortality, but this used a small sample.[108]

A far bigger study dealt with the years 1990 to 2001, when the men classified as current or former RDP increased to 2,348 and women to 3,521.[109] Extraordinarily, the risks for death by suicide among men with RDPS was estimated at more than eight times greater across the life span than for married or formerly married heterosexual men. Among women, having a RDP history had a modest or insignificant positive effect on risk.

A few years on and these results are repeated: men with RDP compared with men with histories of heterosexual marriage had an eightfold greater age-adjusted risk for suicide.[110] This was also nearly twice as high compared to men who had never married and more than four times greater than for all currently or formerly married persons. While the numbers in RDP relationships is small (reducing precision) the elevated risk is present across life. How these findings relate to sexual minorities generally is difficult to assess, given the limits of available data, but it does not so far look good for the 'harm reduction' argument.

If what matters is simply knowing that marriage is there for you then, along with other affirmative interventions and improvements in the social environment for LGBTs which enhance the feel good factor, it may be more important for health benefits than participation – considering how most will probably choose to remain outside.

The general public – in the West, anyway – now overwhelmingly accepts that those homosexually inclined are not to be harmed or shunned, and that discrimination is unacceptable. Rates of 'perceived' discrimination were low (4.9%) and only 3.3% greater than that experienced by heterosexuals in a recent random sample of 7,403 adults.[111]

Parents appear to have grown more accepting, with evidence from the USA of little or no difference now between homosexual and heterosexual youth when it came to rejection, maltreatment or leaving home, although these were still raised for bisexuals.[112] One activist speaks about friends whose parents never spoke to them, or who fled into the 'gay world' because life at home became so uncomfortable "after their sexuality was evident". Now: "I'm glad to say that I hear almost nothing like them when I speak today to younger men" even if they might "still fear their fathers will be disappointed".[113]

Compulsory schooling gives direct access to the young, and here the drive for homosexual affirmation has proceeded farthest and, should claims be right about more LGBTs gladly 'coming out' at younger ages, this is one testimony to the acceptance and sponsorship of sexual minorities in education, health and media. Beyond libraries with their gay penguins and 'LGBT families' in the Early Years Foundation Stage, same sex weddings are in comic books from Archie to X-Men. Batwoman – originally a love interest for Batman – has become a lesbian (earning an award in 2012, from GLAAD, Gay and Lesbian Alliance Against Defamation). In the competition to put more gay models before the young, one of DC Comic's most popular superheroes (*Green Lantern*) was reworked as homosexual for June 2012's issue of *Earth 2* as part of the comic's *New 52* series. With his two marriages and son having been deleted from his biography, children have the inspiration of watching him kissing his boyfriend. It follows Marvel comics, DC's rival, having one of their heroes in the X-Men series *Northstar* marrying his boyfriend. It is hoped that this will "give him [a worried kid] a positive sense of who he is" or "decide I don't need to bully some kind of kid in school."[114] From *South Park* to *Downton Abbey* to *Law and Order* to *Game of Thrones*, numbers of carefully packaged 'gay' characters far exceed their presence in the general population. The popular US sitcom hit *Modern Family* promotes diversity in the US as *Eastenders* does for the UK. There is BBC3 with *Family Guy: 'Family Gay'* to sitcoms about gay and lesbian couples adopting or surrogating children (Channel 4 '*The New Normal*'). The BBC1 *Inside Outside*[115] described how activist Eric Anderson's sperm fertilised an egg of an Egyptian donor, which was then placed inside an Asian surrogate. The resultant twin boys are shown nursed in bed by the father and his partner as he describes how they are "a truly modern family".

This increasing predilection of entertainment for social engineering is credited with causing significant attitude change. Even vice president Joe Biden cited *Will and Grace* for getting him to endorse SSM in 2012. Some may find it disturbing how debate over matters with potentially enormous social implications is replaced by manipulative images from entertainment producers. This might betoken a general retreat from reason in policy making in favour of emotive impressions. As a herd effect is created, public and private bodies are anxious to join the throng. The NHS funded a 'human rights week' (2012), judged important enough to take priority over ambitions of making £20bn in efficiency savings – including 'awareness raising' timelines and photographic exhibitions 'celebrating' transgender and homosexual staff, with conferences and workshops for front-line workers. Newspapers distributed a glossy booklet for Gay History Month (February 2013) sponsored by organisations from Santander to the City of London, to National Grid, Citizens Advice Bureau, Ernst & Young, and so on. A glowering cover figure of indeterminate sex looking like an alien warlord announces: 'OUT, PROUD AND **FIERCE**'. The message was: you don't mess with that!

By early 2014, and as the gay flag flew over Whitehall, television channels competed with celebrations of gay weddings. Along with the unavoidable messages on buses, billboards and in public buildings, compulsory schooling gives direct access to the young, and the news is how "LGBT as an aspect of diversity is well embedded in the curriculum" of more and more schools.[116] In the LGBT week at one London school: "The whole of Year 8 has spent the day creating banners and other materials and this afternoon... over 200 students, walked round the local park displaying their messages: 'some people are gay, get over it', and, 'No matter who we are, we are all human'." Wellington College boasts about a month of LGBT activities in lessons, assemblies and chapel about the difficulties of LGBT people across the world. A head of PE talked about how LGBT week led him to challenge stereotypes in sport and – like someone in the Chinese Cultural Revolution avoiding the re-education camp – thanked the Leadership Team and the Governing School Body for 'enlightening' him.[117] Accompanied by Elton John, children from four years old are told about same sex relationships as part of the International Day against Homophobia and Transphobia. Parents who complained that their children were confused and worried – particularly about being friends with each other – were said to be 'homophobic'.

Ofsted commended schools reviewed and updated all policies "to ensure that they included lesbian, gay, bisexual and transgender (LGBT) pupils" and followed up any staff or pupils with "any anti-gay or anti-transgender attitudes" to make them "change their perceptions.[118] Lessons, books, displays and topics cover all "strands of diversity including sexuality and gender identity" with "role models and resources provided by external organisations [e.g. Stonewall]" imported "to create an inclusive culture" and staff trained (by Stonewall) in how to identify, record, report and tackle homophobia. Even lunchtime supervisors receive anti-homophobia training and, according to teachers, little children are now "very comfortable using the terms 'gay' and 'lesbian' appropriately" to label and applaud themselves and each other. Representatives of *Pride Games* lead sports activities, along with same sex prom couples, visiting gay naval officers, Stonewall DVDs, staff in T-shirts with anti-homophobic slogans, workshops "aimed at eradicating homophobia by indicating to pupils the damage it causes", displays about different sexualities, projects on 'new queer cinema' and meetings with Sir Ian McKellan discussing homophobia with staff, pupils and governors. (In a BBC news clip, he points to a boy and asks, "Has it ever crossed your mind that you might be gay?") Primary school pupils look "at how stories and illustrations have changed in children's books over the past 50 years" and:

> ...explore issues of racism, gender stereotyping and homophobia. At the end of the week pupils make their own storybooks depicting difference and diversity in all its forms and this often illustrates their good understanding and positive attitudes... One girl, for example, wrote a fairy story which ended with two princesses marrying each other. In Year 6 personal, social and health education lessons pupils explore homophobia and stereotyping in the media and learn about gay role models such as actor Sir Ian McKellen and international rugby player Gareth Thomas. Stonewall posters of different families are on display in the school.

Considering the ruthless putdown of critics, is it too soon to ask whether the affirmative interventions and improvements in LGBT's social environment, here or abroad, are related to any decline in their tribulations or improved their health and fortunes? In one test, US researchers set out to find if there were higher rates of psychiatric disorders among LGBs in states with constitutional amendments banning civil unions or SSM and so more 'minority stress'.[119] In US States with constitutional laws banning SSM there were increased levels of general anxiety and alcohol disorders for LGB populations (and for heterosexuals, although not so high). In States without, where there was significantly higher levels of LGB drug use, there was not enough statistical power to test properly the hypothesis – no means of knowing whether symptoms were short-lived or persistent, or varied with negative or positive political campaigns or legislation. The number with diagnosed psychiatric disorders was small anyway.

There are claims made concerning how health has been much improved by the arrival of marriage equality in Massachusetts in 2003. In a study heralded as the first to document general advantages, researchers surveyed

1,211 patients from a community-based health clinic serving sexual minorities. This found a reduction in hypertension, depression, and adjustment disorders for 'gay' men based on billing records for visits (down 13%) and care costs (down 14%) in the 12 months following legalisation compared with the 12 months before, with effects similar for partnered and single men.[120] There is no independent record of actual stress related conditions or comparisons for more objectively defined or verified mental or physical complaints. Such a study would have to be replicated to be accepted as valid.

Questions were raised over the interpretation and promotion of the research. Other factors which may have influenced the results, like the declining economy, were not considered. The seeking of medical treatment for vague conditions might be the first to be affected where resources are squeezed. Otherwise, HIV/AIDS (and related medical visits) went up considerably, and lobby groups have persuaded the Massachusetts Legislature to spend more on the dramatically rising infection rates. Greater accolade and acceptance of same sex relationships might even encourage risks. The HIV/AIDS epidemic came in the wake of an explosion of homosexual activity *after* the removal of prohibitions. There was a brief decrease in HIV positivity as some MSM initially adopted risk-reduction strategies.[121] Despite the flurry of health and educational provisions in an overwhelmingly sympathetic environment, HIV numbers rose again as high risk patterns resumed.[122]

Not least for having had full marriage equality the longest of all, the Netherlands might be the place to credit with being more advanced or homo/bi-sexual friendly and 'pro-gay' as anywhere. In the 1960s, 36% of the population thought that homosexuals should not be 'free to live their life their way', but by 2004 this had dropped to 5%. In 1998, 43% were opposed to same sex marriage, and 22% in 2005. Two-thirds were against the adoption of children by same sex couples in 1980, but by 2002 this was down to a third. There are the 'out and proud' government ministers and honours for contributions to homosexual causes. Children (aged 8–12) with lesbian parents report greater openness about their family, and less frequent encounters with homophobia than in America.[123]

As tolerance, along with homosexuality's presence in the public space, makes for a normalised lifestyle, populations become more open to experimentation. A report has it that 18.2% of Dutch women and 13.4% of men now claim to be (partly) attracted to their own gender, and 12.3% of women and 12.7% of men have had sex with a same-sex partner at least once. Figures for 'consistent' homo/bi-sexuality or attraction, behaviour and self-identification represent a big increase on 1989 and are construed as part of the progress of female sexual emancipation as women's sexual repertoires and numbers of partners grow.[124] The 5.5% of women and 7.9% of men having recently (last six months) had sex with a same sex partner compares to the 1.0% and 1.6% for France. Hence the celebration of how "necessary emancipation processes" are influenced in a "positive way by the increased levels of same-sex experiences", causing "homo-negativity" to further decrease and policies and laws to be even more accommodating.[125]

There appear to be similar movements in New Zealand, particularly with a shift to bisexuality by women, which is high by world standards. Researchers wonder whether this reflects the very heavily feminist and politically correct influences when their respondents were in their early 20s. New Zealand is renowned as a petri dish for single track social movements.[126] More harshly even than in the UK, the conjugal family was castigated and dismissed at the highest levels from the 1980s.[127] With fiscal recognition stripped away as law and language dissolved marriage into cohabitational units, welfare targeted the growing numbers of lone mothers.

Even in the UK, there is excitement in some circles over how women aged 16 to 44 now have 7.7 sexual partners compared to 6.5 in 2001 and 3.7 in 1991, and especially over how 16% have had at least one same sex experience, even if it was kissing, compared with 4% in 1991, while the rate for men had only risen from 6% to 7%.[128] Nowhere does any of this seem to have made a difference to the higher levels of psychiatric problems for those with a history of homosexual contact, with the Netherlands and New Zealand similar to the US, Australia and the UK.[129] A random, nationally representative Dutch household survey recorded high levels of psychiatric problems, including major depression, bipolar disorder ('manic depression') and drug addiction for 125 people reporting only homosexual behaviour compared to 5,873 heterosexuals in the control element of the survey.[130] There was also a 12-month prevalence rate of 21.1% for heterosexually and 35.4% for homosexually experienced men for one or more DSM (Diagnostic and Statistical Manual of Mental Disorders;

American Psychiatric Association) diagnoses, and 22.4% and 34.9% for heterosexual and homosexual women. Those with a history of homosexual contact had higher rates of nearly all measured psychiatric pathologies, not only during adolescence and early adulthood, but in later life, along with generally poorer health. Younger homosexuals have not lowered their risks for suicidality compared to older homosexuals and in comparison with heterosexual counterparts, independently associated as this is with same sex behaviour.[131] In Turkey, homosexual behaviour is not prohibited by law, but attitudes are negative and the police hostile. Yet people with same sex inclinations seem to be at much the same risk for suicidal ideation and behaviour as those in more tolerant places.[132]

As other societies have nonetheless become more accepting of homosexuality over recent time, this should be reflected in the experiences and outcomes for successive generations. The US four cities report catalogues greater openness about sexuality, more experimentation with sexual options, and a fall over time in the age of 'coming out'. With substantial drops in age at the initial or only suicide attempt, there is an increase since 1970 (the year of the Stonewall riots and birth of 'gay liberation') across birth cohorts among those under age 25, not fully explained by 'recency' bias in recollections.[133] One finding from an England and Wales 'snowball' (chain referral) sample of the rates and predictors of mental illness for homo/bi-sexuals was that those under 40 years – the age group with the greatest openness about sexuality – were at the highest risk of mental disorder, harmful drinking and self-harm contemplation.[134] This correlates not only with the growing proportion of men reporting *ever* having had a male partner, but the increase in 'concurrent' (two or more simultaneous) 'partnerships'.[135]

While (according to the ONS) 1.1% of all deaths are from suicide – which makes it quite rare – if 'gay' suicides constitute that oft claimed (never verified) third of all suicides attributed to homophobia, we should still see a difference in the overall suicide rates between more or less 'gay' friendly countries. With the Government's health strategy of 2002 including a target of reducing the number by a fifth by 2010 from the 1995/7 baseline, there were expectations that tackling homophobia might make a contribution to cutting the UK's rate, but this was, in fact, of little or no effect.[136] Comparing rates of suicide in Western countries gives us one of

12.0 per 100,000 males for the Netherlands (2009) compared to the UK's 18.2 (2011). This may seem to be good news, but then there is 17.3 for Norway (2009); 16.4 for Sweden (2010), 16.6 for Denmark (2010), 17.0 for New Zealand (2010) and 17.9 for Canada (2009).[137]

Has the suicidality of 'gay' youngsters declined or their mental health improved or other afflictions attributed to 'homophobia' in its various guises been reversed in Ofsted's LGBT friendly schools? These claim to have overseen a "marked decrease in the use of homophobic language… [after pupils] learnt about the damage homophobia can cause". More staff and pupils may have 'come out' but is that the only purpose? If "pupils who *are or may be* LGBT have rising attendance and achievement" [italics mine], how were these identified and monitored? Complaints are about schools not doing enough and staff being insufficiently trained.[138] Could greater openness mean more insults and hence worse mental health? The four cities US report claims that recent generations have experienced more, not less, early 'anti-gay' harassment, which can be recollections of "being called names" four or more times.[139] While, for SSAY (same sex attracted) Australian youngsters, there were strong relationships between receiving support and youth feeling 'good' or 'great' about their 'sexuality' and family members being more positive, the percentage reporting abuse remained stable. For being treated unfairly because of sexuality, this was higher in 2004 (39%) than in 1998 (29%). And, if "virtually all same sex attracted young Australians experience discrimination" this included a wide range of unverified perceptions or 'feelings' of discrimination, not getting enough "relevant safe sex information", being denied double bed accommodation or even being "brought up straight".[140]

It is acknowledged that there has been encouragement to identify and report 'homophobia' where it might have gone unrecognised or disregarded before, although greater awareness does not exclude a rise. Campaigns and highly vocal interest groups may encourage their clientele to become preoccupied or disturbed by what they would otherwise disregard or shrug off. For all youngsters, a narcissistic focus on feelings and self-esteem "in the classroom is likely to encourage children to feel that they have a mental health problem" or "become more inward looking and less able to cope with the challenges that confront them."[141]

For the Netherlands, blame is directed at those who are still against 'gay' marriage and adoption, or how people may be only accepting of homosexuality as long as it is not too visible. There is also the way that LGBTs are more likely to be found in the media or politics than in sport and how "there is no out-and-proud LGB woman or man among the 125 board members of Dutch companies with stock market quotations."[142] Attraction may not be acted upon due to a prevailing fear of adopting a 'congruent self-identity' because of cultural constrains. The hope for some is that, as this all dies away, there will be equal or greater levels of same sex as heterosexual identification.[143]

7.7   A Voracious Miasma?

With as many or more personal adversities persisting – alongside greater social prominence, recognition and approval – perhaps the causes need re-visiting. It is unfortunate that, before the existence, nature, severity and origins of the evils that were meant to be addressed were even properly identified, it was confidently and opportunistically decided what the remedies were. The truth is that we are far from answers to why sexual minorities have, on average, a different or lower pattern of mental well-being compared to sexual majority populations. Adequate explanation is likely to be neither simple nor limited to politically acceptable hypotheses.[144] Discrimination or victimisation cannot be totally dismissed any more than can other environmental influences. Since the spotlight has been overwhelmingly directed at one factor to explain so many co-morbidities, there may be a failure to recognise that there may be many and perhaps disparate detrimental variables or factors. These, in different circumstances and with various interconnections, might affect a variety of outcomes. A fundamental problem with so many studies relates to causality. When current reports of past events are related to present outcomes, did the 'outcome' influence the report, or did the exposure affect the outcome?[145] The Swedish National Academy for Education conducted an extensive review of educational material, with schools ordered to "integrate gender equality and sexual orientation issues into their operations and everyday tasks". Research was also meant to focus upon how "norms and attitudes make homophobia possible", but in the absence of "statistics or consistent studies which can pinpoint discrimination due to sexual orientation"![146]

Causal diagnosis is problematic not only because of the low quality of much research, but the way that the continually stretching and shifting meaning given to 'homophobia' has created an essentially unfalsifiable hypothesis or explanation.

Victim status is maintained not only through extending the scale of the problem, but the dimensions and manifestations of homophobia. This can be perceived as well as real, in the past as well as the present, contemporary as well as historical – encompassing "the trauma of the journey" out of the closet.[147] As victimhood has been expanded through the concept of the indirect victim, so anyone who has witnessed or heard something unpleasant becomes a candidate for this status. Unlikely ever to be defeated, demands to be free from anything that might conceivably give offence could theoretically swallow the legal and educational systems, art, medicine, religious and professional bodies. Given the vested interests, there is great reluctance to say 'enough is enough', particularly given the emotive appeal to victimhood. Frank Ferudi has observed how victimhood often now becomes part of self-identity, in contrast to people in the past who were not defined by their experiences of being aggrieved or hurt.

Affirmative ventures have now themselves come under attack. Acclamations like "Gay and proud" show that shame is lurking just beneath the surface. Identity politics are effective for achieving rights, but derive their power from collective pain. Even in teaching that explicitly aims to create positive attitudes, heterosexuality is still seen as self-evident and normative. The 'we are all human' and other slogans imply a privileged heterosexual 'we' who have the opportunity to tolerate 'the homosexual' as 'the other'.[148] Thus, 'homo-tolerance' simply reinforces the 'otherness' and 'marginalisation' of non-heterosexuals. Same sex marriage could even enhance the problems of LGBTs as legal recognition makes LGB couples and families more visible, vulnerable to scrutiny and attempts to 'heteronormalise' their relations.

To some this might look like a "semi-permanent state of rage about any remaining imperfection involving those trained to identify grievances, so naturally they are aggrieved."[149] This might include a clinical psychologist who, at LGBT History Month (2013) spoke of:

> … greater presence in the media of positive LGBT role models, greater numbers of significant public figures being open about their sexuality,

politicians, pop stars, actors and generally people of influence ... equal rights to marriage and adoption ...affirmative official statements from professional and scientific bodies that de-stigmatise and normalise non-heterosexual sexuality and identity. It feels safer, more doable, and achievable ... living as an openly LGBT person is less difficult than it used to be.[150]

Despite all this, Kerrigan asks: "then why do I still feel sad?" The reason is that LGBT people are still "at risk of internalizing heterosexist ideas of normality, and negative social messages about their own sexuality" since the "subtle assumption of 'heterosexuality as normality' ... still remains." This denies him much "taken for granted by heterosexual people" and not only encompasses "marriage and having children" but is everywhere in the "ideas, beliefs, biases and attitudes present in society" which permeate "social institutions such as the education system and religious structures". It follows that "psychological difficulty and mental health problems" remain "prevalent in LGBT communities ... as a result of such social processes." Since heterosexism "perpetuates feelings of separateness, difference and of being denied an empowered life experience", then creating equal life opportunities for everyone dictates that we tackle heterosexuality. Similarly, a Danish study muses that mental health issues for homo/bi-sexual men deriving from "anti-gay stigma and consequent adversity in their daily lives" will remain so long as "heterosexual marriage remains the ideal in Denmark".[151]

Chapter Eight

THE AFTERMATH

8.1 SOCIAL OVERHAUL?

The coming of same sex marriage portends a speeding up of change well under way throughout all and every aspect of society. Increasingly the power that pressure groups wield throughout the legislature, education, media and political machinery will move beyond combating the toxicity of homophobia to concentrate on the even greater task of eliminating heterosexism or heteronormality. More than that, "educational efforts, prevention programs, and health services must be designed to address the unique needs of GLB youth",[1] and the wider vision of some might be to bring to fruition the vision set out by gay liberationist Malcolm Macourt back in 1977. Here, as youngsters experiment with various sexual orientations, roles and genders: "each young person becomes aware that each of these life patterns [same-sex partners – opposite-sex partners – partnerships for life or one for a period of mutual growth] is held in equal esteem in society. So that each will feel free to choose the partner or partners with whom they wish to share their lives."[2]

A study commissioned for the BBC advised the corporation to use children's programming to positively "familiarise audiences through incidental portrayal from an early age" with homo/bi-sexuality and family variations as well as validate children who are homo/bisexual.[3] Teachers and governing bodies "will always be expected to be fully aware of their responsibilities under employment law and equalities law...."[4] Section 403(1A)(a) of the Education Act 1996 once imposed a duty on the Secretary of State "to issue guidance" ensuring that pupils "learn the nature of marriage and its importance for family life and the bringing up of children", in response to pro-family pressure. Given animosity towards marriage in public institutions, it hardly went beyond the paper it was printed on, but will now perhaps have a useful lease of life.

Overseen by pressure groups, children can be more widely and comprehensively taught the mechanisms of diverse sexual practices as an integral part of benchmark standards in good sex education and as a necessary corollary of SSM. Pupils may be directed to pressure group websites and – while it is doubtful that material often promoting incredibly dangerous activities can be truly classed as health advice – schools are complying with equality duties. Citing "the right to marry" for making it a place where "it's a great time to be gay", the Massachusetts Department of Public Health helped to produce *The Little Black Book, Queer in the 21st Century* with its 'tips' for boys on how to perform oral sex on anuses, masturbate other males, and 'safely' have someone urinate on you, along with a directory of bars in Boston to meet for anonymous sex. Groups active in Canadian schools are creating 'queer sex ed' curricula conveying practices like fisting to those 13+ of all 'sexualities and orientations'.[5] My Gay Straight Alliance, the education arm of the rights group Egale (like Stonewall) has hundreds of clubs and affiliated school and community groups. Children act out weddings with same sex friends and mass dancing Pink Projects celebrate sexual minorities to Lady Gaga's 'Born This Way'.

As Peter Tatchell here insists: "sex education has an obligation to give all the facts and tell the whole truth about every kind of sex and relationship. …such as anal sex and sadomasochism … schools should adopt a 'live and let live' non-judgmental attitude". The "right to sexual self determination should be promoted in every school, to create a culture of sexual rights where every young person understands and asserts their right to determine what they, and others, do with their body."[6] Others might ask what is being transmitted if any idea of obscenity or perversion is defunct, and sexuality is no longer "integrated into the life of personal affection ... in which the self and its responsibility are centrally involved and indissolubly linked to the pleasures and passions of the body".[7] Such a separation of sex from context is party to that "peculiar negative conception of freedom as isolation and fragmentation of life... to which libertarians of the 1960s were dedicated."

Everybody "must concentrate on their own sexual experience in a vacuum, and that a partner is only a sex aid which happens to prove effective."[8]

Are the interests of equality and justice being served? From anti-bullying campaigns to SSM, all raise the question as to why the welfare or interests of a small minority supplants the well-being or eclipses the interests of all others.

For example: should not bullying *per se* be targeted, not just that which might affect one fraction of the school population, with programmes teaching good behaviour, consideration and tolerance towards all who are different? Tackling serious and specific risks such as suicide, and suicidality preventive strategies, should be population based, remembering that the overwhelming majority of cases will *not* be among sexual minorities.[9] If we take figures for Year 9 age group in the England study, when bullying is at its worst, around 94% is of heterosexual young people.[10] Addressing only LGB bullying leaves this 94% unaddressed. Even if 6% suffered homophobic bullying, this is not *prima facie* evidence that the targets were all homosexual – far from it. A US school study purported to show how a comprehensive pro-gay environment with special protective measures for LGBT pupils was associated with a trivial (and methodologically challengeable) reduction in suicide attempts over 12 months.[11] Someone queried whether this low significance justified "... calling for significant policy changes. I am not sure that's how science is normally done."[12]

Even in the unlikely event that one or other tribulations of a minority might be reduced, are measures acceptable if they expose more to harm? Given the diffusive nature of suicidal thoughts,[13] it may be counter-productive to ever focus on matters of suicide to suggestible youngsters – as happens, with fatal results, when youngsters become involved with 'self-harm' websites.

Moving on to the intensification of the drive to de-heterosexualise society in the wake of SSM and to see what this means for youth, it is useful to return to that report on the sexuality, health, and well-being of same-sex attracted young Australians, exploring how much the dissemination of information on the harms of 'homophobia' was responsible for positive changes in support for same sex attracted young people (SSAY).[14]

More young people here reported being attracted to the same sex and/or identified as 'gay' or lesbian in 2004 than in 1998 and the growing rates seem to have made for earlier sexual activity than heterosexual propensities. However, this was not a completely random sample. After high profile advertising for subjects, 1749 aged between 14 and 21 completed the survey (including nine 'transgendered' youngsters). "Despite the many [hypothesized] social pressures to remain closeted, more than a third (38%) of these young people were in a relationship" even if "not all relationships were same sex ones". With 10% of the 15–18 year old same sex attracted females pregnant, it might well be said that the "picture points to the further complications of making assumptions about the sexual behaviours of SSAY". Similarly, the declaration how "[y]oung people chose their sexual identity for a range of reasons, including what was acceptable in their social groups and not necessarily because of attraction or behavior" is at odds with other claims about "naturally occurring phenomena". The "social changes that have made this more acceptable" are listed as support and positive affirmation for same sex identity and information from schools about homophobia and discrimination, gay and lesbian relationships and safe 'gay' sex, as youngsters were targeted by networks and professional and community development programmes promoting the acceptance of diverse genders and sexual expressions.

While the researchers might have been encouraged about youngsters being same-sex inclined and having earlier sex so, along with the high rates of drug-taking, STIs were five-fold those for youngsters generally (including a 7% rate of hepatitis for the 15–18 year old sub-sample) and at threefold a national secondary school sample. The response was that these young people needed "better sexual health information and support in having safe and protected sex." At the same time as education in the UK is now so much more 'gay friendly', it is emphasised how 'safety' messages and methods must move beyond pregnancy prevention – by providing HIV tests in schools and colleges and counseling to reduce victimisation or the "likelihood of additional violence".[15] The BMA has urged health authorities to introduce HPV (human papilloma virus) vaccinations for young men, given the "alarming increase in anal cancer in gay men", although vaccinating all boys may not yet be possible given the cost.[16]

Social expectations may be stronger factors driving sexual conduct than is currently acknowledged in the face of 'born that way' sloganeering.[17] Perhaps the "recent period of rapid change in sexual practices should be seen, not just as a result of unleashed biological proclivities confronting attenuated cultural prohibitions, but as an active process of social construction and transformation" where, the more society highlights and applauds homosexuality, the more and the earlier will homosexual behavior manifest itself.[18] This is hardly separable from the general sexualisation of society, where sexual behaviour is bound to be as malleable and culturally influenced like other behaviours.[19]

Youth is a very fluid and confused period of development, marked by labile moods and heightened propensities to engage in risky behaviours. There is an increased responsiveness to incentives and emotional cues while the capacity for cognitive and emotion regulation is immature.[20] The complex path to heterosexuality involves leaving sexually segregated and chauvinistic peer groups to negotiate involvement and relationships with the opposite sex. As in some ancient and tribal cultures, youngsters may be involved with (often non-consensual) same sex activities as part of their familiar world. A problem is how the 'rescue' measures which welcome and even glamourise homo-/bi-sexual proclivities may not only be baseless in curative terms, but be *encouraging* the immature to take potentially dangerous steps with the result of a proliferation of ills affecting more people and demanding ever more complex and expensive solutions.[21]

What the *evidence already suggests* is how the earlier a boy 'comes out' to explore and engage in same sex sexual behaviour, the more detrimental it is to mental and physical health – in terms of forced sex, HIV seropositivity and other sexual diseases, abuse, substance use and, later, depression.[22] The more the numbers of sexual partners, the higher the chances of multiple sexual infection acquisition/ transmission, and the earlier the infection, the more time for serious damage.[23] The Terrence Higgins Trust lists as a myth or stereotype that gay men are more likely to get AIDs because of their promiscuity – something that is "individual choice and nothing to do with our sexual orientation."[24] The latter may be factually correct in relation to orientation *per se,* but it does not counter the close statistical association of disease with promiscuity. As it stands: "Public health authorities have failed to warn adequately about the many risks specific to anal intercourse" when it should be "incumbent upon them (as well as on clinicians and sex educators) to be more forthcoming in their details...."[25]

As 4% of youngsters in the NSPCC/Bristol study of sexually associated violence reported a same-sex partner, this accounted for a significant amount of all violence experienced by the male part of the sample.[26] Mounting evidence tells of higher levels of sexual risk for teenagers with same or both sex partners, compared to those with exclusively heterosexual involvement. Not least, 'sexual minority' boys were more likely than girls to report sexual coercion in seven US population-based surveys.[27] For boys in the UK's representative RIPPLE and SHARE studies, the prevalence of unwanted sex, partner pressure, high levels of risk-taking and regret were higher for first homosexual genital contact (oral or anal) than with first intercourse for the exclusively heterosexual group.[28] Same sex encounters were also likely to involve alcohol or drugs and no prior relationship. It is a similar story from the 2005–2007 New York City Youth Risk Behavior Surveys, where large proportions of male and female respondents (one-third) with same or both-sex partners were victims of partner-violence and forced sex at three times national estimates.[29] Bisexually experienced boys who have the earliest sexual debuts are particularly exposed to violence, forced sex and drug and alcohol use. The health outcomes of non-consensual sexual experience are serious in terms of subsequent abuse, psychological and alcohol problems and self-harm as well as serious sexual disease.

As practices pioneered by LGBs are transferred to the heterosexual world, the risks involve (heterosexual) girls as well as boys. 'Whether you're giving, receiving or versatile, the truth is many people, straight, bi and gay enjoy anal sex. Here's how to do it' says a site directed at young people, which offers tips on how to lick the anus and gives reassurance that 'a bit of bleeding (called spotting)' is 'nothing to worry about' so 'long as it's bright red in colour and disappears after 15 minutes…'[30] From here youngsters might visit a Mid-West teens sex show demonstrating 'backdoor business' where a girl's fears about giving in to her boyfriend's demands are allayed and she is shown how to prepare herself. Urged on by magazines and online pornography, more females are complying with male requests as these, in turn, may develop a penchant for an orifice shared with male partners. This is despite the associations with ill health.[31]

High levels of STIs and injury, drug taking, abuse and conflict may take their toll and contribute to serious mental as much as physical health consequences, regardless of familial or wider social acceptance. Among the last things that adolescents need is introduction to risky environments and encouragement to participate in self-destructive behaviour.[32] Preparing adolescents for 'choice' may as much be taking it away.

This is particularly important considering how notions that 'sexual orientation' is inexorably fixed in childhood or tallies with passing attraction and/or behaviour go against the evidence.[33] The Australian Health, Sex and Society research was disappointed when, despite the many who reported feeling same sex attraction at puberty (11–13 years), this did not necessarily "determine the strength or nature of their later identity, attraction or behavior" with "no relationship between age at first realisation, current attraction and gender of sexual partner."[34] The England and Wales snowball sample found that only a quarter of homosexual men reported being aware of their sexual orientation by 10 years (and 8% of bisexual men), although nearly three-quarters stated that they were aware by 15 years.[35] Retrospective data may be problematic because of later interpretations. In turn, sexual activity is an unreliable indicator.[36] Back in the 1990s, a large US study of 36,741 teenagers aged 12 to 18 found that while 1.6% of boys and 0.9% of girls reported some 'homosexual experience' in the previous year, nearly three-quarters of these identified as heterosexual.[37] By 16, same-sex genital contact (touching, oral or anal) was reported by 2.3% of teenagers in the SHARE and RIPPLE studies, but the majority of these (72%) also reported heterosexual intercourse.[38]

The rates of same-sex behaviours were comparable with retrospective reports in national surveys of older UK respondents, which also confirm that most of those with same-sex partners also experienced heterosexual intercourse,[39] raising questions as to whether concepts of early, fixed orientation have much application.[40] Considerable instability is apparent if more than a half of those who experience same sex attraction at age 16 no longer do so at 17,[41] or if 75% of those aged 17-21 changed to opposite sex attraction only.[42] Those with occasional homosexual feelings or behaviour may not regard these as indicative of an underlying nature in the way that pressure groups do. Five waves of longitudinal data on lesbian, bisexual and 'unlabelled' New Zealand women showed how, over 10 years, two-thirds changed identity labels, and a third two or more times.[43] More claimed bisexual/unlabelled identities than relinquished these, although all reported declines in the ratio of same to other-sex behaviour.[44] Equal numbers of men moved in and out of same sex attraction. In another US national survey, only 45% of men who reported MSM *after* the age of 18 years even self-identified as homo/bi-sexual.[45]

Same sex friendships are a part of children's normal development and 'schoolgirl crushes' were once an accepted part of growing up, not indications of a lesbian identity. It is a shame if – as alleged – young children are scared to be close to same sex peers or offer them comfort if they have been exposed to teaching that has effectively collapsed distinctions between sexual behaviour and human attachments. There are those prepared to adamantly state:

> ... that to present this model to young people, or to allow them... to imagine that their transitory adolescent experiments are truly indicative of a settled homosexual disposition, is not only evidence of psychiatric ignorance, but is specifically wicked as well.[46]

All adolescents have to deal with the vicissitudes of life without the coping resources and psychological resilience of maturity. The healthiest, safest adolescents are those who are not sexually involved at all, whether or not they are later going to enter a same or opposite sex oriented lifestyle.[47] These matters may be best postponed to a time when those who have their lives before them are more developmentally able to make more sensible 'choices' and can (hopefully) deal better with possible consequences, and they should not be pushed into an 'orientation' ahead of their years. This would also allow for change over time – given so much volatility in sexual attraction and behaviour, let alone self-identification of orientation.

Preparation for diversity in terms of the overthrow of heteronormality means that, as all information and images "reflect the full range of families", all must come to believe that there is nothing special about a male-female family unit. Teachers have banned Father's Day cards 'in the interests of sensitivity' so as not to offend pupils with single and lesbian mothers.[48] Staff were described as "unafraid to tackle potentially controversial issues" when "one boy from a heterosexual Christian family" queried how a boy who told the class he was born from frozen sperm to two lesbian 'mums' could be without a father, and the teacher abandoned the lesson and created an alternative lesson about different families to ensure that all pupils, regardless of background, were valued. The teacher then discussed the lesson with parents and carers at the end of the day. Might that boy be 'damaged' or suffer 'hurt feelings' by the antagonism directed at his "heterosexual Christian family"? If evidence and social well-being mattered, pupils might be told of the importance or value of fathers – if such lessons are appropriate for primary pupils. Along with lesbian 'how to' exercises, in New York and Massachusetts' schools, those undergoing sex change operations are brought into primary classrooms to tell the children that there are 'different kinds of families.' Complaints by parents are 'inappropriate behavior' from those with no right to object.[49]

8.2   FAMILY-FREE PARENTING

Marriage as just a 'couple relationship' might be finally severed from parenthood but what model or structure, if any, for child rearing do we have in exchange for the old family schema? To replace the way in which paternal obligations and responsibilities once arose from marital commitment, there is a de-institutionalised, de-gendered 'supportive parenting' as a correlate of the 'fact of parenthood'. This is independent of whatever relationships the progenitors may or may not have with each other. In Canada, the amending of all official documentation and legislation in the event of same sex marriage not only eliminated terms like 'husband' and 'wife', but replaced 'natural parent' with 'legal parent'. In Spain, birth certificates now read 'Progenitor A' and 'Progenitor B'. Politicians and commentators tell us how it is "strong relationships between parents" – and whether living together or not – which are "important", not marriage or a "particular family form" (Nick Clegg).

The practice of 'parenting' skills seemingly makes the numbers, sexes and relations of parents irrelevant as this speciality replaces something which human beings have managed within fundamental bonds since the beginning of time. Expert judgment or opinion mediates between parent and child as the source of youth's welfare, as part of a professionalisation of everyday life creating a rising demand for more and more expertise (see Ferudi, op. cit.). On the face of it, the parents' 'partnering' and 'repartnering' need not affect their capacity to 'parent' the resultant children across households or in families of 'all shapes and sizes'. Fathers need not live with their children. Instead, they can drop in to do their spot of 'parenting' in different homes, or children might spend equal time in two (or more) homes or visit their various 'carers' or 'stakeholders'. This 'responsible parent' need have no more to be the biological sire of the child(ren) than be married to or living with the mother(s). Killing two birds with one stone, to "ensure that men stay involved in their children's lives [when relationships break down], they must have more parental leave" which also enables mothers to get back to work even if the father – or substitute(s) – does not live with her.[50]

This is little different from the old Bolshevik policy an admiring feminist once described where, under their social and economic reforms:

> Men and women would come together and separate as they wished, apart from the deforming pressures of economic dependency and need. Free union would gradually replace marriage as the state ceased to interfere in the union between the sexes. Parents, regardless of their marital status, would care for their children with the help of the state… The family, stripped of its previous social functions, would gradually wither away, leaving in its place fully autonomous, equal individuals free to choose their partners on the basis of love and mutual respect.[51]

Presumably, the children are to:

> …understand their parents' needs; the importance of being accepting of sexual orientation and alternative lifestyles; the contingencies of all attachments; the need for each of us to create our own meaning of the universe. Such children are also taught a worldview that is intended to make them accepting of difference and adaptable in a world in which they have no permanent obligations. These "dispositions" are "useful in resigning children who have no choice but to adapt as they are shuffled from household to household." They can learn that "self-gratification is good, that a sense of entitlement is normative, and that acts or omissions need not have consequences."[52]

The belief might be that children can be protected from domestic comings and goings if, through 'joint parenting', they maintain relationships with both parents. However, evidence on peripatetic parenting is that outcomes differ little from those of lone parenthood.[53] Since the children of unmarried or separated parents are likely to have emotional, behavioural and health problems in excess of those with live-in biological married parents, they absorb more resources than other children. So do the parents, considering the costs imposed by living alone in terms of welfare, health, housing, energy and other environmental resources, along with the potential loss of economic productivity.

Even if the best gloss is put upon enlightened looking plans for 'equal parenting' rights when parents break up, there is still the prospect of battles for child time as well as child support, with all the add-ons of double housing, double schools and the children commuting between homes.[54]

The 'fact of parenthood' might seem the obvious and easy way to accommodate the diversity of 'new family forms', but the state has to employ legal machinery to force responsibility on to progenitors or even identify them. Deregulated family culture may not bar a parent directly from family life, but parental obligations are easy to avoid and more or less optional. This fosters fecklessness along with bitterness – demonstrated by excluded fathers' campaigns. Where mothers can ask the state to help them collect money from errant fathers, the costs are borne by taxpayers generally, albeit how notions that absent fathers should contribute to child costs or reimburse the state have been tactically sidelined. When mothers respond to the economics of the situation, the visiting father is likely to be seen as unreliable, inadequate, not worth the trouble, and may become effectively exiled from his children. With men peripherally or accidentally attached to independent mothers, this may not negate male influence and control. Will this be as beneficial as that exercised by the live-in committed father? Overall, it is highly questionable whether ties of kinship can simply emerge out of personal relations or proximity.

The Ministry of Defence is urged to keep DNA samples for all troops in the event of death so that their girlfriends might be able to identify their child(ren)'s father to claim compensation. That unmarried mothers have to appeal for the release of DNA was described by David Cameron as a "dreadful situation" where legal wrangles to establish paternity compound the 'trauma' of losing boyfriends.[55] That none of this would happen if the parents were married goes unmentioned. If a father signs the birth certificate (if the mother agrees to it) this, to the Advisory Board on Family Law, shows an 'appropriate degree of commitment' or might even increase 'feelings' of responsibility. Since:

> We want to do everything we can to promote the involvement of both parents in a child's life. … That may require strengthening guidance or commencing legislation [already] on the statute book....[56]

This was in connection with suggestions that fathers should be *made* to sign birth certificates and enforcement of a 2009 law that threatened mothers with a £200 fine and time in prison if they refused to name the father.

What is missing from all the talk of maintaining the parent-child tie irrespective of the parents' relationships is the issue of what happens when new parental relationships are formed (and other children are born). The problems that a parent's next 'partner' might present for the ex 'partner(s)' appears to be a consideration too far. Would the previous 'partner' always be welcomed in to do his/her spot of 'parenting' by the new incumbent?

The same applies whether children are generated in petri dishes or passing liaisons of convenience. It is not only in heterosexual relationships that children become tools of control. We have lesbians battling it out with the biological father of a 'partner's' child. Said to be betrayed by the man's demands, they expected to control matters to the degree that he formed a "limited but important [*sic*] relationship" with his child and so were unable to "conceive of their child being shuttled, physically but more significantly emotionally between two homes… something that they believe will harm their son and cause significant emotionally damage."[57] How does equal marriage cope with the sort of problems where, as relationships break up, only one parent may be recognised or favoured by the courts, leading to custody and visitation disputes? Since there are not two genetic parents so (marriage or no marriage) one (or more) 'parents' may still have to access the legal procedures available, like second parent adoption – however, this might be criticised as a 'patchwork quilt' of legal security.[58]

How is the presumption that a child born to a married woman is the issue of both the biological mother and her spouse, really transferable to LGB parents? The husband may not always be the father of a child his wife produces and accepts as his own, out of deception or marital obligation, but such obfuscation is hardly possible if the 'husband' is female. In the Netherlands, uncertainty as to whether paternity or maternity could be ascribed to a non-generative 'parent' made it necessary for the partner of a mother to adopt any child they both regarded as their own. Elsewhere, in Canada, the advent of same sex marriage not only led to the concept of natural parent being erased from law – for every child and every couple – but court rulings that children could have three parents. Are these to divide up the 'parenting' between them?

Since no amount of cultural destruction and upheaval can alter the fact that heterosexuals produce children, a medical priority might be to hasten the ability of individuals of the same sex to make their own offspring. As equal marriage increases demands for reproductive technologies, cloning might "clean up the aesthetically unpleasant reality that one of the partners in the same-sex marriage might otherwise be tied through a child to someone of the opposite sex."[59] Men might even be able to fertilise themselves if ovary and womb transplants become successful.

In another case, two lesbian couples, each with children from the partnership of two male homosexuals, prompted a landmark High Court ruling that a sperm donor does not have to have any relationship with a mother to influence a child's upbringing and have a part in its life. Previously, the law refused contact for sperm donors who had no legal or domestic relationship with their biological children. Couples using a sperm donor are now urged to establish the child rearing equivalent of a pre-nuptial agreement or 'co-parenting deal'.[60] Just as gay adoption helped further same sex marriages, so legally recognised triple parenting might eventually help to usher in triple (group) marriage – argued, as it will ingenuously be, as a matter of children's rights or interests.

Writers for the Conservative think-tank Policy Exchange assured us how the law requires people to "look after their children whether married or not" as they justified separating coupledom from procreation. If so, it is doing a very poor job considering the rising toll of fatherless families, the welfare bill and the fortune owed in child support. Publicly recognised marriage was the *sine qua non* for paternal involvement and responsibility, and embodied expectations that both parties would share responsibilities related to the creation of children.[61] Decoupling marriage from "its basic grounding – [how] the people who make the baby are supposed to care for the baby and each other", looks the very opposite of the direction that needs to be moved in if the real crisis of, not least, "the epidemic of fatherlessness" is to be confronted.[62]

If this leads us back to the question of how society "can reliably make men into good fathers while at the same time affirming in its governing family law that children do not need mothers and fathers, and that it is choice … that creates family obligations", then the answer is 'No'. Instead, as regimes seek to abolish the conjugal family, the state increasingly has to intrude and adopt the role of *parens patriae* with results that "range from the inept to the despotic."[63] Government will tell you when you can see the children, whether you can pick them up or not, on what days, whether you can authorise medical treatment and how much you are to spend on them. Particularly where a third party is used for reproduction purposes or a passing 'partner' claims access to a non-related child, the state must employ a plethora of tests and scrutinise the minutiae of family life to determine if they warrant the status of *de facto* parent. With marriage more and more fluid and diverse in its membership, if it is there at all, the state will more and more control parentage. And it is noteworthy how it became a Conservative think tank's assumption that the state, not marriage, determines who looks after children. The supreme irony of free market relations is the destruction of liberty by state power:

> …the sexual revolution is to the family what communism is to the market. Both entail statist assaults on core institutions of civil society, leading to human misery that the state is not equipped to put right … In both cases, citizens lose the buffer of an intermediate form of social order… resulting in their further atomization and defenselessness in the face of state power.[64]

Under a Scottish Government plan all children, from birth up to the age of 18, will be assigned a state guardian – or a health worker to be the 'named person' up to the age of five, after which responsibility would pass to local councils, with teachers likely to take over the role. Start-up costs are estimated at £30 million. Children effectively become wards of a state managing their lives from birth.

All this might suggest that we move completely in the direction Clem Henricson sets out as the culmination of liberal left human rights driven policy on families. Moving from the abolition of tax allowances to the expansion of state-funded childcare to the professional directing and oversight of 'parenting' and to the removal of the need for a father, to proliferating anti-discrimination laws, we end up with direct parenting contracts imposed by the state. Since, in a "well-regulated modern society it is unthinkable that parent-child relationships would be exempt from government control", if this had a significant role in supporting and regulating family relationships, it would ensure 'equality' and end that 'complexity of tensions' within and between families and between families and the state.[65] As the family served as the principal check on state power, G. K. Chesterton predicted that some day the state and family would directly confront one another. What was not perhaps appreciated was how this would be in circumstances where the state ensured that its adversary had been well eroded away to begin with.

If the exclusivity of the parent-child relationship is dissolving, how far will this apply to sexual union? We have seen how adultery does not exist or work the same way for homosexual unions, and is one instance of how SSM has left us with two incompatible understandings of marriage, where the drift is towards the homosexual one.[67] With outlet sex and multiple partners increasingly publicised and therefore expected, the prognosis is that this might easily be imported into heterosexual relations, perhaps to the end of the greater conflict, distress and dissolution which so adversely affect children.

Moreover, if there are really to be 'no outsiders' then no relationship should be denied and there is no reason for public policy to say who or how many a person can or cannot marry. This may initially be strategically sensitive, as calls for 'gay' marriage might once have been. Again the argument will be that little or nothing will change. Again, freedom and autonomy presuppose a level playing field where people enter the relationship(s) of their choice, where the state facilitates moves from one to another product of unconstrained individualism. Facilitating fluid, diverse associations, the law affirms little or nothing beyond self-expression. Loosening or losing its relationship to civil life, it simply reflects the diversity which people make up for themselves.

This returns us to the question of: why any 'marriage' – if a free for all is the only valid form of 'equality'? It may well be believed that a particular area of behaviour should be de-institutionalised and left to everybody's choice and chance, but an institution cannot be supported as well as all deviations from it.

This is illustrated by how the European Court of Human Rights insists that European States adapt their legislation to (its own perception of) the evolution of morals. From now on, when a European State legislates as regards the family, it *"must necessarily take into account developments in society and changes in the perception of social and civil-status issues and relationships, including the fact that there is not just one way or one choice when it comes to leading one's family or private life."* Marking a new stage in the accelerated dissolution of the legal definition of the family, in the case of *Vallianatos and others v. Greece* of November 2013, the Court considered that two men in a homosexual relationship living separately should benefit from the protection granted to families.

It was once solemnly stated (Preamble to the Convention on the Rights of the Child) that the family is recognised and protected as a *"fundamental group of society and the natural environment for the growth and well-being of all its members and particularly children. "* The protection did not target the couple but the family, which "is entitled to protection by society and the State" (Article 16§3 of the Universal Declaration of Human Rights and 23§1 of the International Covenant on Civil and Political Rights) *"while it is responsible for the care and education of dependent children"* (Article 10§1 of the International Covenant on Economic, Social and Cultural Rights). The recognition given by society to the couple derived from its contribution to the common good through the foundation of a family, not by the existence of feelings which come within the scope of private life, just like consensual sexual relations between adults. (See: www.zenit.org/en/articles/the-dilution-of-the-family-in-human-rights.)

The role of LGBT rights in the overthrow of this understanding of the family is inseparable from that emergence of a right to recognition for emotional relationships and coupledom autonomously and independent of any social purpose. No more than the presence of a child or public arrangement does this even make cohabitation necessary since, according to the Court *"individuals of full age, who, (...) are in same-sex relationships and in some cases cohabit"* also lead a family life (§ 49). Thus the Court has abandoned the idea where marriage is the form and the family is the substance, of a unique *"right to marry and to found a family"*. Having established the principle of equivalence under the 'protection of family life' between a same-sex couple without children and a biological family, abstract egalitarian logic reduces the (objective) differences to a simple (subjective) and irrelevant difference of sexual orientation. In turn, as stability is a relative criterion so *"the length or the supportive nature of the relationship"* also cannot be determinative.

Thus, 'family life" under Article 8 of the Convention has come to be characterised by no more than the existence of feelings, which now solicit protection. All this might witness to how, when marriage or the presence of a child is renounced as a criterion of family life, it is difficult to establish other objective, or non-arbitrary, criteria. As decisions now belong to judges, these are contingent and related to cultural developments which, in turn, are meant to act as guides to national courts and legislators. Step by step, legal and political decisions have led the Court to the opposite of the original intention of the authors of the Convention, who wished to protect families from the State, and not to entrust to the State the power to define the family. According to the original conception of the authors of the Convention and other major texts of the post-war period, the State emanates from society which is constituted by families, and therefore the family precedes the State. According to the new conception, it is the State which, through its hold on society, redefines the family according to dominant thinking and demands. Human rights theory might have been founded upon natural law humanism. Now, as an instrument of the implementation of liberal individualism, it reinforces the State's hold over society in exchange for the promise of greater individual freedom.

The early Soviet Union experimented with sexual liberation and marriage's abolition. There was a plunge into barbarism with terrible social distress, destruction and economic costs which threatened its very existence. The state ordered an abrupt turnaround. Less dramatically given this far more advanced or cushioned society, the costs are destined to grow here as well.[66] Marriage's fortunes affect the generations to come and, as a basic building block of society, everything from welfare spending to prison construction to child welfare to inequalities to community cohesion to responsible citizenship. The moral imperatives which involve mutual interdependence and willingness to forgo selfish gratification for the sake of others arise in familial care and generalise to provide the cornerstone of attitudes which underpin social control in all societies. Virtuous citizens are important in a democracy and, if marriage is no more than a matter of any adult's equally valid choices and satisfaction, then a society without norms faces a host of problems.

Ironically, with the weakening of social cohesion and atomisation of social life goes a diminishing sense of personal autonomy. Where no particular lifestyle is a model because all are legitimate, this almost makes social fragmentation a virtue. But while people might be free to choose their lifestyles and relations at will or whim, this freedom also intensifies estrangement and powerlessness. Some might postulate that the consequences of conjugality's defeat must inevitably lead to policy attempts to restore its authority, particularly as the financial costs continue to mount. However, family disintegration has already inflicted massive problems and costs without any attempts being made to grapple with the roots and reverse the trends.

8.3   DEGENDERED MODELS

Where we are moving extends beyond peripatetic parenting and partnering where, entwined with the eradication of heterosexism and heterosexuality is the drive to androgyny. This means a Utopia of sexual or gender identicality whose ambition is people unaware of male/female differences or able to choose whatever they wish to be, whenever they want. The doctrine is that all sexually specific attributes are 'socialised' into people so, along with family, sexes are no longer tangible realities. Instead, these are relative and dynamic "notions" defined by 'rights' where, again, the legal norm itself is an instrument of social engineering. The Council of Europe drafted a definition of gender as meaning: "the socially constructed roles, behaviours, activities and attributes that a given society considers appropriate for women and men." The Strasbourg Court has also applied its powers of defining reality to the terms man and woman, since it: "is not persuaded that ... it can still be assumed that these terms must refer to a determination of gender by purely biological criteria" (Goodwin, 2002 § 100).

If acknowledged at all, problems with male development and place in society can be approached in terms of the consequences of 'gendering'. The answer is that boys be 'constituted differently' or 'gendered' in a different way – something leading to suggestions that schools teach boys baby care and household chores.[71] This would make the absence of positive male role models irrelevant, along with any recognition and place for constructive and specifically masculine contributions and participation.[72] With some UK schools already helping "pupils who may be transgender" as much as homo/bisexual, we hear how:

> ...in the Early Years Foundation Stage in particular many boys dress up in girls 'clothes... and one boy wears his hair long with a ribbon and no one ever teases them. A Year 1 [four-five years of age] boy sometimes wears a tutu all day without comment from his peers. ... Parents and carers are aware that pupils unselfconsciously engage in non-gender stereotypical activities at school and are supportive ... reporting that the school has a 'really inclusive feel'.

Dressing up is harmless enough and for centuries little boys and girls were dressed the same. All habits or conventions are subject to the erosion of time. But, with a process of 'gender liberation' gaining speed, and going well beyond 'gender-neutral' public and school conveniences, it entails deleting words 'girl' or 'boy', 'him' and 'her', along with 'mother' and 'father', 'husband' and 'wife'. Gender 'etiquette' where people are asked with which sex they wish to identify extends to children being enabled to choose to be boy, girl or transgender.

Having led the way on genderless 'parenting' and employment patterns, Sweden is now heading up the move to remove sexual identity. This requires that everything be policed, from the colour and placing of nursery toys to books. This has not escaped criticism for diverting "attention from confronting the crisis of socialization" or avoiding the "inter-generational transmission of values" by using children as vehicles for progressive social change. If schools are ever going to pursue education as something in its own right, a precondition might rather be a general "depoliticization of education and the insulation of schools from the influence of social engineers...."[73]

Furthering moves to de-gender development is that abiding antagonism towards male economic provision which fuels so much antipathy towards the conjugal family. A way to redemption for fathers being pushed with increasing intensity is for them to adopt the caring role or, in the absence of role swap, each 'partner' makes equal contributions to all tasks and brings in equal amounts of income (or women bring in more). As the sexes 'parent' interchangeably, the father's value or place in the family is earned insofar as he imitates mother care as, at the same time, male economic provision is reduced or removed together with the (male) 'marriage premium'.[71] Otherwise, equality or equal contribution is deemed absent and "Edwardian" (Nick Clegg). No consideration can be given to how fathers (or mothers) may differently and uniquely contribute to child development, and in the later or adolescent years as much or more than in infancy. Hence, the suggestions for mothers to take only 14 days of maternity leave as fathers qualify for the remaining 50 weeks, with liberal left politicians pushing for the Swedish option of compulsory paternity leave, together with antenatal attendance. Sweden has seen significant resistance, since many mothers would rather not relinquish the care of infants and want at least one reliable job, not two fragile ones. Employers and colleagues may also see male leave taking as signifying low work commitment and, if they have to, fathers prefer to take leave when children are older, for sports and other activities.[70]

Above all, mothers should work full-time and a lack of child care is the only acceptable reason why they may not do so. Some or many may want to, just as some or many fathers may wish to stay at home to care for children, but choice is not meant to apply. As we saw earlier, the taxation of couple families and especially those with one earner took a further punitive turn in January 2013 as means testing extended up the income distribution. As the depleted child benefit or allowance phases out for one earner families with gross incomes over £50,000 per year, a tax-free Childcare Voucher Scheme worth up to £1,200 per child is promised instead. Eligibility depends upon both parents being in work with individual incomes up to £150,000 (£300,000 total). There are pressures to shift all remaining child benefit into child care. The allocation of child rearing to the domain of Friedrich Engels' 'public industry' will be complete.

Suggestions for the restoration of recognition for marriage to the tax system are all but drowned by this tide. The tiny sums promised nowhere approach the transferable tax allowances of the past or family benefits of other nations and are easily sidelined as an incongruous and unaffordable luxury.

If same sex partners and parents promise to create new and better families than heterosexuals, it is, not least, because they promise to supersede old gender role distinctions as champions of equality. Whilst the Vermont study comparing same sex partners (in and out of civil unions) with married heterosexual couples found infidelity aplenty, what impressed was how: "same sex couples are a model for ways of equalizing the division of housework."[68] Married heterosexual women were more likely to report that husbands paid for more, including rent/mortgage, utilities, groceries, major household appliances, entertainment and eating out, while homosexuals reported sharing costs more equally. Wives also reported doing more household tasks, including taking the children to their activities and appointments. It did not count that husbands dealt with rubbish, garden, household repairs and grocery shopping, fixed and drove the car, and so forth, or that wives may have preferred not to do these tasks. Neither was the man's absence from home when earning to support it an excuse to avoid the housework, since he was only engaged in an oppressive and otherwise irrelevant activity. Elsewhere, same sex partners – like heterosexual cohabiters – have been found to be less likely than opposite-sex married couples to pool their resources, specialise or make relationship specific investments, and were more likely to be financially self-sufficient.[69]

Specialisation and cooperation might be useful features of human society which have advanced wealth and welfare over the centuries but, anxious to abolish these as unjust distributions of 'power', it is hoped that, with movement from opposite to same-sex marriage, there will be future changes towards 'gender-free living'. This has no advantages for children, whilst the loosening of fidelity and commitment are threats to their care and development. Moreover, even at this superficial level, androgyny may be more difficult to achieve than environmental determinists imagine. The researchers for the Vermont project mused that if men still mended cars and women did more child minding, this "raised questions about how women and men are socialized to assume gendered roles in adult relationships, because heterosexuals grew up in the same households as some of the lesbians and gay men".[74]

Perhaps the researchers' intellectual orientation needed re-visiting. Along with obscuring our derivation from male and female, unravelling the sexual membership that has been central to the development of a person is another tremendous venture into the unknown. Obliterating a plethora of beliefs about sexual behaviour, relationships and marriage is perhaps the easiest part of the task. Even at the end of the road for conjugality, there is clearly still a long journey ahead. Conflict looms on so many fronts along with possibly multifarious and far reaching threats to well-being as the family unit with its important and coherent purpose descends into a vortex of smashing atoms. The failure to protect the married family as the foremost community for children, and to discriminate between this and other relationships, has been a great injustice. No one was compelled to cut the remaining threads.

Fig. 1 Number of civil partnerships in the UK by quarter of occurrence, 2005/2011

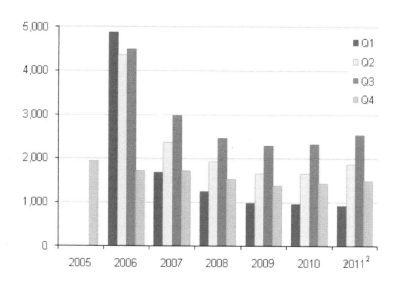

Fig. 2 Number of civil partnership dissolutions in the UK, by quarter, 2007/11
Source: Office for National Statistics

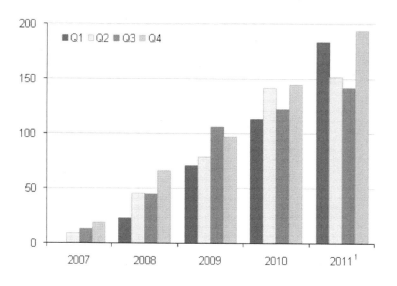

**Fig. 3 Marriage rates for first time married males in selected age groups.
Marriages between different sex 1961–2011**

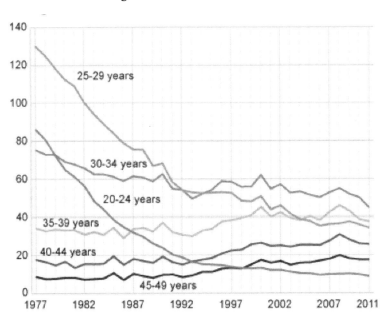

Fig. 4

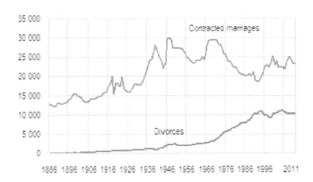

Fig. 5

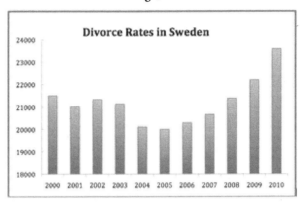

Fig. 6
Marriages Index: Netherlands and Euro area 1997–2009

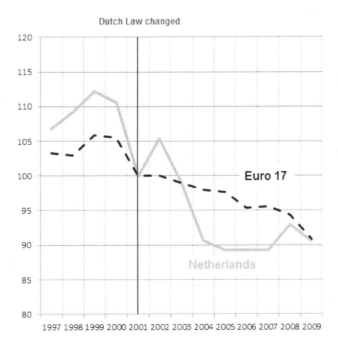

Fig. 7 Marriages and registered partnerships: Netherlands

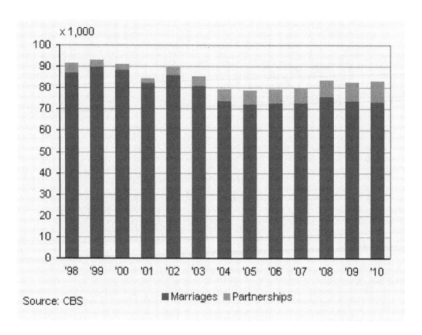

Fig. 8
Marriages Index: Spain and Euro area: 2000–2009

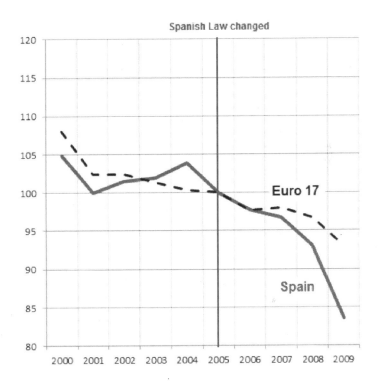

Chapter 1

1. Browning, D. 'What is Marriage? An Explanation', in Mack, D & Blankenhorn, D. eds. *The Book of Marriage: the Wisest Answers to the Toughest Questions,* 2001 Grand Rapids, MI: Eerdmans p.8

2. Gallagher, M. A Reality Waiting to Happen: A Response to Evan Wolfson. In eds. Wardle, L.D. et al *Marriage and Same Sex Unions: A Debate* 2003 Praeger p.11

3. Almond, B. Equal but Different – the Unanswered Questions ed. de Waal, A. 2013 *The Meaning of Matrimony 2013 CIVITAS*

4. Ferudi, F. in ed. de Waal, A. *The Meaning of Matrimony* op. cit.

5. Ivereigh, I. *The Destruction of Conjugality* in *The Meaning of Matrimony* op. cit.

6. West, E. *The Diversity Illusion* 2013 London, Gibson Square p.188

7. Wilson, R.F. The Calculus of Accommodation. The Religious Freedom Project. The Berkeley Center for Religion, Peace and World Affairs. Georgetown University. April 11-12, 2012

8. D'Ancona, M. Cracks in the Coalition marriage *Daily Telegraph* 29.09.2013

9. Ibid.

10. *London Evening Standard* 15.03.2012

11. Scruton, R. Postmodern Tories *Prospect* March 2013

12. Skelton, D. & Flint, R. ed. Gibbs, B. *What's In A Name?* 2012 Policy Exchange

13. O'Neill, B. A Liberal Critique of Gay Marriage in *The Meaning of Matrimony* op. cit. pp.48 & 53

14. Ivereigh, I. The Destruction of Conjugality in *The Meaning of Matrimony* op. cit.

15. D'Ancona, M. Cracks in the Coalition marriage op. cit.

16. O'Neill, B. A Liberal Critique of Gay Marriage in *The Meaning of Matrimony* op.cit. p.42

17. The collapse of the banks. The rise of al-Qaeda. The fall of communism. One man predicted them all. John Gray talks to John Preston *Seven* 24.02.2013

18. Civil Partnerships Survey ComRes, 27 April – 20th May 2012, Table 3, p.12 Equal civil marriage consultation impact Assessment, Government Equalities Office, January 2012 pp. 2 & 5

19. Ibid.

20. *Daily Mail* 14.04.2012

21. Phy-Olsen, A. *Same-Sex Marriage* 2006 Connecticut: Greenwood Press p. 80

22. This is discussed by Booker, C Same-sex marriage: the French connection *Sunday Telegraph* 10.02.2013

23. Government Equalities Office, Civil partnerships on religious premises: A consultation

24. Murray, D. Gay Rites *The Spectator* 01.10.2011

25. A positive step for lesbian, gay and bisexual rights. *HC Hansard* 10.03 2010 col.1062

26. Robbins, M. The irrational and sinister campaign against gay marriage. *Guardian* 20.02. 2012. http://www.pinknews.co.uk/2012/03/11uk-equality-minister-churches-opposition-to-same-sex-marriage-is-dar-age-homophobia/ 11.03.2012

27. Bingham, J. Police chaplain: 'I was dismissed after criticising gay marriage.' *Daily Telegraph* 01.03.13. *BBC News,* 28 October 2011. *The Huffington Post,* 11.09.2012

28. West, E. *The Diversity Illusion* op. cit. p.13

29. Scruton, R. Sacrilege and Sentiment in George, R.P. & Elshtain, J.B., eds. *The Meaning of Marriage* 2006 Dallas: Spence Publishing Company p. 27

30. Parris, M. 'Sweep out religious superstition that will not tolerate me.' *The Times* 23.10.2004

31. Scruton, R. *Sacrilege and Sentiment* op.cit.

32. *Hansard* 21 Jan 2008

33. Skelton, D. and Flint, R. ed. Gibbs, B. *What's In A Name?* op. cit.

34. Araujo, R.J. Marriage, Relationship, and International Law: The Incoherence of the Argument for Same-Sex Marriage. In eds. Wardle, L.D. et al *Marriage and Same-Sex Unions: A Debate* 2003, Praeger p.377

35. Dean, Craig R. executive director of the US Equal Marriage Rights Fund, New York Times, 28.09.1991

36. Skelton, D. & Flint, R. *What's in a Name?* op. cit. p.58

37. Gallagher, M. A Reality Waiting to Happen: A Response to Evan Wolfson. In eds., Wardle, L.D. et al *Marriage and Same Sex Unions: A Debate* op. cit. p.11

38. Phy-Olsen, A. *Same-Sex Marriage* 2006 Connecticut: Greenwood Press p.2

39. Wardle, L.W. Beyond Equality in *Marriage and Same Sex Unions: A Debate* op. cit.

40. Brake, E. Minimal Marriage: What Political Liberalism Implies for Marriage Law, *Ethics* 2010 supra note 36, at 336, 323

41. Browning, D. & Marquardt. What About the Children? in George, R.P. & Elshtain, J. B. eds. *The Meaning of Marriage* 2006 Dallas: Spence Publishing Company p.50

42. George, R. P. Neutrality, Equality, and "Same-Sex Marriage" in *Marriage and Same Sex Unions: A Debate* op. cit. pp.120–132

43. West, E. *The Diversity Illusion* op. cit. p.177

44. *Daily Telegraph* 22.01.2009

45. Gas and Dubois v. France March 2012 (no: 25951/07)

46. Jareborg, M. J. Religious Freedom and Equality: Emerging Conflicts in North America and Europe – a Scandinavian Perspective. The Religious Freedom Project. The Berkeley Center for Religion, Peace and World Affairs. Georgetown University. April 11–12, 2012

47. Murray, D. Gay Rites *The Spectator* 01.10.2011

48. Coren, M. Canadian Crackdown 05.06.2012 *National Review Online*

49. Hom Ombudsmannen mot Diskriminering Pa Grund av Sexuell Laggning Rapport 2004 Stockholm

50. Chester, R. 'The Myth of the Disappearing Nuclear Family' in Anderson, D. & Dawson, G. eds. Family Portraits 1986 London: Social Affairs Unit p.81

51. Girgis, S., George, R. P. & Anderson, R. T. *What is Marriage?* Encounter Books 2012 New York p.265

52. Gas and Dubois v. France March 2012 (no:25951/07)

53. Almond, B. *The Fragmenting Family* 2006 Oxford: OUP. Sugrue, S. Soft Despotism and Same-Sex Marriage in *The Meaning of Marriage* op. cit.

54. George, R.P. Neutrality, Equality, and 'Same-Sex Marriage" in *Marriage and Same Sex Unions: A Debate* op. cit. p.21

55. Scruton, R. Sacrilege and Sentiment in George, R. P. & Elshtain, J. B. eds. *The Meaning of Marriage* 2006 Dallas: Spence Publishing Company p.5

56. Wardle, L.W. Beyond Equality in *Marriage and Same Sex Unions: A Debate* op. cit. p.188

Chapter 2

1. McCarthy, A. Marriage and Meaning, in Watt, H. ed. *Fertility & Gender* 2011 Oxford: Anscombe Bioethics Centre

2. Scruton, R. Sacrilege and Sentiment in George, R. P. & Elshtain, J. B. eds. *The Meaning of Marriage* 2006 Dallas: Spence Publishing Company p. 6

3. Malinowski, B. *Sex and Repression in Savage Society* 1960 (first pub 1927) Routledge and Kegan Paul

4. DeKlyen, M. et al Fathers and preschool behaviour problems. *Developmental Psychology*, 1998 34, 264–275. DeKlyen, M., Speltz, L. & Greenberg, M. Fathering and early onset conduct problems: Positive and negative parenting, father-son attachment, and the marital context. Clinical Child and Family *Psychological Review*, 1998 1, 3–21. Amato, P. & Rivera, F. Paternal involvement and children's behaviour problems. *Journal of Marriage and Family,* 1991 61, 375–384. Flouri, E. & Buchanan, A. Early father's and mother's involvement and child's later educational outcomes. *British Journal of Educational Psychology,* 2004. 74, 141–153. Lewis, C. & Lamb, M. *Fatherhood: Connecting the strands of diversity across time and space 2006* York: Joseph Rowntree Foundation. Ramchandani, P., Stein, A., Evans, J., & O'Connor, T. Paternal depression in the postnatal period and child development: A prospective population study. *The Lancet,* 2005, 365, 2201–2205. A recent study of 192 infants assessed – including with film – father–infant interaction. Disengaged and remote interactions – which could be picked up in the early months of life had implications for later behaviour. Sethna, V. et al Do Early father–infant interactions predict the onset of externalising behaviours in young children? Findings from a longitudinal cohort study *Journal of Child Psychology and Psychiatry* 2012, 53(8)

5. Browning, D. & Marquardt. What About the Children? in *The Meaning of Marriage* op. cit.

6. For a discussion see: Waite, L. & Gallagner, M. *The Case for Marriage: Why Married People are Happier, Healthier and Better-Off Financially* 2000 New York, Doubleday

7. Barker, N. Two Myths about Same-Sex Marriage in *The Meaning of Matrimony* ed. de Waal, A. 2013 CIVITAS p.70

8. Engels, F. *The Origin of the Family, Private Property and the State* 1972 London: ed. Lawrence & Wishart p.141; see Sandall, R. *The Culture Cult: Designers Tribalism and Other Essays* 2001 Westview Press

9. Firestone, S. *The Dialectic of Sex: The Case for Feminist Revolution* 1979 The Women's Press p.222

10. Greer, G. *The Female Eunuch* 1971 Paladin p.235

11. Firestone, S. op. cit. p.197

12. Ibid. pp.193 & 222

13. Engels, F. *The Origin of the Family, Private Property and the State* op. cit. p.145

14. Midgley, M. & Hughes, J. *Women's Choices* 1982 Weidenfeld & Nicholson p.79

15. Midgley, M. & Hughes, J. Ibid. p.80

16. Fortes, M. *Rules and the Emergence of Human Society.* Royal Anthropological Institute of Gt Britain. Occasional Paper 1983, No.39

17. Fortes, M. Ibid.

18. Durkheim, E. *The Division of Labour in Society* (1893) *Rules of the Sociological Method* (1895)

19. Schema, S. *An Embarrassment of Riches* 1987 Collins p. 386 quoting Johan van Beverwijck *Van de Wtnementheyt des Vrouwelicken Geslachts* 2nd edn Dordrecht 1643

20. Daley, J. The Big Society starts with our wedding vows *Daily Telegraph* 13.02.2011

21. Scruton, op. cit. p.33

22. Daley, J. The Big Society starts with our wedding vows *Daily Telegraph* 13.02.2011

23. Fortes op. cit. p.28

24. Sacks, J. 'Social and Moral Concerns we Share: A Jewish Perspective' unpublished paper June 1987

25. The law and its role in marriage, Letters *The Times* 28.03.2013

26. Midgley, M. & Hughes, J. *Women's Choices* op. cit. p.77

27. Scruton, R. Sacrilege and Sentiment in George, R. P. & Elshtain, J. B. eds. *The Meaning of Marriage* op. cit. p.8

28. Scruton, R. *Sexual Desire* 1986 revised 1994 London: Phoenix pp.350 & 355

29. Skelton, D. & Flint, R. ed. Gibbs, B. *What's In A Name?* 2012 Policy Exchange

30. Skelton D. & Flint, R. op. cit. p.58

31. Sugrue, S. Soft Despotism and Same-Sex Marriage in George, R.P. & Elshtain, J.B. eds. *The Meaning of Marriage* 2006 op. cit. p.193

32. Featherstone, L. This is not gay rights versus religious beliefs *Daily Telegraph* 25.02.2012

33. Rauch, J. *Gay Marriage: Why It Is Good for Gays, Good for Straights, and Good for America* 2004 New York: Henry Holt & Co.

34. Skelton, D. and Flint, R. op. cit.

35. Gallagher, M. A Reality Waiting to Happen: A Response to Evan Wolfson. In eds., Wardle, L.D. et al *Marriage and Same Sex Unions: A Debate* 2003 Praeger p.11

36. Zimmerman, C.C. Family and Civilisation ed. Kurt, J. 2008 (original edn 1947) Wilmington, DE: ISI Books

37. Morgan, P. *Family Policies, Family Changes: Sweden, Italy and the UK* 2006 CIVITAS

38. Minutes of evidence, Royal Commission on Marriage and Divorce 16th–17th days. p.428

39. McGregor, O.R. *Divorce in England* 1957 Heineman p. x

40. Wallenstein, J., Lewis, J. M., Blakeslee, S. The Unexpected Legacy of Divorce:

A 25 Year Landmark Study *Hyperion* 2000 xxi-xxii See also: Gallagher, M. T*he Abolition of Marriage*, 1996, Regnery

41. Scruton, R. Sacrilege and Sentiment in George, R.P. & Elshtain, J. B. eds. *The Meaning of Marriage* op. cit. p.20

42. Draper, D., Beighton, L. & Pearson, A. *The taxation of families 2010-11.* 2012 CARE & *The taxation of families – international comparisons* 2012

43. *Supporting Families: A Consultation Document* of 1998 London Home Office

44. Haskins, R. & Dawhill, I. *Work and Marriage: The Way to End Poverty and Welfare.* September 2003 The Brookings Institution Policy Brief Washington, DC. Also Thomas, A. & Sawhill, I. For Richer or for Poorer: Marriage as an Antipoverty Strategy September 2002 *Journal of Policy Analysis and Management.* Similarly, Marsh, A. & Vegeris, S. *The British Lone Parent Cohort and their Children 1991–2001.* DWP 2002

45. Parcel, T. L., Campbell L. A., & Wenxuan, Z. Children's Behavior Problems in the United States and Great Britain *Journal of Health and Social Behavior 2012 53: 165–182*

46. Coote, A., Harman, H. & Hewitt, P. 1990 *The Family Way* Institute for Public Policy Research p.36

47. Tinsley, M. *Parenting Alone: Work and welfare in single parent households* 2014 Policy Exchange

48. Morgan, P. 2007 *The War Between the State and the Family* Institute of Economic Affairs

49. Garner, L. 'Happy Families: Just a game or an ideal way for us to live?' *Sunday Telegraph* 21.01.1990

50. Barker, P. For the children's sake *Guardian* 04.11.1996

51. *Supporting Families* A Consultation Document of 1998 London Home Office

52. Mallon, G.P. and Betts, B. *Recruiting, Assessing and Supporting Lesbian and Gay Carers and Adopters. A good practice guide for social workers.* London: British Association for Adoption and Fostering. 2005 p.22

53. Mallon, G. B. & Betts, B. op. cit. p.7

54. Interviews 2007 in van Acker, E. *Governments and Marriage Education Policy* 2008 Palgrave Macmillan pp. 72, 74, 75

55. Haskey, J. Living arrangements in contemporary Britain: having a partner who usually lives elsewhere and living apart together. Population Trends 2005 122 pp.35–45

56. Wertheimer, A. & McRae, S. Family and Household Change in Britain Research Results Oct 1999 Economic and Social Research Council

57. Popenoe, D. American Family Decline 1960–1990: A Review and Appraisal. *Journal of Marriage and the Family* 1993 55 pp.527–555

58. Wilson, J.Q. in Whelan, R. ed. *Just a Piece of Paper? Divorce Reform and the Undermining of Marriage* 1995, Institute of Economic Affairs p.78

59. Dawson, D.A. Family Structure and Children's Health and Well Being: Data from the 1988 National Health Interview Survey on Child Health Journal

of Marriage and the Family 1991, vol. 53 pp.572–584 Manning, W.D. & Lamb, K.A., Adolescent Well-Being in Cohabiting, Married, and Single-Parent Families, J. Marriage & Family 2003, 56 876–890. See also Pryor, J. & Rodgers, B. *Children in Changing Families: Life after Parental Separation* 2001 Oxford: Blackwell Publishers

60. Ringback Weitoft, G. et al Mortality, Severe Morbidity, and Injury in Children Living with Single Parents in Sweden: A Population Based Study *Lancet* vol 361, 9354 25.01.2003 Unicef, *A League Table of Child Maltreatment Deaths in Rich Nations* 2003 Innocenti Report Card, Issue no. 5. Timms, D.W.G. *Family Structure in Childhood and Mental Health in Adolescence* research report 32 of project Metropolitan, Stockholm, Sweden: University of Stockholm, department of Sociology 1991, 74, 78. Stattin, H. & Magnusson, D. Onset of Official Delinquency *Brit J of Criminology* 1995, 35 pp.417–49

61. Ringback Weitoft, G. et al Mortality, Severe Morbidity, and Injury in Children Living with Single Parents in Sweden: A Population Based Study. *Lancet* vol 361, 9354 25.01.2003 Unicef, *A League Table of Child Maltreatment Deaths in Rich Nations.* 2003 Innocenti Report Card, Issue no.5. Timms, D.W.G. *Family Structure in Childhood and Mental Health in Adolescence* research report 32 of project Metropolitan. Stockholm, Sweden: Univ of Stockholm, department of Sociology 1991, 74, 78. Stattin, H. & Magnusson, D. Onset of Official Delinquency *Brit J of Criminology* 1995, 35 pp.417–49. Tucker, J.S. et al., Parental Divorce: Effects on Individual Behaviour and Longevity *Journal of personality and Social Psychology* 1997 73 pp.381–9. Singh, G. K. & Yu, S. M, US Childhood Mortality, 1950 through 1993: Trends and Socioeconomic Differentials *American Journal of Public Health* 1995. Vol 85 (4) pp.505–12. Jonsson, J O & Gahler, M Fanukt Dissolution, Family Reconstitution and Children's Educational Careers: Recent Evidence from Sweden. *Demography* 1997 34 pp.277–93

62. Duncan, S. & Edwards, R. *Lone Mothers, Paid Work and Gendered Moral Rationalities* 1999 Basingstoke: Macmillan Press Ltd p.34

63. Daly, M. & Wilson, M. Discriminative Parental Solicitude: A Biological Perspective vol.46 May 1980 *Journal of Marriage and Family*

64. Putnam, F.W. Ten Year Research Update Review: Child Sexual Abuse *Journal of the American Academy of Child and Adolescent Abuse* 2003, Vo. 42 pp. 269–278

65. Collishaw, S. et al Time Trends in Adolescent Mental Health *J of Child Psychology and Psychiatry* 2004 45 (8) pp.1350–1362

66. Heard, H. E. The family structure trajectory and adolescent school performance. *J. Fam. Issues* 2007 28, 319–354

67. Cherlin, A.J. Parental Divorce in Childhood and Demographic Outcomes in Young Adulthood. *Demography* 1995 32 pp.299–318 Belsky, J. Steinberg, L. & Draper, P. Childhood experience, interpersonal development, and reproductive strategy: an evolutionary theory of socialization. *Child Dev. 1991 62,* 647–670. Belsky, J. et al & The NICHD Early Child Care Research Network (2007b) Family

rearing antecedents of pubertal timing. *Child Development* 78:1302–21. Draper, P. Harpending, H. Father absence and reproductive strategy: an evolutionary perspective. *J. Anthropol. Res.* 1982 38, 255–273. Bogaert A. F. 2005 Age at puberty and father absence in a national probability sample. *J. Adolesc.* 2005 28, 541–546. Moffitt, T. E. et al Childhood experience and the onset of menarche: a rest of a sociobiological model. *Child Dev.* 1992 63, 47–58. Mendle J et al Associations between father absence and age of first sexual intercourse. *Child Dev.* 2009 80, 1463–1480. Nettle, D., Coall D.A., Dickins T.E. Birthweight and paternal involvement predict early reproduction in British women: evidence from the National Child Development Study. *Am. J. Hum. Biol.* 2010 22, 172–179. Coall, D. A. & Chisholm, J. S. Evolutionary perspectives on pregnancy: maternal age at menarche and infant birth weight. *Soc. Sci. Med.* 2003 57, 1771–1781. Nettle, D., Coall, D. A., Dickins T.E. Early life conditions and age at first pregnancy in British women. *Proc. R. Soc. B* 2011 278, 1721–1727. Ellis, B.J. & Essex, M.J. (2007) Family environments, adrenarche, and sexual maturation: A longitudinal test of a life history model. *Child Development* 78:1799–817. Ellis, B.J. & Garber, J. Psychosocial antecedents of variation in girls' pubertal timing: Maternal depression, stepfather presence, and marital and family stress. *Child Development* 71, 2 2000 485–501. Del Giudice, M. Sex, attachment, and the development of reproductive strategies Behavioral and Brain science 2009 32, 1–67. Andersson-Ellström, A., Forssman, L. & Milsom, I. Age of sexual debut related to life-style and reproductive health factors in a group of Swedish teenage girls *Acta Obstetricia et Gynecologica Scandinavica* 1996, Vol. 75, No. 5 , pp. 484–489. Ellis, B.J. Timing of Pubertal Maturation in Girls: An Integrated Life History Approach. *Psychological Bulletin* 130, 6 2004 920–58

68. Sheppard, P. & Sear, R. Father absence predicts age at sexual maturity and reproductive timing in British men *Biol. Lett.* 2012 8 2 237–240

69. Sergeant, H. *Among the Hoods* 2012 Faber and Faber

70. *Leading Lads* 1999, Topman in association with Oxford University.

71. Laub J.H. & Sampson, R.J. *Shared Beginnings: Divergent Lives*, 2004 Harvard Univ Press & Horney, J., Roberts, J. & Hassell, K.D. The social control function of intimate partners: Attachment or monitoring? 2000, Paper for American Society of Criminology, San Francisco. Dench, G. *The Frog, the Prince and the Problem of Men* 1994 Neanderthal Books & *The Place of Men in Changing Family Cultures* 2011 Institute of Community Studies

72. US Department of Health and Social Services, The Effects of Marriage on Health, 2007. Waite, L. & Gallagher, M. *The Case for Marriage...*

73. Rendall, M.S. et al The Protective Effect of Marriage for Survival: A Review and Update 2011 (2) *Demography* pp.481–506

74. Strohschein L., McDonough P., Monette, G. et al. Marital transitions and mental health: are there gender differences in the short-term effects of marital status change? *Soc Sci Med* 2005 61:2293–303. Kim H.K., McKenry M. The

relationship between marriage and psychological well-being. *J Fam* Issues 2002 23 885–911. Sogaard A.J., Kritz-Silverstein D., Wingard D.L., Finnmark heart study: employment status and parenthood as predictors of psychological health in women, 20–49 years. *Int J Epidemiol* 1994 23 82–90. Johnson, N.J, Backlund, E., Sorlie, P.D., et al. Marital status and mortality: the national longitudinal mortality study. *Ann Epidemiol* 2000 10 224–38. Johnson. N.J., et al. Marital status and mortality: the national longitudinal mortality study. *Ann Epidemiol* 2000 10 224–38. Kiecolt-Glaser, J.K, Newton, T.L. Marriage and health: his and hers. *Psychol Bul* 2001 127 472–503. Johnson, D.R., Wu, J. An empirical test of crisis, social selection and role explanations of the relationship between marital disruption and psychological distress: a pooled time-series analysis of four-wave panel data. *J Marriage Fam* 2002 64 211–24. Rendall, M.S. The Protective Effect of Marriage for Survival: A Review and Update 2011 2. 481–506 See the overview of evidence in *Why Marriage Matters: Thirty conclusions from social sciences.* Institute for American Values and National Marriage Project 2011 University of Virginia

75. Roelfs, D. J. et al The Rising Relative Risk of Mortality for Singles: Meta-Analysis and Meta-Regression *Am. J. Epidemiol* (2011) 174 (4) 379–389

76. Robles, T.F., Kiecolt-Glaser, J.K. The physiology of marriage: pathways to health. *Physiol Behav* 2003 79:409–16. Vogel, J. Economic Problems. Living Conditions and Inequality, 1975–1995 *Levnadsfor hallanden*, 1997 rapport no.91, Statistics Sweden

77. Rsengren, A., Wedel, H. & Wilhemsen, L. Marital Status and Mortality in Middle-aged Swedish Men *American Journal of Epidemiology* 129 pp.54–64

78. Siegler, I.C. & Brummett, B. Consistency and Timing of Marital Transitions and Survival During Midlife: the Role of Personality and Health Risk Behaviors *Annals of Behavioral Medicine* 2013 45

79. Lammintausta, A. et al. Prognosis of acute coronary events is worse in patients living alone: the FINAMI myocardial infarction register. *European Journal of Preventive Cardiology,* Jan 30 2013

80. Sprehn, G.C. et al Decreased cancer survival in individuals separated at time of diagnosis. *Cancer* 2009 Vol 115 (21), pp.5108–5116

81. Hughes, M.E. & Waite, L. J. Marital Biography and Health at Mid-Life *Journal of Health and Social Behavior* 2009 50: 344–358

82. Gahler, M. 'Life After Divorce: Economical and Psychological Well-being among Swedish Adults and Children Following Family Dissolution. Dissertation series 32 (thesis), 1998, Stockholm: Swedish Institute for Social Research. Bjornberg, U Sweden: Supported Workers who Mother, in Duncan, S. and Edwards, R. *Single Mothers in an International Context: Mothers or Workers?* 1997 London: UCL press. Weitoft, G.R., Hagland, B. & Rosen, M. Mortality among Lone Mothers in Sweden: A Population Study, *Lancet* 2000 vol 355 8th April pp.1215–1219

83. Whitehead, M. et al Social Policies and the Pathways to Inequalities in Health:

A Comparative Analysis of Lone Mothers in Britain and Sweden *Social Science and Medicine* 2000, 50 pp.255–70. Burstrom, B. et al Lone Mothers in Sweden: Trends in Health and Socio-economic Circumstances. 1979–1995 *J Epidemiol Community Health* 1999, 53 pp.150–56

84. Meltzer, H., Lader, D., Corbin, T. et al Non-fatal suicide behaviour among adults aged 16–74 in Great Britain 2002 The Stationery Office: London

85. Gunnell, D. et al Why are suicide rates rising in young men but falling in the elderly?—a time-series analysis of trends in England and Wales 1950–1998 *Social Science & Medicine*, 2003 Vol 57(4) pp. 595–611 l

86. Agerbo, E., Stack, S. & Petersen, L.S. Social integration and suicide: Denmark, 1906–2006 *The Social Science Journal*, 2011 Vol 48 (4) pp.630–640

87. Qin, P., Agerbo, E. & Mortensen, P.B. Suicide risk in relation to socioeconomic, demographic, psychiatric, and familial factors: a national register-based study of all suicides in Denmark, 1981–1997 *American Journal of Psychiatry* 2003 160, 765–722

88. Lorant, V. et al, A European comparative study of marital status and socio-economic inequalities in suicide *Social Science & Medicine*, 2005 Vo 60 (11) pp.2431–2441 Agerbo, E., Qin, P., Mortensen, P.O. Psychiatric illness, socioeconomic status, and marital status in people committing suicide: a matched case-sibling-control study. *Epidemiol Community Health* 2006 60:776–781

89. Robins, A. & Fiske, A. Explaining the Relation between Religiousness and Reduced Suicidal Behavior: Social Support Rather Than Specific Beliefs *Suicide and Life-Threatening Behavior* 2009 Vol 39 (4), pp.386–395

90. Gunnell, D. et al Why are suicide rates rising in young men but falling in the elderly?—a time-series analysis of trends in England and Wales 1950–1998 *Social Science & Medicine*, 2003 Vol 57(4) pp.595–611

91. Qin P., Agerbo, E., Mortensen, P.B. Suicide risk in relation to socioeconomic, demographic, psychiatric, and familial factors: a national register-based study of all suicides in Denmark, 1981–1997. *Am J Psychiatry* 2003 160:765–772

92. Durkheim, E. *Suicide: A Study in Sociology* Reprint 1963 (first pub in English 1952) London: Routledge & Kegan Paul, and see Berkman, L.F., Glass, T., Brissette, I. et al. From social integration to health: Durkheim in the new millennium. *Soc Sci Med* 2000. 51, 843–57.

93. Rojas, Y., Stenberg, S. Early life circumstances and male suicide – A 30-year follow-up of a Stockholm cohort born in 1953 *Social Science & Medicine*, 2010 Vol 70 (3), pp.420–427. Hawton, K., Houston, K. & Shepperd, R. Suicide in young people. Study of 174 cases, aged under 25 years, based on coroners' and medical records. *British Journal of Psychiatry* 1999 175: 271–276

94. Eckersley, R. & Dear, K. Cultural correlates of youth suicide *Social Science & Medicine*, 2002 Vol 55 (11) pp.1891–1904

95. Beautrais, A.L. Child and Young Adolescent Suicide in New Zealand *Aust N Z J Psychiatry* 2001 35 pp.647–653 Joop Garssen, J. et al Familial Risk of Early Suicide:

Variations by Age and Sex of Children and Parents *Suicide and Life-Threatening Behavior* 2011 (4) 6. pp. 585–593 & Hawton, K. & van Heeringen, K *The Lancet*, 2009 Vol 373 (9672), pp. 1372–1381. Parker, H. A. &. McNally, R.J. Repressive Coping, Emotional Adjustment, and Cognition in People Who Have Lost Loved Ones to Suicide. *Suicide and Life-Behavior* 2008 Vol 38 (6)

96. Hawton, K. & van Heeringen, K. *The Lancet*, … Op. cit. Houston, K., Hawton, K. & Shepperd, R. Suicide in young people aged 15–24: a psychological autopsy *study Journal of Affective Disorders* 2001 Vol 63 (1), Seminog, O. & Goldace, M. PS56 Risk Of Intentional Self-Harm In Young People With Selected Mental And Chronic Physical Conditions In England pp.159–170. *J Epidemiol Community Health* 2012 66 A59–A60 pp.159–170

97. Qin, P., Agerbo, E., Mortensen, P.B. Suicide risk in relation to socioeconomic, demographic, psychiatric, and familial factors: a national register-based study of all suicides in Denmark, 1981–1997 *American Journal of Psychiatry* 2003 160, 765–722. Fortune, S. et al Suicide in adolescents: Using life charts to understand the suicidal process. *Journal of Affective Disorders* 2007, Vol 100 (1), pp. 199–210. Gunnell, A. et al Suicide and unemployment in young people. Analysis of trends in England and Wales, 1921–1995. *British Journal Psychiatry* 1999 175 263–70. Berkman, L.F., et al. From social integration to health: Durkheim in the new millennium. *Soc Sci Med* 2000 51 843–57

Chapter 3

1. For example: Poster, M. *Critical Theory of the Family* 1978 Seabury Press. Firestone, S. *The Dialectic of Sex* 1979 The Women's Press

2. Ti-Grace Atkinson, head of New York chapter of NOW, 1968. Quoted Kurlansky, M. *1968: The Year That Rocked the World.* 2005 Vintage, First pub: 2004 Jonathan Cape p.317

3. Minogue, K. *Alien Powers* 1985 Weidenfeld and Nicholson

4. Ollendorff, R. The rights of adolescents in Adams, P. *Children's Rights* 1972 Panther p.120

5. Jackson, M. 'Facts of Life' or the eroticization of women's oppression? Sexology and the social construction of heterosexuality, in ed. Caplan, P. *The Cultural Construction of Sexuality* 1989 Routledge pp.76–7

6. The Gay Liberation Manifesto, London 1971

7. Watney, S. *Gay Times* February 1988

8. Molyneux, J. *Socialist Worker* 16.01.1988

9. Tatchell, P. 'Thud', 29th January 1998, http://www.petertatchell.net/lgbt_rights/partnerships/unwedded_bliss.htm

10. Reviwed by Ide, W. Vision in Pink *The Times* 19.03.2004

11. Burke Leacock, E. ed. Intro to Engels, F *The Origins of the Family, Private Property, and the State* ed. Burke Leacock, E. 1972 New York: New World Paperbacks p.44

12. Engels, F. *The Origins of the Family, Private Property, and the State* op. cit. p.139

13. Engels, F. *The Origins of the Family, Private Property, and the State* op. cit. p.139

14. Deputy Prime Minister speech to the Open Society Foundation and the think-tank Demos, Dec 2011 http://demos.co.uk

15. Smart, C. *The Ties that Bind* 1984 Routledge and Kegan Paul p.225 Carol Smart was Professor of Sociology at the University of Leeds (from 1992 in family studies) and before that she was Lecturer and then Senior Lecturer in Sociology at the University of Warwick (1985-92). She is currently Co-Director of the Morgan Centre for the Study of Relationships and Personal Life at Manchester.

16. O'Neill, B. A Liberal Critique of Gay Marriage in ed. de Waal, A. *The Meaning of Matrimony* 2013 CIVITAS p.55

17. Jareborg, M. J., Religious Freedom and Equality: Emerging Conflicts in North America and Europe – a Scandinavian Perspective. The Religious Freedom Project. The Berkeley Center for Religion, Peace and World Affairs. Georgetown University, April 11–12 2012

18. Popenoe, D. Disturbing the Nest: Family Change and Decline in Modern Societies. 1988 New York: Aldine & Gruyter p.156

19. See Morgan, P. *Family Policy, Family Changes* 2006 CIVITAS

20. Lewis, H. *Sweden's Right to be Human,* 1982 Allison and Busby Ltd, p.3

21. Carlson, A. *The Swedish Experiment in Family Politics* 1990 New Brunswick, New Jersey: Transaction & Lewis, H. *Sweden's Right to be Human*

22. Johnson, D. The Real Marriage Problem *Standpoint* April 2012. 41 2012

23. Davies, C. *The Strange Death of Moral Britain* 2006 Transaction p.167

24. *Equality 2000*, the Stonewall Lobby Group Ltd, June 1997

25. The Commission for Human Rights accepted the claim of the BMA that young homosexuals "are less able to access sources of information and advice about safer sexual practice." Euan Sutherland v UK (Application 25186/94. Report of the Commission, 1 July 1997 para 64

26. *Civil Partnership: A framework for the legal recognition of same-sex couples*, DTI Women & Equality Unit, June 2003, p.13

27. *Hansard*, House of Lords debate, Gender Recognition, 11.02.2004, vol., 656 cc 1093–5

28. *Hansard*, House of Commons, 25th January 1999, col. 22 & *The Times*, 2.10.2000

29. *'Gay marriage' in all but name* The Christian Institute 2004 p.13

30. www.christian.org.uk/.../video-holland-discusses-group-marriage-as-next- step/

31. *The Pink Paper* Issue 831, 19.03.2004, pp.18–19

32. Mallon, G.P. and Betts, B. *Recruiting, Assessing and Supporting Lesbian and Gay Carers and Adopters. A good practice guide for social workers* 2005 London: British Association for Adoption and Fostering.

33. See Court of Appeal judgment in case of parent appealing against decision of Camden council to place her children with two men. 'Woman fails to halt adoption by gay couple' *Daily Telegraph* 17.10.2012

34. Key Stage Four PSHE, Coordination Group Publications Ltd 2001 The Study Guide

35. http://www.gmfa.org.uk/sex/how riskyis/fucking

36. Jennings, K. Winning the Culture War at the Human Rights Campaign Fund Leadership Conference 05.03.1995 Massachusetts See also: Brown, M.L. *A Queer Thing Happened to America: And what a long, strange trip it's been* 2011 Equal Time Books

37. Kirk, M. and Madsen, H. *After the Ball: How America Will Conquer Its Fear & Hatred of Gays in the 1990s* 1990 Doubleday: New York p.183

38. Ibid.

39. American Psychological Association (1986) United States Supreme Court Amicus Curiae brief for Bowers v. Hardwick; quote pp. 9-10; at http://www.apa.org/about/offices/ogc/amicus/bowers.pdf. quoted Stanton L. Jones, "Sexual orientation and reason: On the implications of false beliefs about homosexuality", Jan 2012 digitally published at www.christianethics.org

40. Hooker, E. The adjustment of the male overt homosexual *Journal of Projective Techniques,* 1957 21, 18-31 & Hooker, E. "Reflections of a 40-year exploration: A scientific view on homosexuality *American Psychologist* 1993 48 (4), 450-453

41. Stall, R. et al Association of Co-Occurring Psychosocial Health Problems and Increased Vulnerability to HIV/AIDS Among Urban Men Who Have Sex With

Men *American Journal of Public Health* 2003. 93 (6) pp.939–942

42. Dean, L et al., Lesbian, Gay, Bisexual, and Transgender Health: Findings & Concerns, *Journal of the Gay & Lesbian Medical Association*, 2000 4(3): 102–151, pp.102, 116. O'Hanlan, C.A et al., Homophobia As a Health Hazard. *Report of the Gay & Lesbian Medical Association* pp. 3, 5, www.ohanlan.com/phobiahzd.htm

43. Gilman, S.E. et al Risk of psychiatric disorders among individuals reporting same-sex sexual partners in national comorbidity survey *American Journal of Public Health* 2001 91 (6), 933–939 p.933

44. Warner, J., et al Rates and predictors of mental illness in gay men, lesbians, and bisexual men and women: Results from a survey based in England and Wales. British Journal of Psychiatry, 2004 185, 479–485. Chakraborty, A. et al Mental health of the non-heterosexual population of England 2011 *British Journal of Psychiatry* 198: 143–148

45. King, M., & McKeown, E. Mental health and social wellbeing of gay men, lesbians, and bisexuals in England and Wales 2003 London, Mind (National Association for Mental Health)

46. Fergusson, D.M. et al. Is sexual orientation related to mental health problems and suicidality in young people? *Arch Gen Psychiatry* 1999; 56: 876-80. Fergusson, D.M. et al Sexual orientation and mental health in a birth cohort of young adults. *Psychological Medicine* 2005;35(7): 971–981. See also Welch, S., Collings, S.C.D., Howden-Chapman, P. Lesbians in New Zealand: Their mental health and satisfaction with mental health services. *Aust. N.Z.J. Psychiatry* 2000 34, 256-263 and Saphira, M. & Glover, M. New Zealand lesbian health survey. 2000 J. *Gay Lesb. Med. Assn.* 4, 49–56

47. Cochran, S. et al. Prevalence of mental disorders, psychological distress, and mental health services use among lesbian, gay, and bisexual adults in the United States. *J Consult Clin Psychol.* 2003; 71 :53–61. Bailey, J.M. Homosexuality and Mental Illness *Archives of General Psychiatry*, 56, 1999, pp.883–884. King, M. and Nazareth, I. The health of people classified as lesbian, gay and bisexual attending family practitioners in London: a controlled study. *BMC Public Health*, Vol. 6, May 2006, 6:127. Remafeldi, G. et al. The relationships between suicide risk and sexual orientation: Results of a population based study. *American Journal of Public Health* 1998 88 57-60. Conron, K.J., Mimiaga, M.J., & Landers, S. J. A health profile of Massachusetts adults by sexual orientation identity: Results from the 2001–2006 Behavior Risk Factor Surveillance System surveys 2008 Commonwealth of Massachusetts, Department of Public Health. Gilman, S. E., et al. Risk of psychiatric disorders among individuals reporting same-sex sexual partners in the National Comorbidity Survey *American Journal of Public Health,*2002 91, 933–939. Jorm, A. F., et al. Sexual orientation and mental health: Results from a community survey of young and middle-aged adults. *British Journal of Psychiatry*, 2002 180, 423–427. Bostwick, W. B. et al Dimensions of Sexual Orientation and the Prevalence of Mood and Anxiety Disorders in the United

States *American Journal of Public Health* 2010, Vol. 100 (3) pp. 468–475

48. Meyer, I.H. Prejudice, Social Stress, and Mental Health in Lesbian, Gay, and Bisexual Populations: Conceptual Issues and Research Evidence *Psychol. Bull.* 2003 September; 129(5): 674–697

49. Meyer, I. H. Prejudice, Social Stress, and Mental Health in Lesbian, Gay, and Bisexual Populations op. cit.

50. Eskin, M., Kaynak-Demir, H. & Demir, S. Same-Sex Sexual Orientation, Childhood Sexual Abuse, and Suicidal Behavior in University Students in Turkey *Archives of Sexual Behavior*, 2005 34 (2), pp.185–195

51. Ibid.

52. For example: Sandfort, T.G.M., Graaf, R., Bijl, R.V. & Schnabel, P. Same-sex sexual behavior and psychiatric disorders: Findings from the Netherlands mental health survey and incidence study (NEMESIS). Archives of General Psychiatry, 2001 58, 85–91

53. O'Neill, B. A Liberal Critique of Gay Marriage in ed. de Waal, A. 2013 *The Meaning of Matrimony* CIVITAS op. cit. p.42

54. Meyer, I. H. Prejudice, Social Stress, and Mental Health in Lesbian, Gay, and Bisexual Populations...

55. Greenwood, G.L. et al Battering Victimization among a Probability Sample of Men who have Sex with Men. *Amer J of Public Health* 2002, 92(12) 1964–1969.

56. Department of Health National Suicide Prevention Strategy for England 2002 London

57. Mustanski, B. The Sexual Continuum *Psychology Today* April 26, 2012 Referring to: Weinstein, N. et al Parental autonomy support and discrepancies between implicit and explicit sexual identities: Dynamics of self-acceptance and defense *Journal of Personality and Social Psychology* 2012 Vol 102(4), 815–832

58. Don't stick it. STOP IT! Bullying wrecks lives, Mencap, 2007

59. Ferudi, F. *Wasted: Why Education isn't Educating* 2009 Continuum pp.122

60. Johnston, P. *Feel Free to Say it: Threats to Freedom of Speech* 2013 London: CIVITAS

61. Jones, Stanton L. Sexual orientation and reason: On the implications of false beliefs about homosexuality January 2012 digitally published at www.christianethics.org

62. Kantor, M. *Homophobia: the State of Bigotry Today* 2nd edn 2009 Westport, Connecticut & London p.xiii

63. Kantor, M. ibid p.xiv

64. Gower Davies, J. *Mind-Forg'd Manacles* 2012 CIVITAS

65. Scruton, R. Sacrilege and Sentiment in George, R. P. & Elshtain, J. B. eds. *The Meaning of Marriage* 2006 Dallas: Spence Publishing Company op. cit. p.28

66. Almond, B. *The Fragmenting Family* 2006 Oxford: Clarendon

67. Her principal books are *The Autonomy Myth: A Theory of Dependency* (The New Press 2003); *The Neutered Mother, the Sexual Family, and Other Twentieth Century*

Tragedies (Routledge 1995); and *The Illusion of Equality: The Rhetoric and Reality of Divorce Reform* (University of Chicago Press 1991)

68. Katz, J.N. *The Invention of Heterosexuality* 1993 New York: Penguin, pp.186–7 Bronski, M. *A Queer History of the United States* 2011 Beacon Press

69. Almond, B. *The Fragmenting Family* 2006 Oxford: Clarendon p.201 quoting Eskridge, W.N. *Gaylaw: Challenging Apartheid in the Closet* 1999 Cambridge, Mass: Harvard University Press p.11

70. Mason, A. "The scientific baby and the social family: the possibilities of lesbian and gay parenting", in Healey, E., Mason, A. eds. 1994 *Stonewall 25 The Making of the Lesbian and Gay Community in Britain*, Virago Press, London

71. Patten, J. Not even science fiction foresaw the end of fathers *The Spectator* 03.05.2008

72. Alan Doran, Interim Chief Executive, HFEA quoted in Smith, R. The modern family is now so complicated it has taken the fertility regulator 10 pages of legal jargon to define 'mother', 'father' and 'parent' *Daily Telegraph* 28.11.2008

73. *Hansard* 21st January 2008

74. Almond, B. *The Fragmenting Family* op. cit. p. 202

75. Browning, D. & Marquardt. What About the Children? in George, R.P. & Elshtain, J.B. eds. *The Meaning of Marriage* op. cit. p.46

76. Cleland, G. Human-animal embryo split the public *Daily Telegraph* 10.04.2008

77. Cleland, G. Human-animal embryo split the public Ibid.

78. Chapman, J. Minister will rail against tax breaks for marriage. *Daily Mail* 27.02.2007

79. *Guardian* 14.12.2006 & Palmer, A. Bill is not in children's best interests *Daily Telegraph* 10.05.2008

80. Murray, C & Golombok, S Solo mothers and their donor insemination infants: follow-up at age 2 years *Human Reproduction* 2005 vol.20 (6) pp.1655–1660

81. Ibid.

82. Ferri, 1976; Crocket et al., 1993; Dunn et al., 1998; O'Connor et al., 1999; Weinraub et al., 2002

83. Browning, D. & Marquardt. What About the Children? George, R.P. & Elshtain, J.B. eds. *The Meaning of Marriage* op. cit. p.46

Chapter 4

1. Lewis, J. If motherhood is a job, where on earth is my payslip? and Bayley, S. Lust at first sight is likely to lure the unwary into stormy waters *Daily Telegraph* 23.11.2012

2. Gallagher, M. Normal Marriage: Two Views in eds., Wardle, L.D. et al *Marriage and Same Sex Unions: A Debate* 2003 Praeger p.15

3. Browning, D. & Marquardt. What About the Children? George, R.P. & Elshtain, J.B. eds. *The Meaning of Marriage* 2006 Dallas: Spence Publishing Company p.31

4. Skelton, D. and Flint, R. ed. Gibbs, B *What's In A Name?* 2012 Policy Exchange

5. Rauch, J. Gay Marriage: *Why It Is Good for Gays, Good for Straights, and Good for America* 2004 New York: Henry Holt & Co.

6. Equal marriage: The Government's Response 2012 HMSO

7. Harris, C.C. *The Family and Industrial Society* 1982 George Allen and Unwin p.216

8. O'Neill, B. The 'me', 'me', 'me' marriage. Blogs *Daily Telegraph* 12.12.2012

9. Leonard, A.S. On Legal Recognition for Same-Sex Partners in Wardle et al op. cit. p.68

10. Scruton, R. Sacrilege and Sentiment in George, R. P. & Elshtain, J. B. eds. *The Meaning of Marriage* op. cit. p.26

11. http://beyondmarriage.org/full_statement.html

12. Goldberg-Hiller, J. *The Limits to Union: Same-sex marriage and the politics of civil rights.* 2002 The University of Michigan Press p.7

13. Browning, D. & Marquardt. What About he Children? George, R.P. & Elshtain, J.B. eds. *The Meaning of Marriage* op. cit. p.44

14. Coontz, S. "The Heterosexual Revolution," New York Times, 5.07.2005 quoted in Baskerville, S. The Real Danger of Same-Sex Marriage. *The Family in America* (online edn) 2006 Vol 20 (5/6)

15. Gairdner, W.D. *The War against the Family* 1992 Toronto: Stoddart Publishing Company Limited

16. Phy-Olsen, A. *Same-Sex Marriage* 2006 Connecticut: Greenwood Press p.115

17. Moore, C Life, the gift we treasure most, yet refuse to bestow on others *Daily Telegraph* 04.07.2009

18. Stanton Collett, T. in Wardle, L.D. et al *Marriage and Same-Sex Unions: A Debate* 2003 Praeger

19. Tatchell, P. Beyond Equality *New Humanist* 2001 116, 1

20. Polikoff, N. Ending marriage as we know it. 32 *Hofstra Law Review* 201–232

21. Bindel, J. Stop the whingeing about gay people demanding rights *Guardian.* 27.02.2012

22. Tatchell, P. Beyond Equality *New Humanist* 2001 116, 1

23. Sullivan, A. *Virtually Normal* 1995 Picador pp. 202–03, see also Bronski, M. *A Queer History of the United States* 2011 Beacon Press

24. Phy-Olsen, A. *Same-Sex Marriage* 2006 Connecticut Greenwood Press p.3

25. Tatchell, P. Beyond Equality *New Humanist* 2001 116, 1

26. Tatchell, P. Beyond Equality Ibid.

27. Tatchell, P. Beyond Equality Ibid.

28. Bronski, M. *A Queer History of the United States* Beacon 2011

29. Cover, R. *Politicising Queer Issues and Activism: Disciplinarity, Biopolitics and the Means by which Activist Issues Enter the Public Sphere Reconstruction* 10.03.2010)

30. Hari, J. How Gays Helped Make and Remake America: A new history gives them a mission, and it isn't to embrace marriage *Slate* May 23rd, 2011

31. *http://www.sterneck.net/gender/tatchell-beyond/index.php*

32. Brake, E. Minimal Marriage: What Political Liberalism Implies for Marriage Law, *Ethics* 2010 at 336, 323

33. Signorile, M. *Queer in America: Sex, the Media and the Closets of Power*, 1993 Random House

34. Sullivan, A. *Virtually Normal*, Picador, 1996, p.202

35. Sullivan, A. *Virtually Normal* op.cit. pp.202–03

36. Katz, J. Quoted by Blankenhorn, D. *The Future of Marriage* Encounter Books, New York p.149

37. *http://www.sterneck.net/gender/tatchell-beyond/index.php*

38. Ibid.

39. Ibid.

40. Lancaster, R.N. Marriage is not a Timeless, Unchanging Institution in ed. de Waal, A. 2013 *The Meaning of Matrimony* CIVITAS pp.38–39

41. Giddens, A. *Sociology: A Brief but Critical Introduction* 1998 Macmillan London

42. Giddens, A. *The Transformation of Intimacy: Sexuality, Love and Eroticism in Modern Societies.* 1992 Cambridge: Polity p.135 also see: Giddens, A. *The Consequences of Modernity.* 1990 Cambridge: Polity. Giddens, A. *Modernity and Self-Identity. Self and Society in the Late Modern Age.* 1991 Cambridge: Polity

43. Weeks, J., Heaphy, B. & Donovan, C. *Same Sex Intimacies: Families of Choice and other Life Experiments* 2002 Routledge

44. Roseneil, S. Living and Loving beyond the Boundaries of the Heteronorm: Personal Relationships in the 21st Century in McKie, L. and Cunningham in Burley, S. eds. *Families in Society: Boundaries and Relationships* 2005 Bristol Policy Press 241–58 p.247

45. Giddens, A. *Beyond Left and Right: the Future of Radical Politics* 1994 Polity Press: Cambridge p.43

46. Sweden's Action Plan against Poverty and Social Exclusion, 2003 Stockholm: Government Offices of Sweden & Weitoft, G.R, Hagland, B & Rosen, M Mortality among Lone Mothers in Sweden: A Population Study, *Lancet* 2000 vol 355 8th April pp.1215–219

47. Wilson, J.Q. in Whelan, R. ed. *Just a Piece of Paper? Divorce Reform and the Undermining of Marriage.* 1995, Institute of Economic Affairs, p.78

48. Wilkins, R.G. The Constitutionality of Legal Preferences for Heterosexual Marriage. In Wardle, L. et al eds. *Marriage and Same-Sex Unions: A Debate* op. cit. p.234

49. Wilkins, R.G. Ibid.

50. Giddens, A. *The Transformation of Intimacy, Sexuality, Love and Eroticism in Modern Societies* op. cit. pp.14–15, 140. 147–8

51. Leonard, A.S. On Legal Recognition for Same-Sex Partners in Wardle et al eds. *Marriage and Same-Sex Unions: A Debate* op. cit. p.68

52. Sugrue, S. Soft Despotism and Same-Sex Marriage in George, R.P. & Elshtain, J.B. eds. *The Meaning of Marriage* op. cit. p.175

53. Parris, M. It should not be for the state to determine what modern marriage may mean *The Times* 30.10.1995

54. Gallagher, M. Normal Marriage: Two Views. In eds., Wardle, L.D. et al *Marriage and Same Sex Unions: A Debate* op. cit. p.16

55. Parris, M. It should not be for the state... op. cit.

56. Judith Levine, "Stop The Wedding!" Village Voice, 29th July 2003, p.40 cited by Dobson, J.C. Newsletter, September 2003

see www.family.org/docstudy/newsletters/a0027590.html as at 31st March 2004

57. Brake, E. *Minimizing Marriage: Marriage, Morality, and the Law* 2012 Oxford University Press. BEYONDMARRIAGE.ORG (July 26, 2006), http:// beyondmarriage.org/full_statement.html.

58. Bello, M. 'Love is love, whatever you are' *Stella* 22.12.2013

59. Quoted Girgis, S., George, R.P. & Anderson, R.T. *What is Marriage?* p.276, cited in Harvard Journal of Law & Public Policy 2010 Vol. 34

60. Stacey, J. Gay and Lesbian Families: Queer Like Us quoted in *Marriage and the Public Good* 1998 Witherspoon Institute, p.19

61. Robbins, M. *What's wrong with polygamy?* Guardian 20.02.2012

62. Brake, E. Minimal Marriage: What Political Liberalism Implies for Marriage Law *Ethics* 2010 302, 332

63. Blacker, T. Marriage rarely lasts for life – so how about vows fixed to 10 years? *Independent* 21.02.2012

64. Scruton, R *The Meaning of Conservatism* 1981 Pelican

65. Norman, B *A Contractual Basis for Marriage* Unpub manuscript 1996

66. http://beyondmarriage.org/full_statement.html

67. Scruton, R. *Sexual Desire* 1986 rev 1994 London Phoenix: Orion Books p.358

68. Girgis, S., George, R.P. & Anderson, R.T. *What is marriage?* op. cit. p.260

69. Don't judge other families, says Miliband *Daily Telegraph* 01.05.2012

70. Quoted by Piers Paul Read, in response to an imagined objection to his own pro-marriage position: "You may think that the link between people's sex lives and the suffering of children is tenuous". Can Catholicism save Christian England? *The Spectator* 31.03.2010

71. Sullivan, A. Introduction, in Same Sex Marriage: Pro and Con: A Reader, 1st

edn 1997 at xvii, xix

72. Almond, B. *The Fragmenting Family* 2006 op. cit. p.203

73. Cooper, D. *The Death of the Family* London: Penguin 1971 p.151

74. Browning, D. & Marquardt. What About the Children? in George, R.P. & Elshtain, J.B. eds. *The Meaning of Marriage* op. cit.

75. Sugrue, S. Soft Despotism and Same-Sex Marriage in George, R.P. & Elshtain, J.B. eds. *The Meaning of Marriage* op. cit.

76. John Locke Second Treatise of Government (Hackett Pub Co 1980. p.43 quoted Sugrue, S. Soft Despotism and Same-Sex Marriage in George, R.P. & Elshtain, J.B. eds. op. cit. p.178

77. Mill, J.S. *Essay on Liberty* 1992, Everyman edn pp.159–60

78. Wallerstein, J.S. & Kelly, J.B. *Surviving the Breakup: How Parents and Children Cope with Divorce* 1980 Basic Books p.33

79. Scruton, R. *The Uses of Pessimism.* 2010 London: Atlantic Books

80. Gallagher, M. Normal Marriage: Two Views in eds., Wardle, L.D. et al *Marriage and Same Sex Unions: A Debate* op. cit. p.16

81. Giddens, A. *The Transformation of Intimacy* 1992 Polity Press p.63

82. Henricson, C. *A Revolution in Family Policy: Where we should go from here.* 2012 Policy Press

83. West, E. *The Diversity Illusion* 2013 Gibson Sq p.95

84. Almond, B. *The Fragmenting Family* 2006 Oxford Clarendon

85. Scruton, R. Postmodern Tories *Prospect* March 2013

86. Gessen, M. Sydney Writer's Festival 19.05. 2012

87. Mallon, G.P. and Betts, B. *Recruiting, Assessing and Supporting Lesbian and Gay Carers and Adopters. A good practice guide for social workers.* London: British Association for Adoption and Fostering. 2005 p.22

88. Mallon, G.P. and Betts, p.22

89. Stacey, J. 'What is Needed to Defend the Bipartisan Defense of Marriage Act of 1996? : Hearing Before the Subcommittee on the Constitution, Civil Rights and Property Rights of the Senate Comm, on the Judiciary, 108th Cong., Sept. 4th 2003

90. Regnerus, M. How different are the adult children of parents who have same-sex relationships? Findings from the New Family Structures Study, Social Science Research 2012 41: 752-770. See also Moore, Kristin Anderson, Jekielek, Susan M., Emig, Carol, 2002. Marriage from a Child's Perspective: How Does Family Structure Affect Children, and What Can We Do About It? Child Trends Research Brief, Child Trends, Washington, DC.

91. Lerner, R. & Nagai, A.K. No Basis… What the Studies Don't Show Us About Same-Sex Parenting 2001 Marriage Law Project; Washington, D.C see also: Morgan, P. *Children as Trophies? Examining the evidence on same-sex parenting* 2002 The Christian Institute. Schumm, W.R. Re-evaluation of the 'no differences' hypothesis concerning gay and lesbian parenting as assessed in eight early (1979–1986) and four later (1997–1998) dissertations. *Psychological Reports*

2008, 103, pp.275–304

92. Nock, S. cited in *Halpern v. Attorney General of Canada,* No. 684/00 (Ontario Supreme Court of Justice)

93. Belcastro, P.A. et al A Review of Data Based Studies Addressing the Effects of Homosexual Parenting on Children's Sexual and Social Functioning J of Divorce and Remarriage 1993 20(1/2) p.117

94. Marks, L. Same-sex parenting and children's outcomes: A closer examination of the American psychological association's brief on lesbian and gay parenting *Social Science Research* 2012 41, 735–751

95. Jones S.L. *Sexual Orientation and Reason: On the Implications of False Beliefs about Homosexuality* digitally published at www.christianethics.org; an abbreviated version of this essay was published as "Same-sex science" *First Things* February 2012, pp.27–33

96. Stacy, J. & Biblarz, T. How Does the Sexual Orientation of Parents Matter? American Sociological Review 2001, 66 159, p.166. See, for example: Patterson, C.J., 1995. Families of the lesbian baby boom: parents' division of labor and children's adjustment. *Developmental Psychology* 31, 115–123. See also Patterson, C.J., Hurst, S., Mason, C., 1998. Families of the lesbian baby boom: children's contacts with grandparents and other adults. *American Journal of Orthopsychiatry* 68, 390–399. See also Patterson, C.J., 2001. Families of the lesbian baby boom: maternal mental health and child adjustment *Journal of Gay and Lesbian Psychotherapy* 4 (3/4), 91–107

97. Dunne, G. The Different Dimensions of Gay Fatherhood: Exploding the Myths London School of Economics Discussion Paper Series January 2000 p.4 and *Scotland on Sunday* 09.01.2000

98. This is taken up elsewhere: Anderssen, N., Amlie, C., Ytteroy, E.A., Outcomes for children with lesbian or gay parents: a review of studies from 1978 to 2000 *Scandinavian Journal of Psychology* 2002 43, 335–351

99. Patterson, C. in Wardle, L.D. The Potential Impact of Homosexual Parenting on Children 1997 *U.Ill. Law Rev.* 833 1997 quoted in Lerner, R. & Nagai, A.K. No Basis: What the Studies Don't Tell Us About Same-Sex Parenting 2001 Marriage Law Project Washington, D.C

100. Marks, L. op. cit. (note 94) p.744

101. Sarantakos, S., Children in three contexts: family, education, and social development. *Children Australia* 1996 21, 23–31. Sarantakos, S. 2000 Same-Sex Couples Harvard Press, Sydney

101a Hansen, T. A. Review and Analysis of Research Studies Which Assessed Sexual Preference of Children Raised by Homosexuals 2008 www.drtraycehansen.com/Pages/writings-sexpref.html See also Gartrell, N.K., Bos, H.M.W. & Goldberg N.G. Sexual Orientation, Sexual Behavior, and Sexual Risk Exposure *Archives of Sexual Behaviour*, 2011.40 pp.1199–1209

102. Regnerus, M. How different are the adult children of parents who have same-sex relationships? Findings from the New Family Structures Study, Social Science Research 2012 41: 752-770

103. Eggebeen, D.J. What can we learn from studies of children raised by gay or lesbian parents? *Social Science Research* 2012 vol 41 (4) pp. 775–778

104. Mellish, L. et al *Gay, Lesbian and Heterosexual Adoptive Families* 2013 British Association for Adoption and Fostering

105. Mallon, G.P. and Betts, B. *Recruiting, Assessing and Supporting Lesbian and Gay Carers and Adopters* Op. cit.

106. Summarised in Anderson Moore, K. *Marriage from a Child's Perspective: How Does Family Struture Affect Children and What Can We Do About it?* Child Trends Research Brief. Washington, D.C.: Child Trends 2002

107. DiPerna, J.C. Lei, P. Reid, E.E. Kindergarten predictors of mathematical growth in the primary grades: An investigation using the Early Childhood Longitudinal Study–Kindergarten cohort *Journal of Educational Psychology* 2007 Vol 99(2), pp.369–379

108. Potter. D. Same-Sex Parent Families and Children's Academic Achievement *Journal of Marriage and Family* 2012 74: 556–571

109. Gallagher, M.A. Reality Waiting to Happen: A Response to Evan Wolfson in eds., Wardle, L.D. et al *Marriage and Same Sex Unions: A Debate* op. cit. p.11

110. Saletan, W. Does a new study indict gay parenthood or make a case for gay marriage? *Slate* 11.06.2012

111. Osborne, C. Further comments on the papers by Marks and Regnerus *Social Science Research* 2012 4. pp.779–783

112. Sugrue, S. Soft Despotism and Same-Sex Marriage in George, R.P. & Elshtain, J.B. eds. *The Meaning of Marriage* op. cit. p.183

Chapter 5

1. Skelton, D. & Flint, R. ed. Gibbs, B. *What's In A Name?* 2012 Policy Exchange p.34

2. Ibid.

3. David Crawford, Liberal Androgyny and the Meaning of Sexuality in Our Time http://www.communio-icr.com/articles/PDF/crawford33-2.pdf

4. Bennett, W.J. *The Broken Hearth* 2001 Random House with Doubleday p.112

5. Skelton, D. and Flint, R. *What's In A Name?* op. cit.

6. Skelton, D. and Flint, R. Ibid.

7. Skelton, D. and Flint, R. Ibid. p.35

8. Macedo, S. Homosexuality and the Conservative Mind in *Marriage and Same-Sex Unions* Wardle, L.D. et al eds. 2003 Praegar p.103

9. Macedo, S. Homosexuality and the Conservative Mind in *Marriage and Same-Sex Unions* Wardle, L.D. et al eds. op. cit. p.105

10. http://www.lifesitenews.com/news/attorney-for-man-acused-of-incest-asks-if-homosexual-sex-is-legal-why-not;cp http://marriage-equality.blogspot.co.uk

11. Ibid.

12. Behren, P. Do we need a law against incest? *The Guardian* 15.04.2012

13. Hari, J. Forbidden Love *The Guardian* 09.01.2002 and Behren, P. Do we need a law against incest? Ibid.

14. Ibid.

15. Ward, V. Gay marriage law could let fathers marry sons, says Irons. *Daily Telegraph* 05.04.2013

16. Humphreys, J. The Civil Partnership Act 2004: Same-Sex Marriage and the Church of England *Ecclesiastical Law Journal* January 2006 p.289

17. Murray, D. Gay Rites *The Spectator* 01.10.2011

18. Girgis, S., George, R.P. & Anderson, R.T. *Ibid.* pp.254-5

18. Girgis, S., George, R.P. & Anderson, R.T. *What is Marriage?* 2012 Encounter Books pp.254-5, cited in Harvard Journal of Law & Public Policy 2010 Vol. 34

19. DTI Women and Equality Unit, Responses to Civil Partnership: A framework for the legal recognition of same-sex couples, November 2003, p.35

20. Ayesha Yardag, divorce lawyer. Gay marriage bill may mean the death of adultery *Daily Telegraph* 26.01.2013

21. Scruton, R. Don't sacrifice marriage on equality's altar *The Times* 15.12.2012

22. Henderson, A. ed. Sexual Ethics: A Report of the Lesbian and Gay Clergy Consultation Working Group 2004 p.9

23. Pemberton, M. Why Marriage Matters *Daily Telegraph* 22.09.2013

24. Homosexuality Editorial Puts 1st Amendment on Trial *WorldNetDaily* 02.12.2008

25. Pemberton, M. There's no such thing as a 'gay cure'. *Daily Telegraph* 30.04.2012

26. *The Observer* 25.04.1999

27. Bello, M. 'Love is love, whatever you are' *Stella* 22.12.13

28. Holman, R. Lesbian love story that's got me thinking... *Daily Telegraph* 20.12.2013

29. Rosario, M. et al Sexual identity development among gay, lesbian, and bisexual youths: consistency and change over time. *J Sex Res.* 2006;43(1) pp.46–58

30. Quoted in Girgis, S., George, R.P. & Anderson, R.T. *What is Marriage?* op. cit. p.276

31. Anderson, E. *The Monogamy Gap: Men, Love and the Reality of Cheating* 2012 New York: Oxford University Press

32. Eskin, M., Kaynak-Demir, H. & Demir, S. Same-Sex Sexual Orientation, Childhood Sexual Abuse, and Suicidal Behavior in University Students in Turkey *Archives of Sexual Behavior*, 2005 34 (2), pp.185–195

33. Borris, K. & Rousseau, G. *The Sciences of Homosexuality in Early Modern Europe* 2008 London: Routledge

34. Rotello, G. *Sexual Ecology. AIDS and the Destiny of Gay Men.* 1997 Harmondsworth, Middlesex, UK: Dutton

35. Laumann, E.O. et al *The Social Organisation of Sexuality* 1994 paper edn 2000 University of Chicago Press p.283 also Greenberg, D.F. *The Construction of Homosexuality* 1988 University of Chicago Press

36. Rueda and Schwartz, Gays, AIDs and You pp. 60-61 quoted in Gairdner, W.D. *The War against the Family* 1992 Toronto: Stoddart Publishing Company Limited p.377

[Note: Many bystanders regard 'gay' as the expropriation of a word that has no satisfactory substitute or replacement in the English language. (William Blake's 'Gay day' expresses shining happiness, not same sex relations.) Reportedly it means Good As You. Otherwise, 'gay' is derived from the Greek figure Ganymede. Captured to become cup-bearer to the gods, his myth exemplifies man/boy sex. (Thus 'catamite' for the receptive or submissive partner – derived from the Latin version of Catamitus.)

37. Laumann, E.O. et al *The Social Organisation of Sexuality* 1994 paper edn 2000 University of Chicago Press

38. Laumann, E.O. et al Ibid.

39. Reisman, J.A. et al *Kinsey, Sex and Fraud* 1990

40. Laumann, E.O. et al *The Social Organisation of Sexuality* op. cit. p.286

41. Kinsey, A. *Sexual Behavior in the Human Male* 1948. (A 'Lesbian and Gay Veterans Memorial March' put pink triangles on 10% of the graves in Arlington cemetery.)

42. Taylor, T. Review of international organisations' experiences of administering questions on sexual identity/orientation. Data Collection Methodology – Social Surveys Census and Social Methodology. 2008 Division Office for National Statistics

43. Smith, T. Adult Sexual Partners in 1989: Number of Partners, Frequency and Risk. *GSS Topical Report* No 18, 1990 NORC, Univ of Chicago

44. Remafedi, G. et al *Pediatrics* 1992 pp.714–721

45. Integrated Household Survey April 2010 to March 2011 Office of National statistics

46. King, M. et al. A systematic review of mental disorder, suicide, and deliberate self harm in lesbian, gay and bisexual people. *BMC Psychiatry* 2008; 8: 70.

47. Hayes, J. et al., Prevalence of Same-Sex Behavior and Orientation in England: Results from a National Survey *Archives of Sexual Behaviour* published online 06.10.2011

48. Mock, S.E., Eibach, R.P. 2011. Stability and Change in Sexual Orientation Identity Over a 10-Year Period in Adulthood. *Archives of Sexual Behavior* 2011. 40(1)

49. Diamond, L.M. Female bisexuality from adolescence to adulthood: Results from a 10-year longitudinal study. *Developmental Psychology* 2008. 44(1) 5–14. See also: Kinnish, K.K., Strassberg, D.S. and Turner, C.W. Sex differences in the flexibility of sexual orientation: a multidimensional retrospective assessment. *Archives of Sexual Behavior* 2005 34 175–183

50. *The Advocate* 15.08.2006. Whitehead, N. E., & Whitehead, B. K. My genes made me do it! A scientific look at sexual orientation 2007(2nd edn) [Web book] from www.mygenes.co.nz. See also Bell, A.P., Weinberg, M.S. & Hammersmith, S.A. *Sexual preference* 1981 Bloomington, IN: Indiana University Press

51. Stein, T.S. Overview of new developments in understanding homosexuality in: Oldham J.M., Riba, M.B., Tasman, A, eds. *Review of Psychiatry*. Vol. 12. Washington, DC: American Psychiatric Press 1993:9–40

52. *The Advocate* 15.08.2006

53. Mercer, C.H. et al Women Who Report Having Sex With Women: British National Probability Data on Prevalence, Sexual Behaviors, and Health Outcomes. *American Journal of Public Health,* 2007, Vol 97 (6) 1126–1133

54. Lhomond, B. & Saurel-Cubizolles, M. Violence against women and suicide risk: The neglected impact of same-sex sexual behaviour *Social Science & Medicine* 2006 Vol 62 (8) pp. 2002-2013. See also Mercer, C.H. et al Women Who Report Having Sex With Women: British National Probability Data on Prevalence, Sexual Behaviors, and Health Outcomes. *American Journal of Public Health,* 2007, Vol 97 (6) 1126–1133

55. Laumann, E.O. et al *The Social Organisation of Sexuality* op. cit. p.283

56. www.browardpalmbeach.com/2009-08-20/news/those-who-practice-bestiality-say-they-re-part-of-the-next-gay-rights-movement/5/ See also Miletski. H. *Understanding Bestiality & Zoophilia*. 2002 Bethesda, MD: East-West Publishing LLC

57. Ball, C.A. Last Hope: A Response to Professor Teresa Stanton Collett in Wardle, L.D. et al *Marriage and Same-Sex Unions: A Debate* 2003 Westport, CT: Praeger p.164

58. Ball, C. A. Marriage, Same-Gender Relationships, and Human Needs and Capabilities in eds. Wardle, L.D. et al *Marriage and Same-Sex Unions: A Debate*

op. cit. p.139

59. Ball, C.A. Ibid. p.141

60. Civil Partnership: A framework for the legal recognition of same-sex couples, DTI Women & Equality Unit, June 2003, p.9

61. Girgis, S., George, R.P. & Anderson, R.T. What is marriage? *Harvard Journal of Law & Public Policy* 2010 Vol. 34 (1) p.283

62. Morgan, P. T*he War Between the State and the Family: how government divides and impoverishes.* 2007 The Institute for Economic Affairs & Transaction Pub

63. Boswell, J. *Same-Sex Unions in Premodern Europe* 1995 New York: Vintage Books

64. Wilets, J.D. The Inexorable Momentum towards National and International Recognition of Same-Sex Relationships: An International, Competitive, Historical, and Cross Cultural Perspective. In eds. Wardle, L.D. et al *Marriage and Same-Sex Unions: A Debate* op. cit.

65. Horvat, M.T. Rewriting history serve the gay agenda. Autumn 2004 www.traditioninaction.org/bkreviews/A_00br_SameSex.htm See also Same-Sex Unions in Pre-modern Europe *Catholic Family News* October 2001. See also Young, R.D "Gay Marriage: Re-imagining Church History," September 2004, catholiceducation.org

66. Hartney, A.M. *Gruesome Death and Celibate Lives; Christian Martyrs and Ascetics* 2005 Bristol Phoenix Press

67. Lancaster, R.N. Marriage is not a Timeless, Unchanging Institution, ed. de Waal, A. 2013 *The Meaning of Matrimony* CIVITAS pp.26–24

68. Tatchell, P.A. Democracy, not a Theocracy ed. de Waal, A. *The Meaning of Matrimony* op. cit.

69. French, P. *Observer* 22.01.2012

70. Bloch, M. *Feudal Society* 1961 Routledge and Kegan Paul

71. Lynch, J.H. *Christianizing Kinship: Ritual sponsorship in Anglo-Saxon England* 1998 Cornell University Press

72. Juvenal, *Satires ii.* referenced in Sissa, G. *Sex and Sensuality in the Ancient World* 2008 p.158

73. Witte, J. Jr The Tradition of Traditional Marriage in eds. Wardle, L.D. et al *Marriage and Same-Sex Unions: A Debate* op. cit.

74. Phy-Olsen, A. *Same-Sex Marriage* 2006 Connecticut: Greenwood Press

75. Betteridge, T. Introduction and Clarke, D. The Duke of Buckingham and Edward II ed. Betteridge, T *Sodomy in Early Modern Europe* Manchester University Press 2002 pp. 7 & 61; see also Bronski, M. *A Queer History of the United States* 2011 Beacon Press

76. Shepherd, G. Rank, gender and homosexuality in Mombasa in ed. Caplan, P. *The Cultural Construction* op. cit. pp.250-1

77. Dover, K.J. *Greek Homosexuality* 1989 Harvard University Press Cambridge: Mass. See also Halperin, D., Winkler, J. & Zeitlin, E. *Before Sexuality: the*

Construction of Erotic Experience in the Ancient Greek World 1990 Princeton. See also Martii, N. *Homoeroticism in the Biblical World: A Historical Perspective* 1998 Minneapolis: Fortress Press. See also Dover, K. J. *Greek Homosexuality* 1978 Cambridge, M.A. & Sissa, G. *Sex and Sensuality in the Ancient World* 2008 Yale University Press

78. Sissa, G. pp.161 & 159

79. Scruton, R. *Sexual Desire* 1986 rev 1994 London Phoenix: Orion Books p.308

80. Sissa, G. *Sex and Sensuality* op. cit. p.160

81. Ibid. pp.161 & 159

82. Ibid. p.163

83. Hari, J. The Intriguing tale of the gay sheep *Independent* 04.01.2007

84. Richardson, J. and Parnell, P. *And tango makes three*, Simon & Schuster, New York, 2005; 131 de Haan, L. and Nijland, S. *King & King*, Tricycle Press, Berkeley, 2002

85. Stanley, T. Gay, straight or necrophiliac. A penguin isn't a human being. *Daily Telegraph* 09.06.2012

86. Mills, B. The animals went in two by two: Heteronormativity in television wildlife documentaries *European Journal of Cultural Studies* 2013 16:100–114, See also Collins, N 'Tell the truth about gay cuddling chimps, Attenborough Asked' *Daily Telegraph* 09.02.13

87. Engels, F. *The Origin of the Family, Private Property and the State* 1972 London: ed. Lawrence & Wishart p.98

88. Grayling, A.C. Apes and Atheists *Prospect* April 2013

89. Grayling, A.C. States of Mind *Prospect* September 2013

90. Scruton, R. *Sexual Desire* op. cit. pp.350–1

91. Tallis, R. *Aping Mankind: Neuromania, Darwinitis and the Misrepresentation of Humanity* 2011 Acumen p.160

92. Engels, F. *The Origin of the Family, Private Property and the State* op. cit. p.98

93. Ross, T. Same-sex marriages will make our society stronger, says May. *Daily Telegraph* 25.05.2012

94. Quoted by James Kirkup Clegg in gay marriage 'bigots' row. *Daily Telegraph* 12.09.2012

95. Skelton, D. and Flint, R. *What's In A Name?* op. cit. p.42

96. Girgis, S., George, R.P. & Anderson, R.T. *What's In A Name?* op. cit. p.250

97. Skelton, D. and Flint, R. ed. Gibbs, B. *What's In A Name?* op. cit.

98. How does a polyamorous relationship between four people work? (www.bbc.co.uk, 19.08.2013)

99. Krizanovich, K. Till life us do part. Stella 01.12.2013

100. Bello, M. 'Love is love, whatever you are.' *Stella* 22.12.13

101. O'Neill, B. A Liberal Critique of Gay Marriage in ed. de Waal, A. *The Meaning of Matrimony* 2013 CIVITAS p.54

101. O'Neill, B. *A Liberal Critique of Gay Marriage…* p.54

102. Bloom, A. *The Closing of the American Mind* 1987 Simon and Shuster p.175
103. Five different designs included: "We're here, we're queer, we're in your school". The Toronto School Board said: "The images in question were meant to support an individual's right to choose whom they love, regardless of gender … the reason for depicting two women and one man was meant to show that a person can be attracted to more than one gender". As part of its Safe & Positive Space program' this is supposed to affirm and support "all sexual identities, biological sexes, sexual orientations, gender expressions and gender identities." Polygamy and the Toronto School Board's big mistake, blogs, vancouversun.com, 26.09. 2012. Poster not about polygamy: TDSB Yuen, J. *Toronto Sun* 25.09.2012
104. Equality for all (scotsman.com, 2 October 2013)
105. Drucilla Cornell quoted in Gallagher, M. Normal Marriage: Two Views, p.14
106. Stanton Collett, T. Should Marriage Be Privileged? In Wardle, L.D. et al *Marriage and Same Sex Unions: A Debate* 2003 op. cit. p.160

Chapter 6

1. Skelton, D. & Flint, R. ed. Gibbs, B. *What's In A Name?* 2012 Policy Exchange p.12

2. Ross, T. Same-sex marriages will make our society stronger, says May. *Daily Telegraph* 25.05.2012

3. D'Ancona, M. Cracks in the Coalition marriage *Daily Telegraph* 29.09.13

4. Quoted Swinford, S. Rush to bring in gay marriage has harmed Tories, says Minister *Daily Telegraph* 09.11.2023

5. Church leaders intolerant on marriage, says gay minister. *Daily Telegraph* 16.05.2012

6. Skelton, D. & Flint, R. ed. Gibbs *What's In A Name?* op. cit. pp.23–24

7. Attributed to Doris Lessing. Morrison, R. Nurture the boy, save the man. *The Times* 15.08.2001

8. Skelton, D. and Flint, R. ed. Gibbs, B *What's In A Name?* op. cit.. p.32

9. Murray, D. Gay rites. *The Spectator* 01.10.2011

10. Macedo, S. Homosexuality and the Conservative Mind in eds., Wardle, L.D. et al *Marriage and Same Sex Unions: A Debate* 2003 Praeger, p.101

11. Wardle, L.D. Beyond Equality in eds., Wardle, L.D. et al *Marriage and Same Sex Unions* op. cit.

12. Murray, D. Gay Rites *The Spectator* 01.10.2011

13. Rauch, J. Gay Marriage: *Why It Is Good for Gays, Good for Straights, and Good for America* 2004 New York: Henry Holt & Co.

14. Skelton, D. and Flint, R. ed. Gibbs *What's In A Name?* op. cit. p.6

15. Barker, N. Two Myths about Same-Sex Marriage. In de Waal op. cit. p.83

16. Quoting the Centre for Social Justice, Skelton & Gibbs p.22

17. Skelton, D. and Flint, R. op. cit.

18. Bennett, W.J. *The Broken Hearth* p.115

19. Girgis, S., George, R.P. & Anderson, R.T. *What is marriage?* op. cit.

20. Skelton & Flint quoting Lisa Belkin, 'Dutch Views on Same-Sex Marriage', New York Times, 9.11.2009

21. Skelton D. & Flint, R. ed. Gibbs *What's In A Name?* op. cit. p.57

22. Lee Badgett, M.V. Will Providing Marriage Rights to Same-Sex Couples Undermine Heterosexual Marriage? *Sexuality Research & Social Policy* 2004 Vol. 1(3) pp.1–10

23. Lund-Anderson, I. The Danish Registered Partnership Act 1989 in Wintemute, R. & Andenaes, M. Legal Recognition of Same-Sex Partnerships Hart 2001, p.419

24. Frisch, M. & Hviid, A. Childhood Family Correlates of Heterosexual and Homosexual Marriages: *Arch Sex Behav* (2006) 35:533–547

25. Civil Partnership: A framework for the legal recognition of same-sex couples, DTI Women & Equality Unit, June 2003

26. Census 2001: National Report for England and Wales Part 2, TSO, 2004,

Table UV93, p.70

27. Explanatory notes to the Civil Partnership Bill, 30th March 2004, p. 108 footnote 3. See also Population Trends, 115, Spring 2004, ONS, p.70

28. Gallagher, M. & Baker, J.K. Demand for Same-Sex Marriage: Evidence from the United States, Canada and Europe iMAPP, 2006 Vol.3 (1)

29. Andersson, G., et al The demographics of same-sex marriages in Norway and Sweden *Demography,* 2006 43(1), 79–98

30. Noack, T., Fekjær, H., Seierstad, A. (2002): Skilsmisser blant lesbiske og homofile partnere – hvem er mest stabile. Samfunnsspeilet nr. 3, 2002 – cited in Christer Hyggen, C with Skevik, *A Demography of the family in Norway. First report for the project "Welfare Policy and Employment in the Context of Family Change",* drafted for the meeting 12–13 December 2002 in York (UK) NOVA Norwegian Social Research, Oslo

31. Lofquist, D. et al Households and Families: 2010 Census Briefs. Sept. 27, 2011. U.S Census Bureau

32. Andersson, G., et al The demographics of same-sex marriages in Norway and Sweden. *Demography,* 2006 43(1), 79–98. see also Andersson,G et al Divorce-Risk Patterns in Same-Sex Marriages in Norway and Sweden, 2004 soz/conference/papers/p_andersson.pdf http://www.uni-koeln.de/wisofak/fi

33. Statistics Netherlands, "Number of Registered Partnerships Grew Further in 2010" March 15, 2011 at http://www.cbs.nl/en-/menu/themas/bevolking/publicaties/artikelen/archief/2011/2011-3331-wm.htm

34. Kalmijn, M., Loeve, A. & Manting, D. Income dynamics in couples and the dissolution of marriage and cohabitation. *Demography* 2007 44 pp.159–179

35. Lau, Charles, Q. The Stability of Same-Sex Cohabitation, Different-Sex Cohabitation, and Marriage. *Journal of Marriage and Family* 2012 74 pp.973–988

36. Lau, Charles, Q. The Stability of Same-Sex Cohabitation, Different-Sex Cohabitation, and Marriage op. cit.

37. Frisch, M. & Hviid, A. Childhood Family Correlates of Heterosexual and Homosexual Marriages: *Arch Sex Behav* (2006) 35:533–547

38. Frisch, M., Bronnum-Hansen, H. Mortality among men and women in same-sex marriage: a national cohort study of 8333 Danes. *Am J Pub Health* 2009 99:133–137

39. Andersson, G., et al The demographics of same-sex marriages in Norway and Sweden op. cit.

40. Haandrikman, K. *Bi-national Marriages in Sweden: Is There an EU effect?* Research Reports in Demography 2012:2 Stockholm Univ

41. Daugstad, G. and Sandnes, T. Gender and Migration. Similarities and disparities among women and men in the immigrant population. 2008/10 Statistisk sentralbyrå • Statistics Norway Oslo–Kongsvinger

42. Carlson, A. *The Swedish Experiment in Family Politics* 1990 New Brunswick, New Jersey: Transaction & Lewis, H. *Sweden's Right to be Human* 1982 Allen

and Busby, Ltd

43. Eskridge, W.N. & Spedale, D.R. *Gay Marriage: for Better or for Worse?: What We've Learned from the Evidence* 2006 Oxford University Press

44. Ibid. p.176

45. Christer Hyggen, C. with Skevik, A. *Demography of the family in Norway First report for the project "Welfare Policy and Employment in the Context of Family Change"*, drafted for the meeting 12–13 December 2002 in York (UK) NOVA Norwegian Social Research Oslo

46. O'Leary, J. *Will fewer straight people marry if gay people can?* Fullfact.org 12.12.2012 p.50.

47. Duncan, W.C. 'The Tenth Anniversary of Dutch Same-Sex Marriage: How is Marriage Doing in the Netherlands?' iMAPP Research Brief, Vol. 4, No.3. 2011. *Marriages and Partnerships registrations: key statistics,* CBSStartline, 2012 http://tinyurl.com/colyp2o

48. Statistics Netherlands, "Number of Registered Partnerships Grew Further in 2010" March 15th, 2011 at http://www.cbs.nl/en-menu/themas/bevolking/publicaties/artikelen/archief/2011/2011-3331-wm.htm

49. O'Leary, J. *Will fewer straight people marry if gay people can?* op. cit.

50. http://www.belastingdienst.nl/wps/wcm/connect/bldcontentnl/belastingdienst/prive/inkomstenbelasting/nieuw_in_2013/heffingskortingen/algemene_heffingskorting

51. Instituto Nacional de Estadistica, Press release. *Vital Statistics and Basic Demographic Indicators: Preview Data for 2011*, 29th June 2012 p.5

52. Spain's divorce rate soars after rules relaxed *The Guardian* 17.11.2007

53. Quoted Glendon, M.A. *The Transformation of Family Law* 1989 Chicago: University of Chicago Press p.274

Chapter 7

1. The original study informs us that almost 6,900 gay and bisexual men across the UK who had used NHS healthcare services in the last year were surveyed by gay rights charity Stonewall. As this does not tell us about 'gay and bisexual men' generally the figures should not be extrapolated to them. There is nothing about how the sample was recruited or where the comparison with men in general comes from. [Note: Department of Health. Programme Budget 2009–2010. 2010.]

2. www.hpa.org.uk/webc/HPAwebfile/HPAweb_C/1259151891830

3. Rachel Williams, NHS is failing gay and bisexual men, major survey reveals *The Guardian,* 24.04.2012 quoted in Skelton & Flint, p.23 and referring to: Guasp, A *Gay and Bisexual men's Health* Study 2012 Stonewall

4. Skelton, D. & Flint, R. op. cit. p.21

5. Simon Fanshawe quoted in McVeigh, T. Breaking the taboo over the mental health crisis among Britain's gay men *The Observer* 22.08.2010

6. Skelton, D. & Flint, R. op. cit. p.22

7. Macedo, S. Homosexuality and the Conservative Mind in *Marriage and Same-Sex Unions* Wardle, L.D. et al eds. 2003 Praegar op. cit. p.98

8. www.petertatchell.net/lgbt rights/equality not enough/beyond equality.htm

9. Cover, R Politicising Queer Issues and Activism: Disciplinarity, Biopolitics and the Means by which Activist Issues Enter the Public Sphere *Reconstruction* 10.03.2010

10. King, M. et al A systematic review of mental disorder, suicide, and deliberate self harm in lesbian, gay and bisexual people *BMC Psychiatry* 2008; 8: 70

11. Cover, R. Politicising Queer Issues and Activism: Disciplinarity, Biopolitics and the Means by which Activist Issues Enter the Public Sphere *Reconstruction* 10.03.2010) Warner, M. *The Trouble with Normal: Sex, Politics, and the Ethics of Queer Life* 1999 New York: The Free Press

12. See Liu, H., Reczek, C. & Brown, D. Same-Sex Cohabitors and Health: The Role of Race-Ethnicity, Gender, and Socioeconomic Status *Journal of Health and Social Behaviour* 2013 54 25–45. Report 1 of the Council on Science and Public Health (I-09) Health Care Disparities in Same-Sex Households. Cohen, R.A. & Coriaty-Nelson, Z. *Health Insurance Coverage: Estimates From the National Health Interview Survey 2003* Hyattsville, Md: National Center for Health Statistics; 2004. See also Heck, J.E., Sell, R.L. & Sheinfeld Gorin, S. Health Care Access Among Individuals Involved in Same-Sex Relationships *American Journal of Public* Health: 2006, Vol. 96 (6), pp.1111–1118

13. King, M. & Bartlett, A. What same sex civil partnerships may mean for health *Epidemiol Community Health* 2006; 60:188-191

14. Personal Well-being in the UK, 2012/13 30 July 2013 Office of National Statistics

15. Nicoll, A. Are trends in HIV, gonorrhoea, and syphilis worsening in Western Europe? *BMJ* 2002; 324:1324-7. Johnson, A. M., et al. Natsal 2000: Sexual

behaviour in Britain: partnerships, practices, and HIV risk behaviours. Lancet 2001 358 (9296): 1835–42. Wellings, K. et al Sexual behaviour in Britain: early heterosexual experience *Lancet* 2001 358 (9296): 1843–50. Godeau, E. et al Contraceptive Use by 15-Year-Old Students at Their Last Sexual Intercourse: Results From 24 Countries *Arch Pediatr Adolesc Med.* 2008;162(1):66–73

16. Dodds, J.P. and Johnson, A.M. and Parry, J.V. and Mercey, D.E. A tale of three cities: persisting high HIV prevalence, risk behaviour and undiagnosed infection in community samples of men who have sex with men *Sexually Transmitted Infections,* 2007 83 (5). pp.392–396

17. HIV in the United Kingdom: 2010 report Health Protection Agency Chalmer, K. et al Epidemiological Study of Phylogenetic Transmission Clusters in a Local HIV-1 Epidemic Reveals Distinct Differences Between Subtype B and Non-B Infections. *BMC* Infectious Diseases (doi: 10.1186/1471-2334-10-262). Belgium, United Kingdom: Young Gay Men Ignoring Safe Sex, HIV Study Warns U.S. Centers for Disease Control and Prevention *Medical News* 09.09.2010

18. Lansky, A. 2009. Paper presented at the 2009 National HIV Prevention Conference, Centers for Disease Control National Prevention Information Network. 2009, www.cdcnpin.org/nhpc_2009/Public/ListWebcast.aspx (January 29, 2010)

19. Syphilis and Lymphogranuloma Venereum: Resurgent Sexually Transmitted Infections in the UK Health Protect ion Agency 2009 also Table 2: Total number of STI diagnoses and other episodes of care seen at genitourinary medicine clinics, UK & England 2000 – 2009. Sexually Transmitted Infections and Other Sexual Health Information for Scotland, ISD Scotland, 2007, p.5

20. Ibid.

21. Parkin, D.M. The global health burden of infection-associated cancers *Int. J. Cancer* 2006 118 (12): 3030–44 also *Danish Medical Bulletin* 2002 Aug;49(3):194–209 and Changing Trends in Sexual Behavior May Explain Rising Incidence of Anal Cancer Among American Men and Women *Fred Hutchinson Cancer Research Center* 2004.06.07

22. Cohen C.E., Giles, A., Nelson, A., 'Sexual trauma associated with fisting and recreational drugs', *Sex Transm Infect,* 2004, 80:469–70

23. Health Protection Report Vol 6 (22) 1 June 2012

24. HIV infection and AIDS in adolescents: An update of the position of the Society for Adolescent Medicine *Journal of Adolescent Health* 2006 38 88–91

25. Fierstein, H. The Aids awareness industry has turned the virus into a fun, sexy disease *The Times* 01.08.03

26. Mercer, C.H. et al Increasing prevalence of male homosexual partnerships and practices in Britain 1990-2000 AIDS 2004; 18: 1453-8. See also Midgley, C. HIV and the rise of complacency: Is it time to revive the 'Don't die of ignorance' message of the Eighties? *The Times* 15.06.2010. Davies, P. Safer Sex Maintenance among gay men: are we moving in the right direction? *AIDS* 1993, 7. p.280.

see also Marks, G. et al HIV-infected men's practices in notifying past sexual partners of infection risk. Public Health Reports, 1992 107, 100–105. deWit, J.B.F. et al Increase of unprotected anogenital intercourse among homosexual men Public Health Briefs, 1993 83,1451–1453. Pryor, J., & Reeder, G.D. The social psychology of HIV infection. Hillsdale, NJ: Lawrence Erlbaum Associates

27. Cochran, S.D. &. Mays, V.M. Physical Health Complaints Among Lesbians, Gay Men, and Bisexual and Homosexually Experienced Heterosexual Individuals: Results From the California Quality of Life Survey *American Journal of Public Health* 2011, 101 (6) 1133–1138

28. Paul, J.P., et al Suicide attempts among gay and bisexual men: Lifetime prevalence and antecedents. *Am J of Pub Health*, 2002 92 pp.1338–1345

29. *The Lancet* 2013 Vol 381, Issue 9861 pp.101–2

30. Marshal, M.P., et al Sexual orientation and adolescent substance use: A meta-analysis and methodological review *Addiction*, 2008 103, 546–556. See also: Gilman, S. E. et al, Risk of psychiatric disorders among individuals reporting same-sex sexual partners in the National Comorbidity Survey *American Journal of Public Health* 2001 91, 933–939. See also Stall R. D., et al. Alcohol use, drug use, and alcohol-related problems among men who have sex with men: The Urban Men's Health Study *Addiction*, 2001 96, 1589–1601. See also Sandfort, T.G.M. et al, Same-sex sexual behavior and psychiatric disorders. *Archives of General Psychiatry,* 2002 58, 85–91; Sandfort, T.G. et al Sexual orientation and mental and physical health status: findings from a Dutch population survey *American Journal of Public Health*, 2006 96(6), 1119–1125; Wang, J., et al. High prevalence of mental disorders and comorbidity in the Geneva Gay Men's Health Study *Social Psychiatry and Psychiatric Epidemiology* 2007 42(5), 414–420; Thiede, H., et al Regional patterns and correlates of substance use among young men who have sex with men in 7 U.S. urban areas *American Journal of Public Health,* 2003, 93, 1915–1921

31. *The Lancet* 2013 op. cit. also Rosenberg, E.S. et al Number of casual male sexual partners and associated factors among men who have sex with men: results from the National HIV Behavioural Surveillance system *BMC Public Health* 2011, 11, 189. Myers, T HIV, substance misuse and related behaviour of gay and bisexual men *British Journal of Addiction* 1992m 87 209. Purcell D.W., et al Predictors of the use of viagra, testosterone and antidepressants among HIV-seropositive gay and bisexual men', *AIDS,* 2005, 19 Suppl., 1:S57–66. Colfax G, et al EXPLORE Study Team, Substance use and sexual risk: a participant-and episode-level analysis among a cohort of men who have sex with men, *American Journal of Epidemiology,* 2004,159:1002-12; Woody G.E., et al HIVNET VPS 001 Protocol Team, Substance use among men who have sex with men: comparison with a national household survey' *Journal of Acquired Immune Deficiency Syndromes: J AIDS,* 2001, 27:86–90. See also Ross, M.W., Mattison, A.M., Franklin D.R., Jr, 'Club drugs and sex on drugs are associated with different motivations for gay

circuit party attendance in men' *Substance Use & Misuse* 2003, 38:1173–83. See also Schwappach, D.L.B. and Bruggmann, P. An Integrated Model of Care to Counter high Incidence of HIV and Sexually Transmitted Disease in Men who have Sex with Men –Initial Analysis of Service Utilizers in Zurich; *BMC Public Health* 2008, 8. 180 Cochran, S.D. et al. See also Prevalence of nonmedical drug use and dependence among homosexually active men and women in the U.S. population. 2004 *Addiction* 99, 989–998.

32. Myers, T. HIV, substance misuse and related behaviour of gay and bisexual men *British Journal of Addiction.* 1992m 87 209. See also Sullivan, P.S., Salazar, L., Buchbinder, S., Sanchez, T.H. : Estimating the proportion of HIV transmissions from main sex partners among men who have sex with men in five US cities. *AIDS* 2009, 23:1153–1162

33. Leigh, B.C., Stall, R. Substance use and risky sexual behavior for exposure to HIV: Issues in methodology, interpretation, and prevention *American Psychologist*, 1993, 48(10), pp. 1035–1045. See also Mansergh, G. et al The Circuit Party Men's Health Survey: Findings and Implications for Gay and Bisexual Men, *American Journal of Public Health*, 2001 91. 6 pp.953–958. Dennis, G. et al., Methamphetamine and Viagra Use: Relationship to Sexual Risk Behaviors Arch Sex *Archives Sexual Behav* 2011 40:273–279. Spindler, H. H. et al Viagra, methamphetamine, and HIV risk: Results from a probability sample of MSM, San Francisco *Sexually Transmitted Diseases* 2007 38, 586–591. See also Herrick, A.L. Sex While Intoxicated: A Meta-Analysis Comparing Heterosexual and Sexual Minority Youth *Journal of Adolescent Health* 02.09.2010

34. Ellis, D., Collis, I. & King, M. Personality disorder and sexual risk taking among homosexually active and heterosexually active men attending a genito-urinary medicine clinic *J. Psychosom. Res.* 1995 39, 901–910. See also Moffitt T.E., et al A gradient of childhood self-control predicts health, wealth, and public safety *PNAS* 2011;108(7):2693-2698. See also Skegg, K., Nada-Raja, S., Dickson, N. & Paul, C. Perceived "out-of-control" sexual behavior in a cohort of young adults from the Dunedin Multidisciplinary Health and Development Study *Archives of Sexual Behavior*, 2010 39(4), 968–978

35. Koblin, B.A., et al High-risk behaviors among men who have sex with men in 6 US cities: Baseline data from the EXPLORE study *American Journal of Public Health*, 2003 93, 926–932. See also Kalichman, S.C., Heckman, T. & Kelly, J.A. Sensation seeking as an explanation for the association between substance use and HIV-related risky sexual behavior *Archives of Sexual Behavior* 1996 Vol 25 (2) 141-154. See also Kalichman, S.C. et al Sensation Seeking and Alcohol Use as Markers of Sexual transmission Risk Behaviour of HIV Positive Men *Annals of Behavioural Medicine* 2002, 24(3) pp. 229-235 & Dolezal, C. et al Substance Use During Sex and Sensation Seeking as Predictors of Sexual Risk Behaviours among HIV+ and HIV–Gay Men *AIDS and Behaviour* 1997 Vol 1 (1) pp.19–28

36. Mayer, K.H., Colfax, G. & Guzman, R. Club Drugs and HIV Infection: A

Review *Clinical Infectious Diseases* 2006 42, 10. pp.1463–1469

37. Fethers, K. et al., Sexually transmitted infections and risk behaviours in women who have sex with women *Sexually Transmitted Infections* 2000 76. 5 pp.345–349. See also Mercer, C.H. et al Women Who Report Having Sex With Women: British National Probability Data on Prevalence, Sexual Behaviors, and Health Outcomes *American Journal of Public Health,* 2007, Vol 97 (6) 1126–1133. Cochran, S.D. et al. Prevalence of nonmedical drug use and dependence among homosexually active men and women in the U.S. population *Addiction* 2004 99, 989–998. See also Drabble, L. & Trocki, K. Alcohol consumption, alcohol-related problems, and other substance use among lesbian and bisexual women *Journal of Lesbian Studies* 2005 9(3), 19–30. See also Fethers, K. et al Sexually transmitted infections and risk behaviours in women who have sex with women *Sexually Transmitted Infections* 2000 76(5) pp.345–349. See also Richters, J. et al, HIV risks among women in contact with Sydney's gay and lesbian community *Venereology,* 11(3):35–38 (1998); Richters, J et al Women in Contact with the Gay and Lesbian Community: Sydney Women and Sexual Health Survey 1996 and 1998 *National Centre in HIV Social Research* 1999 University of New South Wales. See also Wilsnack, S. C., et al Drinking and drinking-related problems among heterosexual and sexual minority women *Journal of Studies in Alcohol and Drugs,* 2008 *69,* 129–139; earlier Lewis, C.E. Drinking patterns in homosexual and heterosexual women *J Clin Psychiat* 1982 43 277–9. See also Cochran, S.D. et al Estimates of alcohol use and clinical treatment needs among homosexually active men and women in the U.S. population *Journal of Consulting and Clinical Psychology* 2000, 68(6), 1062–1071. See also Mercer, C.H. et al Women Who Report Having Sex With Women: British National Probability Data on Prevalence, Sexual Behaviors, and Health Outcomes American Journal of Public Health: 2007 Vol. 97 (6), pp.1126–1133

38. Pathela, P., Schillinger, J.A. Sexual Behaviors and Sexual Violence: Adolescents With Opposite-, Same-, or Both-Sex Partners *Pediatrics* 2010 Vol. 126 (5) pp.879 -886 Loosier, P.S., Dittus, P.J. Group Differences in Risk Across Three Domains Using an Expanded Measure of Sexual Orientation *J Prim Prev.* 2010;31(5):261-272

39. Stall, R. et al Association of Co-Occurring Psychosocial Health Problems and Increased Vulnerability to HIV/AIDS Among Urban Men Who Have Sex With Men *American Journal of Public Health* 2003 93 (6) pp. 939–942. Greenwood, G.L. et al Battering Victimization among a Probability Sample of Men who have Sex with Men *Amer J of Public Health* 2002, 92(12) 1964–1969

40. Island, D. and Letellier, P. *Men Who Beat the Men Who Love Them: Battered Gay Men and Domestic Violence* 1991 New York: Haworth Press. See also Turell, S.C. A Descriptive Analysis of Same-Sex Relationship Violence for a Diverse Sample *Journal of Family Violence* 2000 15 3 281–293

41. Jaden, P., Thoennes, N. & Allison, C. J. Comparing violence of the life span in

sample of same-sex and opposite-sex cohabitants *Violence and Victims* 1999 14(4), 413–425. See also Plichta, S. B. & Weisman, C.S. Spouse or partner abuse, use of health services and unmet need for medical care in US women *J Women's Health* 1995 4, pp.45–54 and Straus, M.A., Gelles, R.J. *Physical Violence in American Families* 1990 New Brunswick, NJ: Transaction Pub. Waldner-Haugrud, L.K. Sexual coercion in lesbian and gay relationships: A review and critique *Aggression and Violence Behavior* 19991 4, 139–149. See also Bagshaw, D., et al Reshaping Responses to Domestic Violence – Final Report, Partnerships Against Domestic Violence, 2000 Department of Human Services, South Australia, University of South Australia, Commonwealth of Australia. See also Turrell, S.C. A descriptive analysis of same-sex relationship violence for a diverse sample *Journal of Family Violence* 2002 15(3), 281–293.15(3), 281–293. See also Alexander C.J. Violence in gay and lesbian relationships *J Gay Lesb Soc Serv* 2002;14:95–8

42. Greenwood, G.L. et al *Battering Victimization....* op. cit.

43. Rachel Williams, NHS is failing gay and bisexual men, major survey reveals, *The Guardian,* 24.04. 2012 referring to: Guasp A *Gay and Bisexual men's Health Study* 2012 Stonewall

44. Chan, C. Domestic Violence in Gay and Lesbian Relationships ... p.3 relying on Vickers, L. 'The second closet...'

45. Turrell, S. C. A descriptive analysis of same-sex relationship violence... op. cit.

46. Turrell, S. C. A descriptive analysis of same-sex relationship violence... op. cit.

47. Stanley, J.L. et al Intimate Violence in Male Same-Sex Relationships *Journal of Family Violence* 2006 Vol 21 (1), pp.31–41

48. Stanley, J.L. et al *Intimate Violence...* op. cit.

49. Saukko P. and Knight, B. Knight's *Forensic Pathology* (3rd Edn) 2004 London: Arnold Publishers

50. The UK gay men's sex survey, Vital Statistics 2010 Sigma

51. Johnson, A.M. & Wellings, K. et al *Sexual Attitudes and Lifestyle* 1994. See also Mercer, C. H., Hart, G. J., Johnson, A.M. & Cassell, J.A. Behaviourally bisexual men as a bridge population for HIV and sexually transmitted infections? Evidence from a national probability survey *International Journal of STD and AIDS,* 2009, 20, 87–94

52. Rosenberg, E.S. et al Number of casual male sexual partners and associated factors among men who have sex with men: results from the National HIV Behavioural Surveillance system *BMC Public Health* 2011, 11, 189

53. www.latrobe.edu.au/arcshs/assets/downloads/reports/private_lives_report_pdf

54. Altman, Dennis *The Homosexualization of America, the Americanisation of Homosexuality.*1982 quoted ibid.

55. Kurdek, L.A. Relationship Outcomes and Their Predictors: Longitudinal Evidence from Heterosexual Married, Gay Cohabiting and Lesbian Cohabiting Couples *Journal of Marriage and the Family* 1998, 60 pp.553–568

56. Weatherburn P., Hunt, A., Hickson, F., Davies, P. *The Sexual Lifestyles of*

Gay and Bisexual Men in England and Wales (Project SIGMA) London: HMSO, 1992; 10–12 and Hickson, F.C.I. et al Maintenance of open gay relationships: some strategies for protection against *HIV AIDS* Care 1992; 4: 4

57. Weatherburn, P. et al *The Sexual Lifestyles....* op. cit.

58. Rosenberg, E. S., et al. Number of casual male sexual partners and associated factors among men who have sex with men: results from the National HIV Behavioral Surveillance system *BMC Public Health* 2011 11, 189

59. McWhirter, D. P. & Mattison, A.M. *The Male Couple: How relationships develop* 1984 Prentice-Hall pp.252–3

60. Davidovich, U. et al Increase in the share of steady partners as a source of HIV infection: A 17-year study of seroconversion among gay men *AIDS*, 2001 15, 1303–1308. See also Sullivan, P. S. et al Estimating the proportion of HIV transmissions from main sex partners among men who have sex with men in five US cities *AIDS*, 2009 23, 1153–1162

61. Adimora, A.A., Schoenbach, V.J. & Doherty, I.A. Concurrent Sexual Partnerships among Men in the United States *American Journal of Public Health 2007*

62. Wheldon, C.W. & Pathak, E.B. Masculinity and Relationship Agreements among Male Same-Sex Couples *Journal of Sex Research* 2010 vol 47 (5) pp. 451–459

63. www.washblade.com/2003/8-22/news/national/nonmonog.cfm

64. Bradford, J., Ryan, C., & Rothblum, E.D. National lesbian health care survey: Implications for mental health care *Journal of Consulting and Clinical Psychology*, 1994 62, 228–242. See also D'Augelli et al Predicting the suicide attempts of lesbian, gay, and bisexual youth *Suicide and Life-Threatening Behavior* 2005 35(6), 646–660

65. Bell, A.P., & Weinberg, M.S. *Homosexualities: A study of diversity among men and women* 1978 New York: Simon & Schuster. See also Hendin, H. Suicide and homosexuality *Suicide in America* 1995 pp.129–146). New York: W.W. Norton. See also Bartholow, B.N. et al Emotional, behavioral, and HIV risks associated with sexual abuse among adult homosexual and bisexual men *Child Abuse and Neglect,* 1994 18, 745–761. See also Remafedi, G., Farrow, J.A., & Deisher, R.W. Risk factors for attempted suicide in gay and bisexual youth. *Pediatrics,* 1991 87, 869–875

66. Macedo, S. Homosexuality and the Conservative Mind in *Marriage and Same-Sex Unions* Wardle, L.D. et al eds. 2003 Praegar p.98

67. Wardle, L.D Image, Analysis, and the Nature of Relationships: Macedo begs the question in Wardle et al eds. p.116

68. Horn, E.E. et al Accounting for the physical and mental health benefits of entry into marriage: A genetically informed study of selection and causation *Journal of Family Psychology,* 2013 Vol 27(1), 30–41

69. Liu, H., Reczek, C. & Brown, D. Same-Sex Cohabitors and Health: The Role of Race-Ethnicity, Gender, and Socioeconomic Status *J of Health and Social*

behaviour 2013 54 25–45

70. Parsons, J.T. et al., Alternatives to Monogamy Among Gay Male Couples in a Community Survey: Implications for Mental Health and Sexual Risk *Archives of Sexual Behaviour* 2011. 40(6)

71. Kurdek, L.A. Relationship Outcomes and Their Predictors: Longitudinal Evidence from Heterosexual Married, Gay Cohabiting and Lesbian Cohabiting Couples *Journal of Marriage and the Family* 1998, 60 pp.553–568 [Note: Unfortunately, the samples here were self-selected and therefore unrepresentative and measures were obtained from self-reports, with the problem of self-presentation bias.]

72. Levinger, G. A socio-psychological respective on marital dissolution. *Journal of Social Issues* 1976 53 21–47

73. Levinger, G. Ibid.

74. Oswald, R. F. Inclusion and belonging in the family rituals of gay and lesbian people *Journal of Family Psychology*, Vol 16(4), Dec 2002, 428–436

75. Skelton D. & Flint, R. op. cit. p.24

76. Andrew Sullivan, Virtually Normal, p184 quoted Skelton D. & Flint, R. p.24

77. Johnson, B. et al *A Social Scientific Response to the Regnerus Controversy* June 20, 2012 Institute for Studies of Religion Baylor University

78. Andersson, G., et al The demographics of same-sex marriages in Norway and Sweden *Demography*, 2006 43(1), 79–98. see also Andersson, G. et al Divorce-Risk Patterns in Same-Sex Marriages in Norway and Sweden, 2004 soz/conference/papers/p_andersson.pdf http://www.uni-koeln.de/wisofak/fi

79. Reiss, R. *Cruise Control: Understanding Sex Addiction in Gay Men*, 2005 Alyson Books: New York

80. Marshal M.P. et al *Sexual orientation and adolescent substance use: a meta-analysis and methodological review* Addiction *2008* Vol 103 (4), pp.546–556

81. Michael P. Marshal, Assistant Professor of Psychiatry at the Western Psychiatric Institute and Clinic of UPMC, who led the study. 25 March 2008 UNIVERSITY OF PITTSBURGH MEDIA RELEASE 'GAY YOUTH REPORT HIGHER RATES OF DRUG AND ALCOHOL USE' University of Pittsburgh researchers report findings in journal *Addiction*

82. Hillier, L., Turner, A, & Mitchell, A. The second national report on sexuality, health, and well-being of same-sex attracted young Australians 2005 Melbourne, Australia: Australian Research Center in Sex, Health, and Society

83. Hillier, L., Turner, A, & Mitchell, A. (2005) *The second national...* See also Hillier, L., De Visser, R., Kavanagh, A. & McNair, R. The association between licit and illicit drug use and sexuality in young Australian women. *Medical Journal of Australia*, 2003 179, 6, 326–327 and Murnane, A. 2000 Beyond perceptions: A report on alcohol and other drug use among gay lesbian and queer communities in Victoria. Melbourne: Australian Drug Foundation

84. Perilla, J. et al A working analysis of women's use of violence in the context of learning, opportunity, and choice *Violence Against Women* 2003 vol. 9, no. 1 pp.10–46. quoted in Chan, C. Domestic Violence in Gay and Lesbian Relationships Australian Domestic and Family Violence Clearinghouse undated, p.10

85. Brown, C. Gender-Role Implications on Same-Sex Intimate Partner Abuse *Journal of Family Violence* 2008 Vol 23 (6) pp.457–462

86. Chan, C. Domestic Violence in Gay and Lesbian Relationships ... p.3 relying on Vickers, L. 'The second closet...'

87. Chan, C. *Domestic Violence in Gay and Lesbian Relationships* ... pp.7–8

88. Hendin, H. Suicide among homosexual men. *American Journal of Psychiatry*, 1992 149, 1426–1427. See also Hendin, H. Suicide and homosexuality *Suicide in America* 1995 pp.129–146). New York: W.W.Norton. Hillier, L., Turner, A. & Mitchell, A. The second national report.... op. cit.

89. See Hendin, H. *Suicide in America* 1995 New York, NY: W.W. Norton

90. Scruton, R. *Sexual Desire* op. cit. pp.307–8

91. Scruton Ibid. p.309–310

92. Solomon, S.E. et al Money, Housework, Sex, and Conflict: Same-Sex Couples in Civil Unions, Those Not in Civil Unions, and Heterosexual Married Siblings *Sex Roles* 2005 Vol. 52, (9/10). 561–575 [Note: Ranging from completed questionnaires by both members of all three types of couples to one from six possible respondents. Completed sets for civil union couples were 82%. For same-sex couples not in civil unions 58% and for heterosexual married couples 52%. The disadvantage of using snowballing or personal contact means that at each stage representativeness is lost, although recruiting through siblings and friends has the advantage that different couple types are similar on ethnicity, age, and childhood factors.]

93. Spears, B. & Lowen, L. Beyond Monogamy: Lessons from Long-term Male Couples in Non-Monogamous Relationships www.thecouplesstudy.com p.72

94. Savage, D. *New York Times Magazine* June 2011

95. Scruton, R. *Sexual Desire* op. cit. p.306

96. Scruton, Ibid. p.307

97. King, M. & Bartlett, A. What same sex civil partnerships may mean for health *Epidemiol Community Health* 2006 60:188–191

98. Becker, Gary, S. A. *Treatise on the Family* 1991 Cambridge: Harvard University Press

99. Zavodny, M. Is There a 'Marriage Premium' for Gay Men? Discussion Paper No. 3192 November 2007 IZA Bonn: Germany and Ginther, D.K. & Zavodny, M. 'Is the Male Marriage Premium Due to Selection?' *Journal of Population Economics* 2001 14: 313–328

100. Lee Badgett, M.V.W. *When Gay People Get Married: What Happens when Societies Legalise Same-Sex Marriage* 2009 New York: NYUP referenced in Skelton & Flint p.22

101. "Dutch Same-Sex Couples Less Likely to Marry" Radio Netherlands

Worldwide, March 27th, 2011 at:
www.rnw.nl/english/bulletin/dutch-gay-couples-marry-far-less

102. Michael Bronski, Sexual Ceiling: The queer community's fight for same-sex marriage, combined with revived AIDS hysteria, is short-changing GLBT youth by stifling discussion of gay sexuality The Boston Phoenix, March 23rd, 2005

103. Solomon, S.E. et al *Money, Housework, Sex, and Conflict....* op.cit.

104. Yiannopoulos, M. The idea of Gay Marriage is ludicrous. 19.09. 2011, http://yiannopoulos.net/2011/09/19/the-idea-of-gay-marriage-is-ludicrous/#more-544

105. Posner, R. A. *Sex and Reason* 1992 Cambridge, Massachusetts: Harvard University Press p.312

106. Frisch, M., Brønnum-Hansen, H. Mortality among men and women in same-sex marriage: a national cohort study of 8333 Danes. *Am J Pub Health* 2009 vol 99(1) pp.133–137

107. Frisch, M. & Brønnum-Hansen, H. Ibid.

108. Qin, P., Agerbo, E., Mortensen P.B. Suicide risk in relation to socioeconomic, demographic, psychiatric, and familial factors: a national register-based study of all suicides in Denmark, 1981–1997 *Am J Psychiatry* 2003 160:765–772

109. Qin, P., Agerbo, E., Mortensen P.B. Ibid.

110. Mathy, R.M., Cochran, S.D., Olsen, J., & Mays, V.M. The association between relationship markers of sexual orientation and suicide: Denmark 1990–2001. *Social Psychiatry and Psychiatric Epidemiology* 2009 Soc Psychiatry Psychiatr Epidemiol first pub online 2009 2011 46:111–117

111. Chakraborty, A. et al Mental health of the non-heterosexual population of England *Br J Psychiatry* 2011 198 pp.143–8

112. Loosier, P.S., Dittus, P.J. Group Differences in Risk Across Three Domains Using an Expanded Measure of Sexual Orientation *J Prim Prev.* 2010;31(5):261–272

113. Bronski, M. The Bridge to Manhood: A gay man talks about disappointing-and loving-his father, http://www.beliefnet.com/Love-Family/2004/06/The-Bridge-To-Manhood.aspx#ixzz1vt6O123R

114. Twice married superhero comes out of the closet *Daily Telegraph* 02.06.2012

115. 10.12.2012

116. No Place for Bullying, Ofsted June 2012, No. 110179

117. Young, T. Status Anxiety: A lesson in satire *The Spectator* blog 26.02.2011

118. No Place for Bullying, Ofsted op. cit.

119. Hatzenbuehler, M. L. et al The impact of institutional discrimination on psychiatric disorders in lesbian, gay and bisexual populations: a prospective study. Am J Public Health 2010, 100 pp.452–9

120. Hatzenbuehler, M. L. et al Effect of Same-Sex Marriage Laws on Health Care Use and Expenditures in Sexual Minority Men: A Quasi-Natural Experiment *American Journal of Public Health,* 2012, Vol. 102 (2) pp.285–291

121. Francis, A.M. The economics of sexuality: The effect of HIV/AIDS on

homosexual behavior in the United States *Journal of Health Economics* 2008 27(3), 675–689

122. Kelly, J.A., et al. Situational factors associated with AIDS risk behavior lapses and coping strategies used by gay men who successfully avoid lapses *American Journal of Public Health* 1991 81, 1335–1338

123. Bos, H.M., & van Balen, F. Children in planned lesbian families: Stigmatisation, psychological adjustment and protective factors *Culture, Health, & Sexualities* 2008 10, 221–236

124. Bakker, F. & Vanwesenbeeck, I. (2006) Seksuele gezondheid in Nederland 2006 [Sexual Health in the Netherlands 2006]. Delft, the Netherlands: Eburon. Quoted in ibid. also: Kuyper, L., Vanwesenbeeck, I. High levels of same-sex experiences in the Netherlands: prevalences of same-sex experiences in historical and international perspective *Journal of Homosexuality* 2009 56(8):993–1010

125. Quoted in ibid. also: Kuyper, L., Vanwesenbeeck, I. High levels of same-sex experiences in the Netherlands: prevalences of same-sex experiences in historical and international perspective *Journal of Homosexuality* 2009 56(8):993–1010

126. Diamond, Lisa M. Female bisexuality from adolescence to adulthood: Results from a 10-year longitudinal study *Developmental Psychology* 2008 44(1) 5–14. See also: Kinnish, K.K., Strassberg, D.S. and Turner, C.W. Sex differences in the flexibility of sexual orientation: a multidimensional retrospective assessment *Archives of Sexual Behavior* 2005 34 pp.175–183

127. Morgan, P. *Family Matters: Family Breakdown and its Consequences* 2004 New Zealand Business Roundtable

128. Women becoming the more adventurous sex *Daily Telegraph* 26.11.2013 from National Survey of Sexual Attitudes and Lifestyles 2013

129. de Graaf, R., Sandfort, T.G.M., & Have, M. Suicidality and sexual orientation: Differences between men and women in a general population-based sample from the Netherlands *Archives of Sexual Behavior* 2006 35, 253–262

130. Sandfort T.G., et al Same-sex sexual behavior and psychiatric disorders: findings from the Netherlands Mental Health Survey and Incidence Study (NEMESIS) *Arch Gen Psychiatry* 2001 58:85–91. Sandfort, T. G. M., et al. Sexual orientation and mental and physical health status: findings from a Dutch population survey. *American Journal of Public Health,* 2006. 96(6), 1119–1125

131. de Graaf, R., Sandfort, T.G.M., & ten Have, M. Suicidality and sexual orientation … ibid.

132. Eskin, M., Kaynak-Demir, H. & Demir, S. Same-Sex Sexual Orientation, Childhood Sexual Abuse, and Suicidal Behavior in University Students in Turkey *Archives of Sexual Behavior* 2005 34 (2), pp.185–195

133. Paul, J.P., et al Suicide attempts among gay and bisexual men: Lifetime prevalence and antecedents *Am J of Pub Health,* 2002 92 pp.1338–1345

134. Warner, J., et al Rates and predictors of mental illness in gay men, lesbians, and bisexual men and women: Results from a survey based in England and Wales

British *Journal of Psychiatry* 2004 185, 479–485

135. Johnson, A. M. et al Natsal 2000: Sexual behaviour in Britain: partnerships, practices, and HIV risk behaviours *Lancet* 2001 358 (9296): 1835–42. Wellings, K. et al Sexual behaviour in Britain: early heterosexual experience *Lancet* 2001 358 (9296): 1843-50. Godeau, E. et al Contraceptive Use by 15-Year-Old Students at Their Last Sexual Intercourse: Results From 24 Countries *Arch Pediatr Adolesc Med.* 2008;162(1):66–73

136. Dept. of Health National Suicide Prevention Strategy for England 2002

137. "Suicide rates per 100,000 by country, year and sex (Table)". World Health Organization 2011

138. Jenkin, M. Most teachers not trained to deal with anti-gay bullying, report finds LGBT campaign group SchoolsOUT calls for UK schools to better equip teachers to tackle homophobic bullying following Ofsted report *PinkStarNews* 20.06.2012

139. Paul, J.P. et al Suicide attempts among gay and bisexual men: Lifetime prevalence and antecedents *Am J of Pub Health*, 2002 92 pp. 1338–1345

140. Hillier, L., Turner, A. & Mitchell, A. (2005) The second national report... op. cit.

141. Ferudi, F. *Wasted* 2009 Continuum pp.105 190–1

142. Kuyper, L., Vanwesenbeeck, I. 2009 High levels of same-sex experiences in the Netherlands: prevalences of same-sex experiences in historical and international perspective *Journal of Homosexuality* 56(8):993–1010

143. Bakker, F. & Vanwesenbeeck, I. (2006) Seksuele gezondheid in Nederland 2006 [Sexual Health in the Netherlands 2006]. Delft, the Netherlands: Eburon quoted in Kuyper, L., Vanwesenbeeck, I. High levels of same-sex experiences in the Netherlands....

144. US Department of Health and Human Services (1994) Bibliography with abstracts of substance abuse studies on lesbians, gay men, and bisexuals. (DHHS Publication No. 94-2097) Washington, DC: US Government Printing Office.

145. Hom Ombudsmannen mot Diskriminering Pa Grund av Sexuell Laggning Rapport 2004 Stockholm

146. It is significant that a fourfold higher incidence of psychosis, which involved independent, clinical diagnosis, not subjective reporting, is unrelated to any accounts of discrimination. Chakraborty, A. et al Mental health of the non-heterosexual population of England *Br J Psychiatry* 2011 198 pp.143–8

147. Ibid.

148. Hellesund, T. Deadly identities? : Homosexuality, adolescence and parasuicide *Ethnologia scandinavica* 2007 37: 35–46

149. Moore, C This Equality obsession is mad, bad and very, very dangerous. *Daily Telegraph* 02.02.2013

150. Kerrigan, K. "If it's OK to be gay, then why do I still feel sad" The Power of Heterosexism 2013 LGBT History Month Magazine

151. Qin, P., Agerbo, E., Mortensen, P.B. Suicide risk in relation to socioeconomic, demographic, psychiatric, and familial factors: a national register-based study of all suicides in Denmark 1981–1997 *Am J Psychiatry* 2003 160:765–772

Chapter 8

1. Garofalo, R., Wolf, R.C., Kessel, S. The association between health risk behaviors and sexual orientation among a school-based sample of adolescents *Pediatrics.* 1998;101:895–902

2. Macourt, M. *Towards a Theology of Gay Liberation* 1977 SCM Press Ltd p.24

3. Ward, V. BBC told to put more gays on children's TV *Daily Telegraph* 14.12.2012

4. Helen Grant, Parliamentary Under-Secretary at the Department for Culture, Media and Sport 19.10.2012

5. www.xtra.ca/public/Toronto/Planned-Parenthood_to_bolster_sex_ed-12457. aspx hhpt://teenhelth source.com/about-us/
http:/teenhelth source.com/sex/fingering-fisting-101/

6. http://www.petertatchell.nett/sex education/schoolsex.htm

7. Scruton *Sexual Desire* op. cit. pp.346-7

8. Midgley, M. & Hughes, J. *Women's Choices* 1983 London: Weidenfeld and Nicholson p.138

9. Hawton, K., Houston, K. & Shepperd, R. Suicide in young people. Study of 174 cases, aged under 25 years, based on coroners' and medical records. *British Journal of Psychiatry* 1999 175: 271-276

10. Robinson, Joseph P., Espelage, Dorothy L., and Rivers, Ian 'Developmental Trends in Peer Victimization and Emotional Distress in LGB and Heterosexual Youth, *Pediatrics* 2013 pp.423-30. They make use of data come from the Longitudinal Study of Young People in England LSYPE; http://www.esds.ac.uk/doc/5545/mrdoc/UKDA/UKDA_Study5545_Information.htm

11. Hatzenbuehler, M.L. The Social Environment and Suicide Attempts in Lesbian, Gay, and Bisexual Youth *Pediatrics* 2011 Vol. 127 (5) pp.896–903

12. Schuum, W. R. Complexities of the Social Environment *Pediatrics* published online April 18, 2011

13. Baller, R.D. & Richardson, K.K. The "Dark Side" of the Strength of Weak Ties: The Diffusion of Suicidal Thoughts *Journal of Health and Social Behavior* 2009 50: 261–276

14. Hillier, L., Turner, A. & Mitchell, A. (2005) The second national report on sexuality, health, and well-being of same-sex attracted young Australians. Melbourne, Australia: Australian Research Center in Sex, Health, and Society

15. Pathela, P., Schillinger, J.A. Sexual Behaviors and Sexual Violence: Adolescents With Opposite-, Same-, or Both-Sex Partners *Pediatrics* 2010 Vol. 126(5) pp.879-886

16. Laurance, J. *The Independent* 16.01.2013

17. See Baumeister, R.F. (2000) Gender differences in erotic plasticity: The female sex drive and socially flexible and responsive *Psychological Bulletin,* 126(3), 347–374

18. Laumann, E.O. et al The Social Organisation of Sexuality 1994 paper edn 2000 University of Chicago Press p.109

19. Hansen, T. A Review and Analysis of Research Studies Which Assessed Sexual Preference of Children Raised by Homosexuals 2008 http://www.drtraycehansen. com/Pages/writings-sexpref.html. See also Gartrell, N.K, Bos, H.M.W & Goldberg N.G Sexual Orientation, Sexual Behavior, and Sexual Risk Exposure *Archives of Sexual Behaviour* 2011 40. pp.1199-1209

20. Somerville, L.H., Jones, R.M. & Casey, B.J. *A time of change: Behavioral and neural correlates of adolescent sensitivity to appetitive and aversive environmental cues* Brain and Cognition 2010 72 (1), 124–133

21. LaBarbera, P. The Gay Youth Suicide Myth *Insight* Family Research Council February 1994

22. Friedman, M.S., et al Gay-related development, early abuse and adult health outcomes among gay males *AIDS and Behavior* 2008 12, pp.891–902. See also Marshal M.P. et al Sexual orientation and adolescent substance use: a meta-analysis and methodological review *Addiction* 2008 Vol 103 (4), pp.546–556

23. Pathela, P., Schillinger, J.A. Sexual Behaviors and Sexual Violence.... op. cit. Hillier, L., Turner, A. & Mitchell, A. *The second national report....* op. cit.

24. 'Challenging myths and stereotypes about LGB people' Out in School 2009 http://www.tht.org.uk/~/media/BE7585FBDDEC45A2965641ADE84842D2. ashx

25. Brody, S & Weiss, B *Heterosexual Anal Intercourse* .... op. cit.

26. Barter, C. et al Partner exploitation and violence in teenage intimate relationships University of Bristol and the NSPCC September 2009

27. Saewyc, E., Skay, C., Richens, K. Sexual orientation, sexual abuse, and HIV-risk behaviors among adolescents in the Pacific northwest. *Am J Public Health.* 2006;96:1104–1110. See also Diamond L.M., Lucas, S. Sexual-minority and heterosexual youths' peer relationships: Experiences, expectations, and implications for well-being *J Res Adolesc* 2004;14:313–340

28. Parkes, A. et al Comparison of Teenagers' Early Same-Sex and Heterosexual Behavior: UK Data From the SHARE and RIPPLE Studies *Journal of Adolescent Health* 02.09.2010

29. Pathela, P., Schillinger, J.A. *Sexual Behaviors and Sexual Violence....* op. cit.

30. www.TheSite.org/sexandrelationships/havingsex/styles/analplay

31. Brody, S. & Weiss, B. Heterosexual Anal Intercourse: Increasing Prevalence, and Association with Sexual Dysfunction, Bisexual Behavior, and Venereal Disease History *Journal of Sex & Marital Therapy* 2011 Vol 37(4) pp.298-306

32. Rosenberg, E.S. et all Number of casual male sexual partners and associated factors among men who have sex with men: results from the National HIV Behavioural Surveillance system *BMC Public Health* 2011, 11, 189

33. Wellings, K. Field, J. et al *Sexual behaviour in Britain* The National Survey of Sexual attitudes and Lifestyles, 1994 Penguin

34. Hillier, L., Turner, A. & Mitchell, A. (2005) The second national report op. cit.

35. Warner, J., et al Rates and predictors of mental illness in gay men, lesbians,

and bisexual men and women: Results from a survey based in England and Wales British *Journal of Psychiatry* 2004 185, 479–485

36. Calzo, J.P. Retrospective recall of sexual orientation identity development among gay, lesbian, and bisexual adults *Developmental Psychology* 2008 44(1) pp. 1658-1673

37. Remafedi, G. Demography of Sexual Orientation in Adolescents *Pediatrics* 1992 89, 4 pp.714–721 also Wellings, K et al, *Sexual Behaviour in Britain* 1994 Penguin

38. Parkes, A. et al *Comparison of Teenagers...* op. cit.

39. Mercer, C.H., Fenton, K.A., Copas, A.J. Increasing prevalence of male homosexual partnerships and practices in Britain 1990–2000: Evidence from national probability surveys *AIDS* 2004;18:1453–1458

40. Pathela, P., Schillinger, J.A. *Sexual Behaviors and Sexual Violence....* op. cit. Garofalo, R. et al *Sexual orientation and risk...* op. cit.

41. Savin-Williams, R.C. & Ream, G.L. Prevalence and stability of sexual orientation components during adolescence and young adulthood *Archives of Sexual Behavior* 2007, 36, 385–394

42. Parkes, A. et al Comparison of Teenagers' Early Same-Sex and Heterosexual Behavior: UK Data From the SHARE and RIPPLE Studies *Journal of Adolescent Health* 02.09.2010

43. Dickson, N., Paul, C. and Herbison, P. Same-sex attraction in a birth cohort: prevalence and persistence in early adulthood *Social Science and Medicine* 2003, 56 1607-1615

44. Diamond, L.M. Female bisexuality from adolescence to adulthood: Results from a 10-year longitudinal study *Developmental Psychology* 2008 44(1) 5-14. See also Kinnish, K.K., Strassberg, D.S. and Turner, C.W. Sex differences in the flexibility of sexual orientation: a multidimensional retrospective assessment *Archives of Sexual Behavior* 2005 34 175–183

45. Laumann, E.O. et al ibid.

46. Barnhouse, R.T. *Homosexuality: A symbolic confusion* 1977 New York: Seabury Press pp.153-4

47. Joyner, K. & Udry, J.R. (2000) You don't bring me anything but down: Adolescent romance and depression *Journal of Health and Social Behavior*, 41(4), pp. 369–391

48. Father's Day Cards Banned *Daily Telegraph* 20.06.2008

49. David Parker and others v. William Hurley and others. United States, District Court of Massachusetts, Feb 23, 2007

50. Dept Prime Minister speech to the Open Society Foundation and the think-tank Demos December 2011 http://demos.co.uk

51. Goldman, W. Z. *Women, The State and Revolution, Soviet Family Policy and Social Life, 1917-1936* Cambridge University Press 1993 p.3

52. Sugrue, S. Soft Despotism and Same-Sex Marriage in George, R.P. & Elshtain,

J.B. eds. *The Meaning of Marriage* 2006 Dallas: Spence Publishing Company p.190

53. For example: Amato, P.R., Kane, J.B. & James, S. Reconsidering the 'Good Divorce' *Family Relations* 2011, 60 (5) 511–524

54. Concern over 'flaws' in shared parenting plan *The Times* 19.07.2012

55. Mother wins DNA battle over dead soldier *Daily Telegraph* 27.11.2012

56. Hennessy, P. Fathers 'to sign birth records' *Daily Telegraph* 17.06.2012

57. Britten, N. Son caught in middle as lesbians accuse gay father of breaking access deal *Daily Telegraph* 07.02.2012

58. Pawelski, J.G., Perrin, E.C., Foy, J.M., Allen, C.E., Crawford, J.E., Del Monte, Kaufman, M. et al The effects of marriage, civil union, and domestic partnership laws on the health and well-being of children *Pediatrics* 2006 118, 349–364

59. Sugrue, S. *Soft Despotism....* op. cit. p.184

60. Sperm donors can seek more parental rights *Daily Telegraph* 01.02.2013

61. Ball, C.A. Marriage, Same-Gender Relationships, and Human Needs and Capabilities in eds., Wardle, L.D. et al *Marriage and Same Sex Unions: A Debate* 2003 Praeger

62. Gallagher, M. A Reality Waiting to Happen: A Response to Evan Wolfson. In eds., Wardle, L.D. et al *Marriage and Same Sex Unions: A Debate* 2003 Praeger p.11

63. Gallagher, M. Normal Marriage: Two Views in eds., Wardle, L.D. et al pp.17–18

64. Sugrue, S. *Soft Despotism....* op. cit. pp.195 & 174

65. Henricson, C. *Government and Parenting* 2003 Joseph Rowntree Foundation and *A Revolution in Family Policy: Where we should go from here* 2012 Policy Press

66. Johnson, D. The real marriage problems ed. *Standpoint* April 2012 Issue 41

67. Regnerus, M. Yes, Marriage Will Change – and Here's How *Public Discourse* 07.05.2013

68. Solomon, S.E. et al Money, Housework, Sex, and Conflict: Same-Sex Couples in Civil Unions, Those Not in Civil Unions, and Heterosexual Married Siblings *Sex Roles* 2005 Vol. 52, (9/10) 561–575

69. Solomon, S.E., Rothblum, E.D. & Balsam, K.F. Pioneers in partnership; Lesbian and gay male couples in civil unions compared with those not in civil unions and married heterosexual siblings *Journal of Family Psychology* 2004, 18 pp.275–286

70. Morgan, P. *Family Policy: Family Changes* 2006 Institute for the Study of Civil Society. Haas, L. *Equal Parenthood and Social Policy: A Study of Parental leave in Sweden* 1992 Albany, NY: State University of New York Press

71. Teach boys about child care and chores, urges girls schools leader *Daily Telegraph* 30.03.2013

72. Mac an Ghaill, M. & Haywood, C. Understanding boys': Thinking through boys, masculinity and suicide (available online 26th August 2010) *Social Science and Medicine* online 26th August 2010

73. Ferudi, F. *Wasted* 2009 Continuum pp.105, 190–1 & 216

74. Solomon, S.E. et al *Money, Housework, Sex, and Conflict....* op. cit.